FRANCO'S
FRIENDS

PETER DAY

FRANCO'S FRIENDS

HOW BRITISH INTELLIGENCE HELPED BRING FRANCO TO POWER IN SPAIN

Biteback Publishing

First published in Great Britain in 2011 by
Biteback Publishing Ltd
Westminster Tower
3 Albert Embankment
London
SE1 7SP

ISBN 978-1-84954-098-8

10 9 8 7 6 5 4 3 2 1

A CIP catalogue record for this book is available from the British Library.

Set in Caslon and Preussische
Cover design by Namkwan Cho

Printed and bound in Great Britain by
TJ International, Padstow, Cornwall

CONTENTS

ACKNOWLEDGEMENTS

My research for this book has been sustained by the ever patient and resourceful staff of the National Archives at Kew and by frequent recourse to the London Library, supplemented by the Churchill Archives, Cambridge University Library, National Maritime Museum and the British Library. Particular thanks are due to the Imperial War Museum for use of material from their sound archive. I have benefited too from the dedication of volunteers at the Croydon Airport Society, the British Airways Museum and the Fernhurst Society, the West Sussex county record office and the George Müller Charitable Trust in Bristol. Many individuals have been generous with their time and knowledge, among them Mrs Jeane Pollard, Colin Davis, Henry and Julia Watson, Michael Petre, Mrs Geraldine Petre-Guest, Philip Bebb, Professor June Cumbrae-Stewart and Tristan Hillgarth. I have reason to be especially grateful for the editing skills of Sam Carter and Hollie Teague in imposing order and clarity.

I would like to thank the following for their permission to reproduce photographs: the Garland Collection at the West Sussex Record Office (Hugh and Diana Pollard and Dorothy Watson); the Fernhurst Society (Spread Eagle pub); Getty Images (Juan March, Juan de la Cierva, General Francisco Franco); Tristan Hillgarth (Captain Alan Hillgarth); the National Portrait Gallery (Douglas Jerrold by John Gay) and the Croydon Airport Society (*Dragon Rapide*, Cecil Bebb, George Bryers and Gordon Olley).

PROLOGUE

The sharp tang of orange cut through the whisky fumes in the cramped, stifling cabin of the *Dragon Rapide*. The sea breeze was buffeting the little plane as it flew a few hundred feet above the Atlantic waves breaking over shipwrecks on the north African shore. There was no obvious cause for alarm, and Diana Pollard was reluctant to shout over the racket from the twin engines to ask, but she knew that if Bebb the pilot was chewing oranges he was worried.

She had only met him four days ago but she had quickly grown to admire the sandy haired, freckled young aviator. He was confident and competent and he didn't need regular shots from a hip flask to calm his nerves, unlike the radio operator they had left behind in Casablanca.

The two Spaniards had stayed there too and now Diana's father, Hugh, was making the decisions. He was just as partial to a drink, but he could handle himself. She had watched through the half-open study door as he took a revolver from the gun cupboard, cleaned and checked it as always before slipping it beneath the shirts in his valise. The thought of it caused her as much apprehension as reassurance.

Beside her Dorothy Watson shifted in her seat, reaching for the cigarette packet that she kept tucked in the elastic of her underwear. Uncouth. But then she was the girl who looked after their chickens at home and she really was a good sort, always cheery and ready to play the game.

She had seemed quite oblivious to the risks they were running that lunchtime as they danced the tango in the desert with lecherous Spanish legionnaires from the fort at Port Juby, carefree and dangerously flirtatious. She had heard an edge in her father's voice as he told the commandant that they really must be going and it had dawned on her that there was a limit to his powers of protection if things turned nasty.

Dorothy was peering over her shoulder at the fashion photos in the copy of *Vogue* open on her lap. She caught her father's eye and tugged the magazine away, a little too quickly. He had hidden documents inside those pages and she had not dared even to look at them.

That he trusted her with them she took as a great compliment. He had never included her in one of his adventures before and she was determined not to let him down. Her father's life was largely a mystery to her. He was an army man, but not the sort to march around in uniform, barking orders. Small wars and skirmishes were his speciality, and when they couldn't be had he was busy experimenting with firearms and solving crimes for Scotland Yard.

Truth be told, she rather wished he had not involved her in this mission of his. She took after him a little, with her foxy good looks and fearless riding to hounds, but she was only nineteen and just out of convent school. Nevertheless, she had formed a poor opinion of the Spaniards they encountered, even the rather dashing Luis Bolin with his Clark Gable moustache and tanned good looks.

This was their show, she knew that much. But after histrionics in Bordeaux, Biarritz and Lisbon they had opted to stay behind and it was the English who were taking the lead. Her father had warned her they would both be shot if they were caught but no one was going to call her a coward. Her mother's worried face kept appearing in her mind: 'Here we go again, oh dear, they may none of them come back.'

It had all begun a few days earlier with a hushed phone call taken in Hugh Pollard's study. Luis Bolin needed an aeroplane, a reliable man and two platinum blondes to deflect attention from their real purpose. 'Can you fly to Africa tomorrow with two girls?' Hugh was asked. 'Depends on the girls,' came the predictable reply. 'You can choose.' By teatime Hugh Pollard was shaking hands in the Sussex countryside on an escapade that would change the course of history.

CHAPTER 1: PLOTTERS

Nobody seems have to have told Luis Bolin that the best way to keep a secret is not to let on that you know one. Lunch at Simpson's in the Strand was conducted with such ostentatious secrecy that everyone in the London restaurant realised plotting was afoot. His guest, the punctiliously English Douglas Jerrold, was wryly amused by his old friend's antics as they ate roast saddle of mutton, at four shillings each, drank claret, and conspired in cavalier fashion. MI6 cannot have remained in ignorance of that lunch 400 yards from the Prime Minister's residence in Downing Street. Indeed the chief guest is reputed to have been one of their agents.

The three men at the table, plotting a military coup that would depose the lawfully elected Spanish government which counted Britain as its ally, had connections at the highest levels of British politics, commerce and the aristocracy. The plane that flew General Francisco Franco to join his troops in Morocco was owned by Britain's foremost tobacco baron. He was a pillar of the banking community with widespread financial interests. The Spaniard who arranged the flight knew most of the Air Force top brass. The plotters had easy access to the royal households of Britain and Spain.

Love is blind, friendship closes its eyes, so the old saying goes. Franco's British friends did that. They chose to overlook the brutality and the repression that went on for forty years, the Fascist philosophy and the collaboration with Hitler and Mussolini.

MI6 did not so much close its eyes as demurely avert them. They were known within the Foreign Office as 'The Friends', people whose true identity was never acknowledged. Their dirty tricks could be disowned.

The deputy director of MI6 was in touch with the conspirators and two of the principal actors in the drama, Hugh Pollard and Arthur Loveday, acted as agents. Pollard was involved in revolutions on three continents; the violent suppression of the IRA's murderous campaign for Irish independence; and had a hand in some of the blackest propaganda of the First World War.

Loveday boasted that he had been behind the exposure of a Communist plot that justified Franco's pre-emptive coup. The evidence he revealed was almost certainly fake – the Spanish equivalent of the Zinoviev letter.

They also had a role to play in one of the greatest intelligence coups of the Second World War. Their contacts and influence paved the way for the wholesale bribery of the highest echelons of Spain's military government, the pay off for persuading Franco not to enter the war on Hitler's side.

When the war was over it was payback time. To meet the bill the intelligence services, Foreign Office and the Treasury collaborated with their Spanish friends in a breathtaking piece of financial chicanery.

The instigator of the Simpson's lunch was Luis Antonio Bolin, whose superficial charm masked a vicious streak. Handsome, dark-eyed and with greying hair, Bolin was, according to Hugh Pollard's daughter Diana, 'a bit stagey', reminiscent 'of a Hollywood film star rather than a real person'.[1] He became press chief to General Franco in the bloody conflict in which propaganda was a frontline weapon. He was notorious for his bullying death threats to journalists who did not toe the Nationalist line and his defence of his side's worst excesses.

Bolin was the grandson of a British diplomat, Charles Toll Bidwell, who had served in Panama and the Balearic Islands before becoming British consul in Malaga in 1881.[2] Bolin had been a newspaper correspondent in France in the First World War and press attaché at the Spanish embassy in London in 1920. He had studied law at the Middle Temple and lived in Britain for twenty years, so he was quite at home, with his wife Mercedes, five-year-old son Fernando, and baby daughter Marisol in Hornton Street, Kensington as part of the Anglo-Spanish social scene. As London correspondent of the Spanish newspaper *ABC* and the magazine *Blanco y Negro,* he took his orders, for work and revolution, from the editor and proprietor, the Marqués de Luca de Tena.[3]

Bolín's lunch companion was the inventor Juan de la Cierva whose autogiro aircraft were the forerunners of the helicopter. His father, also Juan, had been leader of the Spanish Conservative Party and Minister of War. Franco was one of the army officers he sent to avenge a shocking series of defeats by the Moroccan tribal leader Abd el-Krim. King Alfonso of Spain had long been a friend of the family.

From the age of fourteen La Cierva had been building aeroplanes. The first was powered by a company of small boys, running along pulling on the end of a rope. He moved to London and in 1925 demonstrated his autogiro at Farnborough, the home of His Majesty's Balloon Factory and cradle of British aeronautical research. The Air Minister, Sir Samuel Hoare,was so impressed he ordered four immediately. The American version was feted at the White House.

La Cierva had contacts at the very top of the Air Ministry and in politics. His business partner and financial backer was Air Commodore James Weir, a governor of the Bank of England. According to Bolín's account, La Cierva was at dinner at Weir's home on the evening that the orders came through to launch the revolt and Bolín telephoned him there to discuss it. La Cierva rushed to Bolín's house to hammer out the details over glasses of whisky.[4]

James Weir's older brother, Lord Weir, also had shares in La Cierva's company. He was personal adviser to the Air Minister, responsible for increasing production of Spitfire and Hurricane fighters,[5] and he had the ear of Winston Churchill through membership of an exclusive dining club. During the summer of 1936 the two men kept up a spirited correspondence about the need for re-armament.[6]

Completing the trio was Douglas Jerrold, an enigmatic figure: director of the respected publishing house Eyre and Spottiswoode; editor of the *English Review*, journal of high Toryism; war hero; devout Catholic and the pivotal connection between the Spanish Nationalist cause and the British establishment. He associated himself with the Anglo-German Fellowship and The Link, two organisations condemned for their pro-Hitler leanings prior to the outbreak of the Second World War, yet he was no Nazi and deplored anti-Semitism. His firm was one of three permitted to publish the authorised version of *The Bible* but also, in an apparent aberration, published the notorious anti-Semitic forgeries *The Protocols of the Elders of Zion*. Brendan Bracken, Winston Churchill's close friend and wartime personal assistant, was a fellow director.

Jerrold was born in Scarborough in 1893 and hankered after the glories of an earlier age. He persisted in wearing an old-fashioned black coat, with starched shirt collar and pinstripe trousers. His father was district auditor for the local government board, but he followed in the footsteps of his grandfather Blanchard Jerrold and great-grandfather Douglas W. Jerrold, both playwrights and men of letters. Douglas senior was one of the founding contributors to *Punch* magazine and a close friend of Charles Dickens; Blanchard a newspaper editor, *bon viveur* and friend and collaborator of the French artist Gustave Doré.

The young Douglas had won a scholarship to read modern history at New College, Oxford, and there began his career in political journalism and a number of influential friendships. He abandoned university at the beginning of the First World War to join the Royal Naval Division – a military unit formed of naval reservists – and saw action at Gallipoli and on the Somme where he was shot and lost the use of his left arm, a disability he overcame with grim humour and determination. After the war he wrote the history of the division, with a foreword by Churchill, who had been First Lord of the Admiralty.

He was described as a large man with a small head, who could be gloomy and difficult yet maintained a wide social circle through membership of some of London's best known gentlemen's clubs, among them the Athenaeum, the Carlton and the Authors' Club at No 2 Whitehall Court, Westminster, where he had a flat.[7] No. 2 Whitehall Court was also the base for Mansfield Cumming, the first director of MI6.

Jerrold reacted vehemently against the intellectual flirtations of the 1920s and 1930s with Socialism and Marxism. It was the era when the Cambridge spies – Blunt, Burgess, Maclean and Philby – were recruited by Soviet intelligence. Indeed, one of Philby's first assignments was the assassination of Franco, a mission in which he manifestly failed. Jerrold acknowledged the defects of industrialisation and the iniquities of capitalism but saw the solution in a return to Christian and human values in a corporate state, achieved not through democracy but by a kind of benign dictatorship. He admired Mussolini and thought he might steer the Conservative Party in the same direction by promoting Lord Lloyd, former high commissioner to Egypt and the Sudan. A lunch organised by the *English Review* in November 1933 to launch this campaign, supported by fifty to sixty MPs, was well attended but foundered, as Jerrold ruefully admitted, because their protégé was more interested in taking part in change than leading it and because 'the audience consisted of devoted subscribers of the *English Review* who have never read a line of what had been written there'.

Nothing daunted, Jerrold proclaimed in his magazine the following month:

> There is no folly more fashionable than the saying that the English will never tolerate a dictatorship. Under constitutional reforms of a very flimsy character the English have invariably insisted on being governed either by a close oligarchy or a virtual dictatorship … It is because the party machines have notably failed to govern that they are losing the public confidence, and unless Parliament under universal franchise can fulfil the indispensable task of leadership, a dictatorship is not only inevitable but necessary.[8]

He hoped to join Parliament himself, but the Conservatives would not offer him a seat. England may not have been ready for his vision but in Spain, he felt, the need was crying out to be met. Looking back, in 1950, he wrote:

> Any merely competent clerk in any foreign office in the world must have seen, the moment the Spanish Civil War broke out, an event of immense consequence to Europe... For four and a half years events in Spain were side-line news. The expulsion of the Jesuits, the confiscation of property, the secularisation of education, the legalisation of divorce – these sure signposts to revolution were passed amid the world's indifference... Spain, to the most cursory glance, was either going to the Left, to become a western outpost of Bolshevism, or to the Right, to become, with our ancient ally Portugal, a Christian and civilised outpost, but still an outpost, of authoritarianism. For England this was a vital matter. Even if our leaders were wholly ignorant of the moral and political issues at stake, not one of them was unaware of the importance of Gibraltar, or of the almost equal military importance of a neutral Spain in the event of a new Anglo-German war fought out on French soil.[9]

In 1933, through Eyre and Spottiswoode he had published anonymously a volume entitled *The Spanish Republic: A Survey of Two Years of Progress*. His collaborators on the project were Luis Bolín and the Marqués del Moral. The Marqués, born and brought up in Australia, with a Spanish father and an English mother, had been an intelligence officer for Lord Kitchener during the Boer War and returned to intelligence duties briefly during the Second World War.

The book's foreword claimed that it was only concerned with facts and had no political motives. It went on to explain that under General Primo de Rivera's mild and constructive dictatorship freedom and order reigned supreme throughout the land, and all systems and communications, including rail, road and telephones, were immensely improved ... the efficiency of the administration increased a thousandfold, national finance was set upon a sound basis, terrorism was stamped out, beggars disappeared from the streets and sanitation proceeded at a great pace.

This had been thrown away by a gullible electorate seduced by the promises of agents of the freemasonry of the Grand Orient and the Soviet who were driving the nation to chaos and ruin, characterised by strikes, riots and bombings. It painted a bleak picture of the horrors endured by the Church, business and land-owning classes at the hands of Socialists and anarchists.[10]

The Spanish Republic had been written with the encouragement of the historian Sir Charles Petrie, a monarchist who shared Jerrold's admiration for Mussolini and distrust of Hitler. Petrie had worked during the First World War in the Cabinet Office, where he got to know the author John Buchan, who was in charge of government propaganda. The war had interrupted his university education and at Oxford in the 1920s, as president of the Oxford Carlton Club, he made the acquaintance of many of the leading Tories of the day.

Jerrold had interviewed King Alfonso XIII of Spain after he vacated the throne in 1931 and Petrie was in frequent contact with the King, whom he regarded as 'the greatest Spaniard of the twentieth century'.

The book was followed by the formation of the Spanish Committee in London. Apart from Petrie and Jerrold, its English members included the Tory MP Sir Victor Raikes. He had a link to Stewart Menzies, then deputy director of MI6, through membership of the strongly pro-appeasement Imperial Policy Group. Their secretary, Kenneth de Courcy, was a friend of Menzies and fellow White's Club member.[11]

The Spanish Committee was supported by King Alfonso XIII and the Duke of Alba, whose British title Duke of Berwick arose through direct descent from King James II of England and his mistress Arabella Churchill. The Duke became Franco's ambassador in London during the Second World War.[12]

This group evolved into the Friends of Nationalist Spain. De Courcy is said to have been a founder member and a friend of

Jerrold. The intelligence analyst Stephen Dorril identifies Jerrold as a member of MI6.[13]

Jerrold's autobiography *Georgian Adventure,* published in 1937, is a lament for the loss of a supposedly gilded Edwardian era: from the disappearance of the music hall to the breakdown of the social order, in a machine age of ennobled cads and ruffianly millionaires. The world had gone from a fool's paradise in 1914 to a fool's hell, the rotten foundations of which had been laid in 1920 and whose intellectual fabric was worthless. His interest in Spain had been heightened by his encounter with the King and his certainty that the Spanish people, any more than the British, would not allow themselves to be 'racketeered' into Communism. He was appalled by the statistics of church arsons, bombings and murder in the early months of 1936. During that time he had, he said, dined on three occasions with Spanish women widowed in left-wing violence. So, apparently without difficulty, he turned to arms dealing from his publishing office in Fetter Lane, just off Fleet Street – the newspaper hub of London. He was visited by a mysterious Spaniard who said that his friend Luis Bolin had recommended Jerrold as the only man in London who could help in his quest for fifty Hotchkiss machine guns and 500,000 rounds of ammunition. Jerrold casually replied that it might be possible, agreed a price and within twenty-four hours was able to tell Bolin that the deal could probably go ahead. Jerrold does not explain how he achieved this feat but his friend Hugh Pollard would have been a likely contender for the role of arms dealer. The offer was never taken up. Clearly, though, Bolin was impressed by Jerrold's debut in the murky world of private military procurement. It was two weeks later that he summoned Jerrold, at a matter of a few hours' notice, to lunch at Simpson's.

CHAPTER 2: FRONT MAN

For a bookish political philosopher, Douglas Jerrold had some surprising contacts. Over lunch with Bolin he came up with three names of military men ready for adventure, no questions asked. He had no hesitation in recommending Hugh Bertie Campbell Pollard as the best of them. Pollard had been in the spying game years before the Secret Service Bureau, forerunner of MI5 and MI6, was founded in 1909.

He was one of the first recruits to the Legion of Frontiersmen, founded in 1904 by Roger Pocock, a former constable in the Canadian North-West Mounted Police. He recruited 'men trained by military service ... by working, hunting or fighting in wild countries or at sea ... who are not prepared, by reason of temperament or vocation, to submit themselves to the ordinary routine of military discipline, except in time of war'.

A host of military men signed up, among them Admiral Prince Louis of Battenberg and Sir John French, later commander in chief of the British Expeditionary Force in the First World War. From the ranks of writers and explorers there were Sir Arthur Conan Doyle, Rider Haggard, Edgar Wallace and Erskine Childers.[14]

One of Pollard's first missions, at the age of twenty, was to Morocco accompanied by his friend Alan Ostler, a *Daily Express* journalist. In 1908 Mulai Hafid had just overthrown his brother and seized power as Sultan. Pollard reported to Pocock on 28 August:

> Ostler and I have been in Fez for a fortnight, and have had a very good time. I have interviewed the Sultan twice, and been to tea etc.

with all his ministers. Wazir Hafid presented us each with a bag of silver dollars, about £7 worth, and is a real tough nut.

Of the first Europeans to arrive in the capital, Fez, after the coup, four were members of the Legion. They had denounced a rival Frenchman as a spy and got him expelled. Pollard continued:

> Please send me a good bundle of application forms, tracts etc and I will wipe in about seven men for certain: two here, three in Alcazar and two in Tangier; these are all vice-consuls and big pots. I am sure the Sultan will be interested. Can you have a silver badge of the Legion sent out? I will pay the cost of it and guarantee to present it to his Shereepian majesty. A man who has done what he has, i.e. pinched a kingdom! is certainly down for our Honorary List. Further, he will have in a year or so lots of jobs going, and all Legion members will be interested in getting these for our unemployed (provided they are capable).

Pollard's letter was forwarded by Pocock to the Foreign Office who were aghast at the idea of amateurs trespassing on their territory – and very much the wrong type of amateur at that. The War Office, however, was in favour of the League and encouraged them.[15]

By 1910 Pollard was in Mexico working as a land agent. His first task, as described by him, had all the elements of a Wild West novel. He was instructed to recover a debt from a notorious bandit on the Guatemalan border, saddled up his horse, packed a shotgun and revolver and set off fearing the worst. Yet by dint of his quick wits he tricked this desperado into settling the debt. His next adventures took on the character of Indiana Jones. He fell in with a couple of Englishmen whose idea of a good night out in Mexico City was to tour the more disreputable bars in search of one of the local bullfighters and chop off his pigtail – an adornment that marked out their profession. After one successful scalping in a bar the trio decided to try their luck in a brothel:

When we arrived everything was in full swing. People of all nationalities, and girls of every shade of colour, from a Haiti half-breed to a blonde Flamande, were seated in the gallery. At a big table on the patio sat two toreros and their jackals, with several ladies. Then we took a hand. The table went over bodily as Trott and Pulteney tackled a bull-fighter apiece … with the flash of a knife the whole complexion of matters changed. From the door came the hoarse challenge of the police… It was time to move. A straight blow or two cleaned up the remainder, and we went in a body for the gallery stairs. From the ballrooms and the private rooms came Americans and Britishers, Germans and Swedes, all ready for a scrap, and all pleased at the excitement.

From the balcony they showered the police with giant flowerpots; and then shooting broke out. They made their escape by breaking through a barred window and dashing across the rooftops, accompanied by the pick of the girls.[16]

He reported from the frontline on the revolution in which Francisco Madero deposed the long-serving President Porfirio Diaz. When Diaz secretly fled Mexico City, Pollard was on the train that took him to Vera Cruz and joined in the shooting when they were ambushed by a band of rebels. First Secretary Thomas Hohler reported from the British embassy in Mexico City:

Preparations were made with the utmost secrecy for the departure of President Diaz, one or two Englishmen being invited to assist, and giving all the aid that was possible; and he left the city by the inter-oceanic railway at 4 o'clock on the morning of 26 May, arriving at his destination at 4pm, after a brush with the revolutionaries or bandits at a place called Tepeyahualco. He is reported to have led the troops who were escorting him himself. The assailants were easily beaten off.[17]

Diaz spent his last night on Mexican soil at the home of Mr J. S. Body, chief representative of Lord Cowdray. According to Body, he and one other employee were the only Englishmen informed in advance of the escape plan. Lord Cowdray's close friendship with Diaz had led to his company, S. Pearson and Co., winning huge oil concessions and major engineering contracts in Mexico which made him one of the richest men in England. As a sign of his gratitude, he offered Diaz lifelong use of one of his English mansions – Paddockhurst in Sussex.[18] The president declined the offer, opting for warmer climes, but Hugh Pollard lived for some time in properties on the Cowdray estate.

Pollard was the son of a distinguished surgeon, Joseph Pollard, and his wife Helen. The Pollards could trace their lineage back to the twelfth century. In more recent times they had been Quaker gentleman farmers and tradesmen in Hertfordshire. Joseph was house surgeon to Joseph Lister, fellow Hertfordshire Quaker and pioneer of antiseptic surgery. He had a practice just off Harley Street and did research into skin diseases. He was also a pioneer of the use of mild anaesthesia in childbirth.

He had been an army doctor and became a prominent freemason, Grand Provincial Warden of Surrey and member of the Parthenon and Earl of Mornington Lodges.[19] The family lived prosperously in Queen Anne Street, Marylebone, with five servants.[20] Hugh attended Westminster School as a boarder then spent a year being privately educated in Germany.[21]

Hugh Pollard's father would only pay for him to go to university with a view to entering a profession like medicine or the law.[22] Pollard opted for journalism and adventure, having first spent some time as an apprentice at the Armstrong Whitworth engineering works in Newcastle upon Tyne and two years studying at the School of Practical Engineering at Crystal Palace, qualifying for membership of the Institution of Mechanical Engineers.[23] In documents he completed in the 1940s for the Special Operations Executive he also claimed to have studied at King's College, London and to have served in the Northumberland Hussars and Yeomanry as an officer cadet. He said he was fluent in French, Spanish and German. He also mentioned that his politics were Conservative and Unionist

– 'extreme Right' – and that his private income was inadequate and diminishing.[24]

The date of his conversion to Catholicism is not known but in 1915 he married Ruth Gibbons, daughter of a Staffordshire master lockmaker and ornamental ironwork manufacturer, at St James's in Spanish Place, Marylebone.[25] Its connections to Spanish ambassadors in London date back to Elizabethan times. Among its artefacts is the personal standard of King Alfonso XIII who abandoned his throne in 1931. Pollard would later play a part in trying to re-establish the Spanish monarchy.

Douglas Jerrold was one of the witnesses at the marriage ceremony. He had known Pollard since before the First World War. Jerrold was editing the *New Oxford Review* magazine. Pollard had got into the technical press, working as an assistant editor of *The Cinema* and then technical editor of *Autocycle*. Jerrold says of Pollard at that time:

> He looked, and occasionally behaved, like the German Crown Prince and had a habit of letting off revolvers in any office which he happened to visit. When I asked him once if he had ever killed anybody he replied: Never accidentally.[26]

Pollard's younger sister, Rosamund, married Sydney 'Sammy' Davis, one of the famous Bentley Boys who raced their huge 4.5 litre engine machines without thought for their safety. He won the 1927 Le Mans twenty-four hour race. Pollard was more of a hunting man but had no objection to partying with the fast set.

Pollard joined the 25th Cyclists Battalion of the London Regiment before the outbreak of the First World War, rising to the rank of captain.[27] He organised motorcycle despatch riders in London before being sent to France, attached to the Royal Engineers and responsible for bridge building, road maintenance and trench digging during the second battle of Ypres.[28]

His experience of sitting on courts martial, where men were sometimes accused of deliberately shooting themselves in order to be invalided out of the trenches, precipitated his post-war study of ballistics.[29]

He briefly managed his father-in-law's Wolverhampton factory, which had been turned over to grenade production, and in 1916 transferred to the War Office intelligence directorate's department MI 7B, responsible for dropping propaganda leaflets over Germany from unmanned balloons. His capacity for tall tales made him a welcome addition. He combined war service with the role of special correspondent of the *Daily Express*, whose proprietor, Lord Beaverbrook, became Britain's first Minister of Information in 1918.

The Legion of Frontiersmen credited Pollard and Ostler with inventing a phantom Russian army joining the Allies on the Western front. The seal of authenticity was provided by Pollard inventing quotes from a railway cleaning lady complaining about 'them Roosians' leaving the snow off their boots for her to sweep up.[30]

This was a mild foretaste of what was to come. John Buchan, author of the spy thriller *The Thirty-Nine Steps*, became the government's director of information. He was one of a number of authors commissioned to write propaganda books for a foreign audience. His contribution was *The Battle of the Somme*; Sir Arthur Conan Doyle had already penned *To Arms*; Pollard wrote *The Story of Ypres*.[31] Not surprisingly it is a story of allied heroism in the face of brutal bombardment by the Hun, overlaid with dark hints of barbarity by German cavalry against the local peasants.

Pollard was related, on his mother's side, to the Montagu merchant banking family. His father was their family doctor. Ivor Montagu recalls that Hugh was his favourite cousin:

> His slightly cynical air and knowing smile, his constant traveller's tales, made him the hero of his younger kinsmen. What adventures he had had! What places he had been to, and what events he had seen. In the First War he was with Intelligence, and presented me with pieces of the first Zeppelins that had been brought down. How we laughed at his cleverness when he told us how

his department had launched the account of the German corpse factories and of how the Hun was using myriads of trench-war casualties for making soap and margarine. He explained that he had originally thought up the idea himself to discredit the enemy among the populations of Oriental countries, hoping to play upon the respect for the dead that goes with ancestor worship. To the surprise of the authorities it had caught on, and they were now making propaganda of it everywhere. The tears ran down his cheeks as he told us of the story they had circulated of a consignment of soap from Germany arriving in Holland and being buried with full military honours.'[32]

Whether Pollard was the originator of this preposterous untrue story, it was certainly put out by his department and believed. *The Times* published it in April 1917.[33]

After 1918 Pollard spent a year with the Ministry of Labour and was then seconded to the Royal Irish Constabulary in Dublin, responsible for putting down the Sinn Fein and Irish Republican Army war of independence. He talked of being involved in dirty tricks, among them brokering a deal to sell a consignment of light artillery and Hotchkiss machine guns to the IRA. Then he made sure the guns were intercepted and confiscated, thus depriving the opposition of the arms and the funds they had raised from American sympathisers to pay for them.[34]

Ivor Montagu, who had been amused by the anti-German propaganda, was shocked by Pollard's approving accounts of the murderous repression practised by the Black and Tans – so called because they were recruits from the First World War wearing part-khaki army uniform and part-police surplus.

At the beginning of November 1920 the Black and Tans sealed off the town of Tralee after two policemen had been abducted and murdered. For about a week the population found themselves under siege, with reprisal raids late at night in which suspected Sinn Fein members were shot and their homes set alight. There was a backlash in the British Press at the excesses of the troop and police reaction.

Then on Saturday 13 November, as things were beginning to calm down, *The Times* carried a two paragraph report saying that a small group of press men had been ambushed on the road between Castleisland and Tralee. Pollard was one of the government officials accompanying them. Their military escort had fought off seventy attackers, killing two and wounding seven. The following day some Sunday papers carried a photograph and report of the 'Battle of Tralee.' A Pathé newsreel was said to exist.

It quickly became clear that the photo was a fake. Readers identified the street as Vico Road in Dalkey, a quiet seaside Dublin suburb. There were rumours that the newsreel had been withdrawn after one of the IRA 'corpses' in the road was seen to move.

A subsequent investigation by the Labour Party condemned the entire incident, which had caused outrage in the Commons, as a fabrication.[35]

A week later, on 20 November, came Bloody Sunday. In early morning raids the IRA murdered fourteen British intelligence officers and agents at their homes. That afternoon British forces opened fire on the crowd at a Gaelic football match at Croke Park, killing a similar number, and that evening three Irish prisoners were killed, supposedly while trying to escape.

In December, in the House of Commons, the Irish Nationalist MP Jeremiah McVeagh demanded to know who was responsible for the official issue of the photograph; whether a government armoured car and soldiers were lent for the purpose of preparing the picture; and what action the government proposed to take. The Attorney General, Mr Denis Henry, replied, lamely:

> I know nothing as to the circumstances in which the picture in question was taken. It was not issued officially or with the knowledge of any responsible official. The hon. gentleman knows much more about the photograph than I do.[36]

Unabashed, Pollard continued to contribute to a weekly summary of events in Ireland, of doubtful veracity, and in 1922 he published a book, *The Secret Societies of Ireland: Their Rise and Progress*. It set out to describe the origins of Irish nationalism back to the seventeenth century, making play of the associations of some groups with Bolshevism and others with Germany during the First World War. It concluded with an apologia for the failings and excesses of British Intelligence, attributed blame to the Roman Catholic Church in Ireland for lack of authority and indulged in some crude denigration of the Irish character.

During the 1920s and 1930s Pollard was sporting editor of *Country Life* magazine and author of a series of books with a hunting and shooting theme. He rode with Lord Leconfield's hunt based at Petworth House in Sussex.

His interest in guns had started at school when he was a regular visitor to gun shops and got to know Robert Churchill, whose establishment in Orange Street, behind the National Gallery, held a royal warrant from King Alfonso of Spain. Pollard played the role of Mycroft, the older brother, to Churchill's Sherlock Holmes, according to Churchill's biographer Macdonald Hastings.

In 1924 Pollard had published a pioneering scientific pamphlet on the use of microscopic comparison to match bullets to the guns that fired them. The pair became Scotland Yard's principal forensic experts in firearms cases.

In one sensational trial, of the society heiress Elvira Barney, aged twenty-six, for the murder of her bi-sexual lover Michael Stephen, Pollard and Churchill gave evidence that might have sent her to the gallows. Stephen had been found dead on the stairs of Elvira's Mayfair flat after a night out at the Café de Paris. Neighbours reported hearing a lovers' tiff and then a shot.

Elvira claimed that the Smith and Wesson revolver had gone off accidentally as they wrestled for control of it. The two experts said that was impossible but she was acquitted after a dramatic closing speech by her defence counsel.[37]

According to Hastings, who became a friend of Pollard, he could be found at his Sussex home surrounded by instruments and armaments, antique weapons and armour, enjoying his own cooking and homemade wine (with gunpowder potency), writing, experimenting and inventing unlikely devices like the Pollard Scentmeter for tracking foxes.[38]

Hugh and Ruth Pollard had two daughters, Diana, born in 1916, and Avril in 1919. Diana was nineteen and had only recently completed her education at the Convent of the Holy Child Jesus in St Leonards-on-Sea on the Sussex coast when Douglas Jerrold and his Spanish friends came knocking at their door.

At the age of sixty-five Diana made a little-known tape recording for the Imperial War Museum sound archives, recalling that day and the events that followed. Pollard was a gentleman farmer at Hoewyck Farm, a rambling red-brick building tucked away down a single-track lane near Fernhurst, Sussex but, according to Diana, not wealthy. He had a very small private income and her mother had some money.

> There would be summonses and things like that always around the place. Not vast extravagances – they never had enough money to meet things they'd like to do.

She is hazy about her father's past:

> I never really heard him give us a coherent account of these events, which used to irritate us rather. He used to go off to shooting parties. He was a sporty chap and army basically. Not regular army but there were so many wars and so many troubles, he was always on the fringe of that kind of thing. Troubles and revolutions and wars – if there was some kind of exciting job he could take, he would probably have said: Yes, I'll go and look.
>
> I remember that summer's day fairly distinctly. My father came out and he was rather excited and I think my mother knew straight away – one of these things was blowing up. He said ... would we be willing to act as cover, pretend to be rich tourists, just about a week ... as company with whoever was there and dump a plane in North Africa, no question of going further ... and then come back by boat.

So, you know, you are eighteen and you don't have any particular wish for adventure but it would have been a stupid thing to say No – that was rather like being cowardly. They wanted another girl because one girl wouldn't be enough. We had some battery chickens and Dorothy Watson … [looked after them]. She was a very nice girl, and she was pretty, so they said: There's another ready made one. My mother was very worried. I saw the face: Here we go again, oh dear. They may none of them come back. She didn't think it at all suitable. We hadn't got summer clothes. We had to get Dorothy a passport, I think in a day. Within twenty-four hours we had to be at Croydon. My sister was too young to go.

She remained, even at sixty-five, cautiously vague about the motives behind the mission while slipping in occasional dismissive references to Spanish anarchists and Socialists.[39]

Her account chimes in pretty well with that given by Jerrold and Bolin. According to Bolin, Pollard asked for more details of the mysterious escapade and he replied:

There is nothing more that I can add, except that what I have in mind is something to which, if you only knew it, I think you would not object on principle. The trip will, I trust, be a pleasant one, and you and the young ladies who might honour us with their company will be my guests the whole way there and back.[40]

This pompous and not very convincing assurance persuaded Pollard to demand life insurance for all concerned and that he should pack a gun. All that remained was to recruit Dorothy Watson, who was tracked down to a local pub and who, despite a knowledge of geography so hazy that she was not sure where Africa was, agreed without protest. Jerrold, who claims never to have known her surname, recorded:

Dorothy, I had noticed, kept her cigarettes in her knickers. She couldn't, she explained, afford a handbag. Obviously she was the type that went to Africa.[41]

The pub where they met was probably the Spread Eagle at Fernhurst, which had recently been transformed from a village inn to a brick and plaster mock-Tudor roadhouse under the licensee Jack Edwards. Dorothy was living there in 1936 and she was still there two years later when she married Harry Gauntlett, a member of a well-known local family who ran a horticultural nursery business at Chiddingfold. Her father did not approve. Dorothy was twenty-nine at the time of the trip to Spain – a lively, adventurous girl who was mad about horses. She had grown up in west London and Reigate, Surrey with her older brother Barnard and parents Reginald, a bank worker, and Mary, a clergyman's daughter. Dorothy was only seventeen when her mother died of liver cancer in 1924. Her father later remarried. Neither Dorothy nor Diana was especially blonde, but that was the smallest and most innocuous white lie in a saga of deception.

The day after Pollard's first meeting with Luis Bolin he took him to lunch at his Mayfair club, The Savile, and that afternoon Bolin went to Croydon to finalise the arrangements for the flight. Earlier he had collected £2,000 cash – a staggering amount of money, equivalent to around £75,000 in 2010 – from the Fenchurch Street branch of Kleinwort's Bank, courtesy of the bank's Spanish director, José Mayorga. It had been deposited there by the coup's financier, Juan March. The bulk of it was handed over that afternoon, Thursday 9 July, to Captain Gordon Olley to hire a *Dragon Rapide* and crew for the trip. Bolin was fearful that Olley might tip off the police. Instead he demanded an indemnity of £10,000 against the possible loss of the plane, even though he was supposedly in ignorance of the purpose of its journey. Luckily Juan de la Cierva and the Duke of Alba were willing to stand surety.[42]

With that much money at stake, surely Olley would keep his mouth shut.

CHAPTER 3: BACKGROUND

In 1930 Douglas Jerrold departed from his normal high-minded political journalism to publish *Storm Over Europe*, a racy and amusing novel set in a fictitious Ruritanian state. It opened with King George Adolphus being bundled off the throne in a coup d'état after a series of sordid domestic scandals. The King flees to Paris with a bevy of mistresses. Despite being set in a country on the Austro-Hungarian border, the names of places and characters had a Spanish ring to them. The country was divided between industrial wealth and rural poverty, governed alternately by self-interested barons and a rag-bag of subscribers to the League of Free Thought, whose policies, fuelled by anti-Catholic feeling and the quest for social justice, included subsidies for bread, coal and houses, the enfranchisement of boys and girls and the institution of compulsory divorce.

After fifteen years of descent into anarchy the Royalist leader D'Alvarez engineers a coup, telling his supporters:

This is no petty domestic squabble. The fight before us is one which has to be fought out all over Europe sooner or later. The threat to our civilisation was never graver. Genghis Khan at the gates of the Carpathians, the Turks at the gates of Vienna, may have provided more spectacular examples of dangers threatening the very existence of our culture and faith. But the danger today is infinitely greater. That the authority of governments is provisional and temporary, that the sanctity of marriage and the institution of the family are superstitious relics of tribal religion, that the authority of the word of God as taught by the Church is a delusion based on error and bolstered up by a lie, that man is self-sufficient to his own salvation in this life and that there is no hereafter – these are the doctrines of the new priesthood, which, if they are taught and believed, will shatter, as they are intended to do, the very framework of society.[43]

Jerrold's tongue in cheek account was recognisably similar to the Spanish Nationalists' list of grievances that led to their coup in 1936 and in one respect at least he was remarkably prescient. In 1931, the year after the book was published, King Alfonso XIII of Spain voluntarily vacated his throne to make way for a Republican government. He was married to Princess Victoria Eugenie, granddaughter of Queen Victoria, but had a string of mistresses and several illegitimate children. They fled to Paris.

The King had little alternative. In 1923 he had acquiesced in a coup d'état that brought to power the military dictator General Miguel Primo de Rivera. Spain had become a third-rate and peripheral country, corrupt and feudal, living on the past and lost glories of a once great South American empire. The last vestiges of colonial power, including Cuba, had been lost in a war with the United States in 1898. That military humiliation was compounded by a creeping loss of control over Morocco, to the French and to rebellious local tribesmen. From that confrontation Francisco Franco first emerged in 1912–1913 as a brave and ruthless army officer, barely out of his teens, who believed in the efficacy of the bayonet charge and was prepared to lead it from the front rather than consign others to their death from the safety of his own lines.

Spain remained neutral in the First World War but Franco had seen plenty of action repressing the Moroccan revolts. In June 1916, when his commanding officer was badly wounded during an assault, he took control, despite a serious stomach wound that might have killed him, and 'showed incomparable bravery, gift for command and energy deployed in combat'. The King promoted him to Major at the age of twenty-three. His survival and daring led his Moorish troops to believe he was blessed with *baraka*, a mystical quality of divine protection that rendered him invulnerable.[44]

Franco was to return to Morocco in 1920 as second in command of the newly formed Spanish Legion, a desperate band of misfits, murderers, criminals and foreign veterans of the First World War who were subject to savage discipline and encouraged to be brutally ruthless in return for the chance of a new life. They were nicknamed The Bridegrooms of Death. These were the men Franco would unleash on his fellow countrymen in 1936 in the pursuit of power.

The left-wing journalist Arthur Koestler, describing their progress through southern Spain at the start of the Civil War, wrote:

> The shadows of the Middle Ages seemed to have come alive, the gargoyles were spouting blood, Goya's *Disasters* were made to look like topical records: once more a mercenary horde, the foreign Legionaries of the *Tercio*, killed, raped and plundered in the name of a holy crusade, while the air smelt of incense and burning flesh.[45]

While Franco was instilling discipline in his new army, Spain was being torn apart by civil disturbances and strikes in what came to be regarded as three years of Bolshevism. Spain had prospered through its neutrality in the First World War, able to trade its agricultural goods, raw materials and limited industrial products. Anarchists and Socialists found eager support among factory workers, on starvation wages, and landless agricultural labourers. Pitted against them were industrialists, aristocratic landowners and a politicised Catholic movement that represented the peasantry and small farmers. With lacklustre Conservative and Liberal politicians unable to maintain order, Primo de Rivera seized power.

Spain was crucial to British strategic interests and the balance of power in the western Mediterranean and North Africa. The British ambassador, Esmé Howard, a Catholic who had worked in the 1890s for the social reformer Charles Booth, founder of the Salvation Army, believed in a fusion of imperial federation and state Socialism. He acknowledged the damage done by industrial strife but blamed the *juntas des defensa* – 'trades unions' of middle-ranking army officers – and political corruption for rendering Spain's parliamentary system bankrupt. He was dismayed to find the British mining company Rio Tinto bribing politicians and journalists to take their side in a labour dispute.[46]

He wrote in his memoirs:

The Extreme Right prescribed a military government, while the Extreme Left wished to adopt the Dictatorship of the Proletariat and the Soviet system. All that could be said was that Parliamentary Government as we understand it in England was becoming more and more discredited, and this naturally encouraged revolution in one sense or another.[47]

In a report to the Foreign Secretary, Lord Curzon, in 1920 he was even more forthright:

If I had to paint an impressionist painting of Spain in 1920, for which accurate and detailed drawing was not required, it would be an easier task. I could then take a large canvas and produce a stage in a state of chaotic welter on which various politicians would prominently figure pulling strings in different directions and to no purpose across a background of strikes, bombs and outrages, and apparent general discontent, of committees of military officers springing suddenly into the foreground and retiring as suddenly into obscurity for no apparent reason, of railway companies carrying on systematic sabotage against themselves in order to force the country and Government into raising rates, of banks and profiteers indulging in wild speculations in foreign exchanges, undermining all the advantages the country obtained by her policy of neutrality throughout the war, of regionalism in an extreme form increasing in certain provinces and extreme centralisation clinging to straws of hope in maintaining itself, of governments coming and going without serious programmes of reform, and, above this turmoil, of King Alfonso the only stable element apparently in it all, serenely trying now this expedient, now that, to carry on against great odds until some sane, wise and strong man should emerge on the stage to put all these tragi-comedians into their right places and allow the play to proceed to the benefit and content of the public in the house.[48]

These comments led the Foreign Office assistant secretary Gerald Villiers to the conclusion that 'a dose of *fascismo* would do Spain a world of good'. He did not think that Primo de Rivera was of the same calibre as Mussolini but his commitment to closer relations with Britain demonstrated a rather statesmanlike grasp of the needs of his country. Villiers recognised that Fascist-style regional security forces were potential troublemakers but commented:

On the whole I think one is justified in believing that the bloodless revolution will effect some purification of and improvement in the highly diseased Spanish body politic.[49]

Primo de Rivera's reforms succeeded in enraging his opponents while alienating his supporters. His attempt to streamline the convoluted and hierarchical military system offended senior officers who owed their exalted ranks to the old order; his well-intentioned programme of public infrastructure works led to a collapse of the currency; and the landowners were disaffected by attempts to introduce arbitration committees for farm workers' wages and working conditions.

Primo de Rivera resigned in 1930 and in elections the following year Socialists and liberal Republicans triumphed. The King took the hint and departed before he could be deposed, but did not abdicate. In his place, the Second Republic was a loose-knit group with a programme of reform which represented a direct challenge to the old authority of Church and Army. It raised expectations among the impoverished rural and industrial labourers that were incapable of being met. The rich and land-owning classes blocked change at every turn and damaged the economy by shifting their wealth abroad.

The Left forced through arbitration panels on rural pay, limits to working hours and security of tenure. Farmers were legally forbidden to take their land out of cultivation – a device they had used to thwart the reforms. The new government walked a tightrope of economic and social reform, beset by a wave of strikes from workers and the constant threat of an army coup. Against the background of the worldwide Great Depression it was a task doomed to fail.

The Catholic Right formed *Acción Popular,* led by José María Gil Robles, to frustrate the reforms with legalistic objection and convince the country that the Republic was:

> A Godless, rabble-rousing instrument of Soviet Communism poised to steal their lands and dragoon their wives and daughters into an orgy of obligatory free love.[50]

There were powerful groups on the Right actively contemplating armed insurrection. The Carlists were traditionalist, theocratic, with their own Bourbon pretender to the Spanish throne and a fanatical militia, the *Requete,* whom Franco would use to terrorise his opponents in the Civil War; the Royalists, loyal to Alfonso XIII and his heir Don Juan, had wealth and the support of many senior army officers; the Fascists were admirers of Hitler and Mussolini, who subsidised them, with the Falange providing the shock troops who would provoke street fighting with the Left.

In this polarised and hate-fuelled atmosphere some Catholic Church leaders called on their followers to take up arms against the regime. They were outraged when the Minister of War, Manuel Azaña, refused to call out the Civil Guard to deal with a wave of church arson. He declared: 'All the convents in Madrid are not worth the life of one Republican.'

This resentment boiled over in an attempted military coup, sparked initially by two small but horrific acts of violence that were a microcosm of the wider confrontation. At the end of 1931 in the remote village of Castilblanco in Extremadura the Civil Guard opened fire to disperse a crowd of striking farm workers, killing one man and injuring two. The crowd beat and stabbed the four Guards to death with stones and knives, mutilating the bodies. The head of the Civil Guard, General José Sanjurjo, a veteran of violent suppression of Moroccan tribesmen, declared it the worst outrage he had ever seen and blamed it on the Socialists. Soon after, the Civil Guard opened fire again, at a workers' protest in northern Castile, killing four women and a child. Sanjurjo was sacked for what was seen as a reprisal attack and transferred to the border and customs police.[51]

The General's humiliation became a rallying point for the disaffected right and he was persuaded to launch a hurriedly conceived and poorly planned coup which the Republican government had little difficulty suppressing. Franco, while sympathetic to the cause, kept himself aloof from the proceedings. Sanjurjo was sentenced to death, reprieved and jailed, then further reprieved and removed himself to exile in Portugal, a military dictator in waiting.

Although the coup failed, a new right-wing coalition, led by Gil Robles of *Acción Popular,* triumphed in elections in November 1933, defeating a disunited opposition amid allegations of widespread electoral fraud, which was a common feature of an archaic electoral system. Results hung on small shifts in voting patterns, often achieved by crude intimidation at the ballot box.

Gil Robles propped up a government formed by the second-largest party, the Radicals. In the next three years a violent backlash from the Left served to justify Fascist retaliation on the Right, with the blue-shirted Falange taking to the streets.

As the violence escalated, further elections were called in February 1936. In exile in Rome, King Alfonso warned of a Communist coup whoever won. The British ambassador in Madrid, Sir Henry Chilton, reported rumours that the Soviet Union had sent one million pesetas to support the Communists.[52] Chilton's own sympathies were not difficult to discern. He allowed the Duke of Alba to deposit his most precious possessions at the embassy for safekeeping. The Duke was president of the custodians of the Prado Museum and had a superlative art collection of his own. Chilton also committed himself to providing refuge in the embassy to forty leading Spanish monarchists whom he regarded as personal friends.[53]

There was astonishment among the right-wing parties when it transpired that the Republicans and Socialists had emerged from the elections with a majority. However, the Socialist leader Largo Caballero decided not to back the new Republican government, believing that without his support they would have to give way to a fully-fledged Socialist administration. He toured Spain prophesying the coming of the Red Revolution and was flatteringly described by the Russian official newspaper *Pravda* as the Spanish Lenin. Sir Henry Chilton warned that he might depose the President and set up a Soviet-style republic.

New labour laws required firms to reinstate and compensate strikers dismissed during an uprising in 1934. Businesses faced new customs duties and tariffs and in June a bill was introduced in the Cortes – the Spanish Parliament – for state control of mines, a direct threat to the British owners Rio Tinto and Consett Steel. There were strikes, sabotage and bomb outrages. At the beginning of July Joseph Mitchell Hood, the British manager of a lace factory in Barcelona, was murdered. On the streets there were increasing signs of a real war, with bombings and the assassination of public officials.

Franco was stuck in the military and political backwater of the Canaries. President Azaña posted him there as military commander and moved General Manuel Goded to Majorca. Britain's military attaché, Colonel Frederick Beaumont-Nesbitt, reported that the Spanish army's two most brilliant officers had been despatched 'to a safe distance'. General Emilio Mola, who would in due course organise the Franco coup, was removed from the key command of Morocco and put in charge of an infantry brigade.[54]

By late March 1936, with municipal elections pending, Chilton reported increasing unrest resulting from the release of political prisoners and criminals under an amnesty. There were persistent rumours of a coup, to be led by an unnamed but distinguished general. In London Evelyn Shuckburgh at the Foreign Office noted resignedly:

There is nothing more we can do except wait for the coup d'état, or the revolution, or whatever is to come.[55]

Sir Arthur Bryant, the right-wing historian and widely read contributor to *The Illustrated London News*, wrote to his friend the Prime Minister, Stanley Baldwin, in April 1936:

> In Spain things are far worse than is realised here. In the big towns and show places it is hidden away. But everywhere else revolution is beginning. I travelled 5,000 miles in Spain and except in Catalonia saw on the walls of every village I visited the symbols of the hammer and sickle, and in the streets the undisguised signs of bitter class hatred fomented by increasing agitation of Soviet agents.[56]

But these events were subordinate to a bigger picture. The Foreign Office was acutely conscious of the weakness of Spain and France, both militarily and because of the political divisions caused by the 'mumps and measles' of world society – Fascism and Communism. It regarded Fascism as an urgent, short-term problem; Communism as a long-term one.[57]

In the words of Sir Robert Vansittart, permanent secretary at the Foreign Office: 'Wherever troubled waters exist, Russia is the compleat angler.'[58]

The Versailles Treaty that followed the First World War was dismissed by Field Marshal Ferdinand Foch, the French commander of Allied Forces, with the words:

'This is not peace. It is an armistice for twenty years.'

For the French it did not go far enough. They wanted a border on the left bank of the Rhine, giving them access to the coalfields of the Saar, but had to settle for a temporary administration by the newly formed League of Nations. They wanted massive reparations to rebuild their shattered land. Britain too, needed reparations, not least to repay its £4 billion war debt to the United States – a debt that remains unpaid to this day. As a result Germany was faced with punitive repayments to the Allies which Winston Churchill, who took part in the peace negotiations, described as 'malignant and silly to an extent that made them futile'.[59]

The Prime Minister, Lloyd George, feared that if pushed too far Germany might succumb to the Communist revolution which had already befallen Russia. France was most afraid of the Teuton while he was most afraid of the Slav, he said.[60]

While Germany nursed the resentment which fostered Nazi-ism, Britain and France continued in distrustful alliance while observing with some alarm the rise in Italy of the Fascist dictator Benito Mussolini. He had been on the payroll of Sir Samuel Hoare, MI5 and MI6's representative in Rome, to the tune of £100 a week as an informant at the end of the First World War.[61]

Sir Samuel had previously been MI6's man in Russia, supplying intelligence on the murder of Rasputin and the rise of the Bolsheviks. As Foreign Secretary in 1935 he figured prominently in the diplomatic manoeuvring over Mussolini's attempts to colonise Abyssinia. Hoare and the Prime Minister of France, Pierre Laval, made a secret deal giving Mussolini most of what he wanted. Hoare's argument was that by placating his old informant he kept him from a closer alignment with Hitler. When the deal was leaked by a French newspaper there was a public outcry. Hoare and Laval were obliged to resign. Mussolini went ahead with his conquest and, with League of Nations sanctions ineffectual, the emperor Haile Selassie took refuge in Britain.

Douglas Jerrold's close friend Sir Charles Petrie had a meeting with Mussolini in June 1936, the month before the Spanish uprising. He wrote afterwards:

Undoubtedly the most important discussion I personally ever had with the Duce was in June 1936, at the end of the Abyssinian war and a week or two before Neville Chamberlain announced the abandonment of sanctions. I had always been opposed to sanctions, and there could be no doubt that British prestige had suffered a serious rebuff in consequence of the Italian victory. Nevertheless, Britain was an infinitely greater Power than Italy, and Mussolini could only have access to his new conquest by leave of the British Navy: therefore the prudent course for him to adopt was to let bygones be bygones, and not to 'rub it in' where Great Britain was concerned; it was the tradition of British diplomacy to accept the fait accompli, and he would find that the Italian conquest of Abyssinia would prove no exception. Otherwise he would see himself compelled to go in with Hitler, and on Hitler's terms, for Italy was not strong enough to stand alone. Mussolini listened most attentively, and made no serious criticism. When the discussion was over he walked from his desk across the great length of the room to the door with his arm round my shoulders, and our leave taking could not have been more cordial.[62]

Hitler had come to power in Germany in January 1933 and rapidly set about consolidating his position in a one-party state, intensifying his persecution of the Jews, and defying the Versailles Treaty by founding the Luftwaffe and re-introducing conscription. British policy was based on an assumption that no major conflict would arise within ten years. Britain regarded France as incapable of mounting a military defence and was dismayed by the signing of a French pact with Russia. The Bolshevik menace still outweighed the Fascist one and in 1935 an Anglo-German naval agreement effectively gave Hitler more scope for re-armament. In March 1936 Hitler's troops re-occupied the Rhineland. In May, in France, the combined left-wing forces of the Popular Front won the election and the Socialist Leon Blum became Prime Minister although the Communists did not join the government.

In November 1935 Ramsay MacDonald's National Government in Britain had given way to a Conservative-led administration with Stanley Baldwin as Prime Minister. He argued that the electorate had shown themselves to be massively against re-armament, as had the Labour Party.

But by 1936 Britain's main ally, France, and her neighbour Spain had Popular Front governments apparently under the sway of the Comintern. How far Stalin was committed to exporting the revolution, rather than establishing a bulwark against Fascism, is open to question but in Britain there was still the strong memory of the murder of the Tsar and his relatives, so closely related to the British royal family. The General Strike and the Jarrow hunger marches raised the spectre of Britain going the same way. According to historian Professor Michael Alpert:

> The dominating concerns in Britain were to try to repair the breach with Italy; to keep the USSR out of Western Europe and to guard vital Mediterranean routes. The recent Anglo-German naval treaty and the removal of sanctions against Italy were hopeful signs of a general settlement. Britain was resolved not be drawn into European wars ...[not] to support Popular Fronts which might sign alliances with the Soviet Union or frighten the Germans and Italians by appearing to be combining against them. In addition, the British armed forces and the defence industries had been run down. Economies had been made in the defence of the Mediterranean bases of Gibraltar, Malta and Suez.
>
> The consequence of all this was the refusal of Britain to give France guarantees over the Rhineland, and weakness towards Italy. Both Left and Right opinion wanted to reduce British commitments abroad...
>
> Britain needed Spanish goodwill in order to safeguard the essential Mediterranean route past Gibraltar. It was a cardinal point of British policy that the Balearics and the Canaries should never be allowed to fall under hostile control, and that the Moroccan side of the Straits of Gibraltar should be occupied by a weak yet friendly Spain. Above all, Spain must be kept out of European alliances.[63]

During the summer of 1936 the Foreign Secretary, Anthony Eden, canvassed the views of his senior ministerial and civil service colleagues about reforming the League of Nations to make it more effective. On 20 July, the day after Franco arrived in Morocco to launch his coup, the Cabinet Secretary, Sir Maurice Hankey, concluded his five-page response with the words:

With France and Spain menaced by Bolshevism, it is not inconceivable that before long it may pay us to throw in our lot with Germany and Italy, and the greater our detachment from European entanglements the better.[64]

CHAPTER 4: THE PROMOTER

Juan March has been described as the most mysterious man in the world, the Spanish Rockefeller and the uncrowned King of the Balearic Islands. He claimed to be the seventh richest man in the world. He had worked for Britain's secret services as an agent of the director of naval intelligence, Captain Reginald 'Blinker' Hall, during the First World War.

March had passed on information for anti-submarine warfare but there were always suspicions that he was playing a double game, provisioning the German U-boats and then betraying them. He was also believed to have run a protection racket for merchant shipping, offering insurance against German attack. Those who chose not to subscribe ran the risk that he would tip off the nearest U-boat as soon as the ship sailed, and collect a 'finder's fee' from Germany for lining up a soft target. The Germans did not necessarily sink the ships; sometimes they captured and impounded them and their cargoes.

March was born on 4 October 1880 in Santa Margarita, Majorca, the son of a poor pig farmer. Although widely believed to be illiterate, he did attend a local school before working for his father and then branching out on his own into farming and property. Smuggling was not an uncommon route out of poverty in Majorca and March made no secret in later years that his first fortune was built on running contraband from North Africa to mainland Spain, particularly tobacco. By 1916 he owned his own shipping line. Very early in March's career a business associate was found murdered. He clearly had most to gain from the death and suspicion naturally fell on him. Yet police and judicial inquiries went nowhere and that was how he acquired a reputation for ruthlessness and a willingness to pay those in authority not to stand in his way.

He turned from poacher to gamekeeper, with a legal monopoly of tobacco supply in Spanish Morocco. In the 1920s, as he fought a running battle with the dictator Primo de Rivera, he bought newspapers to make sure his side of the story was prominently told in Spain. His wealth and power became evident for all to see on his island base. His magnificent residence in the Plaza Almoina in the capital, Palma, faced the Gothic cathedral and the Almudaina Palace, traditional home of Majorcan royalty. It was built on the site of the former Santo Domingo Convent during the Second World War. The March Palace now holds the family trust's collection of modern sculpture, including works by Rodin and Henry Moore, and a library of more than 2,000 manuscripts and 60,000 books

In 1922 March became Majorca's representative in the Cortes, the Spanish Parliament. He was rumoured to have spent £10,000 – equivalent to £200,000 at 2010 prices – getting himself elected. On the Saturday night before the vote he threw a party in the main square for the entire island, with a barbecue consisting of four lambs, ten suckling pigs and 100 chickens.[65]

The British ambassador at the time, Esmé Howard, recorded that the incident explained the discontent of the Right as well as the Left with the conduct of parliamentary elections in Spain. A highly respected parliamentary leader had lost his seat to the immensely rich smuggler king, Don Juan March, whose objective was to get the concession for building a railway from the north to the south of Spain.[66]

That railway line was a continuing scandal for the next twenty years. It was alleged that March had involved members of the Spanish royal family in corrupt commission payments which led to a British company winning the contract. It was to run from Santander on the northern coast via Burgos to Valencia on the Mediterranean, a distance of 430 kilometres. Work began in 1924 and was never completed. It was an era in which the dictatorship of Primo de Rivera planned great public works. With great public works there were great opportunities for private backhanders and Juan March was the master at manipulating them.

The railway contract went to the Anglo-Spanish Construction Company, who deputed a young manager to oversee it from London. It was a testing initiation for David Eccles because the Spanish government simply failed to pay its bill, on grounds of impropriety in the awarding of the original contract. By early 1936 the debt stood at £1.75 million (£65 million at 2010 prices) and despite court orders in their favour, the company could not extract payment. Eccles led a deputation in January 1936 to complain to Sir George Mounsey, a senior figure at the Foreign Office. In the course of the meeting, the delegation told Sir George that the Royalists and right-wing parties were expecting victory in forthcoming elections and were not likely to mount a coup before that date. By implication, a coup was to be expected if they lost.[67]

Like Hugh Pollard and Alan Hillgarth – wartime head of intelligence in Madrid – Eccles was the son of a doctor. William McAdam Eccles lived at 124 Harley Street and Hillgarth's father Willmott Evans at 121. David Eccles married Sybil Dawson, daughter of the King's physician, Lord Dawson, who lived around the corner in Wigmore Street.

Eccles, who became a minister in Winston Churchill's post-war Conservative government, was an ardent Franco supporter. He went on to play an important role in liaising with the Spanish General during the Civil War and was an intelligence officer in Madrid and Lisbon in the Second World War where his duties included extensive bribery to keep Spanish mineral supplies and Portuguese wolfram (tungsten ore), an ingredient in steel making, out of German hands. He also had a hand in ensuring that the Duke and Duchess of Windsor did not fall prey to Nazi overtures during their convoluted progress from France, via the Iberian peninsular, to their wartime quarantine in the governorship of the Bahamas.[68]

In 1931, when Juan March was re-elected to the Spanish Parliament, the Republican government prevented him from taking his seat on grounds of moral incompatibility. He spent the next sixteen months in prison, though his confinement was less arduous than might be expected. He could receive visitors, serve them coffee and brandy and meals prepared by his personal chef, or call on the services of two secretaries.[69] At first he was held on unspecified allegations of high treason and then accused of corruption. It was alleged that he paid one million pesetas to the Queen of Spain in order to get his tobacco monopoly.

This was embarrassing for Britain because Queen Ena – real name Victoria Eugenie of Battenberg – was granddaughter of Queen Victoria, a cousin of King George V and maintained close ties with her homeland. March, in his defence, insisted that the money was for a Red Cross hospital in the Balearics and Queen Ena was their Spanish patron. The embarrassment was compounded in 1933 when Señor March, tiring of his captivity, simply bribed a warder to take him out of the prison and transport him safely to British territory in Gibraltar, where he announced that his escape had been necessary for the sake of his health. The British Foreign Office feared a highly public rift with Spain if the Republican government tried to extradite him.

The British ambassador in Madrid, Sir George Grahame, sent a colourful account of March's character:

> This man is an astonishing figure. Many people say that he is the richest man in Spain and has occult power of the most extensive description; in fact, there is something of an Al Capone about him. He is portrayed as a kind of melodramatic arch-ruffian and is said to have killed someone in Africa with his own hand! A list of those who have received bribes from him in the course of his career would probably astound the world. He was known already twenty years ago as the Smuggler King.[70]

Sir George's predecessor Esmé Howard had plenty of experience of March's smuggling activity in the 1920s. Spanish customs patrol ships regularly arrested feluccas – small sailing boats – and motor launches, flying the British flag but owned by Juan March. He paid British Gibraltarians to act as cover by registering the boats and sailing under British protection to reduce the chances of getting caught. Howard had the job of extricating the British sailors, knowing full well who was behind it and knowing also that the Foreign Minister with whom he had to deal, Santiago Alba, was simultaneously acting as Juan March's legal adviser.

American *Time* magazine reported in November 1933:

A character from Cervantes is illiterate Juan March, richest man in Spain. He rolled up to the yellow stucco Rock Hotel at Gibraltar last week with his jailer and a carload of friends, thumbed his nose at the Government of Spain and went to bed. Sallow Castilians slapped their thighs and swore that Por Dios, Juan had done it again! Every packet of rank, loose-rolled Canarias that Spaniards smoke puts a few centesimos in the pockets of Juan March. Never able to read or write, he laid the foundation of his fortune by selling bootlegged cigarettes made from smuggled tobacco. Last week he decided that he had been in jail long enough, walked out the front door, climbed into a car full of friends and drove off, taking one of the lesser wardens with him.

March had been granted the tobacco franchise in Morocco by Primo de Rivera in the belief that the Spanish government would benefit from the proceeds. March had carried on as before, bribing officials and obtaining illicit tobacco supplies from Moorish tribesmen in exchange for weapons which they then used against the Spanish army. To escape the wrath of Primo de Rivera, March fled to France disguised in a monk's habit. He had returned after the dictator resigned, believing he would be immune from prosecution as a member of the Cortes.

So there was some relief in Britain when Señor March decided to move on from Gibraltar. He was bent on revenge. He had been bribing the Republicans and they had turned against him. He could see that a right-wing coup was imminent and he knew Franco well because he had been Captain General of Majorca, March's island power base. The tobacco baron set up in Biarritz where he began plotting against his Republican accusers by financing the military coup. He organised credit and provided bases for operations in Biarritz, Lisbon, Rome and London. He paid for fuel for the rebel army and sent a message of total support to Franco at the end of June 1936. As proof, he provided an insurance policy of one million pesetas each for the coup leaders plus, for Franco, the equivalent of a year's salary paid into a foreign bank to support his family if needed. March is estimated to have provided backing in the Civil War of anything up to 1,000 million pesetas.[71]

It was March who provided the funds to hire the *Dragon Rapide* that flew from Croydon to collect Franco.

March's London representative in the 1930s was Arthur Frederic Loveday. He worked for Antony Gibbs & Co., founded in 1788 to export wool to Spain. It had developed in the Victorian era into a major trading conglomerate in Spain and South America, with its own merchant bank. Arthur Loveday's family were owners of Wardington Manor north-east of Banbury, Oxfordshire.

After his retirement at the end of the Second World War, Loveday declared his role in British intelligence in his *Who's Who* entry. Born in 1878, he had spent most of his early adult life in South America and it was there he met his wife Mary. His brother-in-law Albert Bennett was Controller of Propaganda for Central and South America at the Ministry of Information during the First World War. Loveday remained in Chile working as a correspondent for *The Times* while simultaneously supplying intelligence, for which he was awarded an OBE in 1919. He moved to Spain in 1921 and continued as a businessman, journalist for the *Morning Post* and British intelligence agent throughout the 1920s and 1930s. He was chairman of the British Chamber of Commerce in Spain in 1932–33.

From 1936–39 he was secretary of the Spanish Children's Repatriation Committee, on which Douglas Jerrold also served. It was a controversial group, partly a propaganda front for Franco, challenging the justification for bringing refugee children caught up in the Spanish Civil War to Britain.

Loveday claimed responsibility for uncovering the Communist plot which, retrospectively, was used to justify the Nationalist coup. In his book *World War in Spain,* published in 1939, he declared:

> The sparks that set light to the conflagration and fixed the date of the rising of the Army officers were two; the discovery of the secret document containing the complete details for the proletarian communist rising with the establishment of a Soviet Spain under the dictatorship of Largo Caballero, and the murder of the leader of the opposition in the Cortes, Señor Calvo Sotelo, under the most savage conditions by uniformed Government police.
>
> As regards the secret document detailing the instructions and outlining the procedure for the proletarian rising timed to start on some date in June or July, 1936, its authenticity was doubted by some people, and the apologists of the Spanish Government attempted to discredit it, saying it was invented subsequently as an excuse for the Civil War. But there need no longer be any doubt about it in the minds of students of history. It was stolen from the anarchist headquarters and a copy brought to England by the writer of this history in June, 1936, a month before the Civil War broke out. Subsequently, during the course of the war, copies of it were found at Communist-Socialist headquarters in Majorca, Seville and Badajoz, after their capture by General Franco's army. The internal evidence of the document's authenticity is so great as to be overwhelming, for, not only were many of the plans and policies laid down in it actually fulfilled, but some of the very people indicated by name for various positions, actually and subsequently filled them.[72]

These documents purported to be the record of a meeting in Valencia on 16 May 1936 at which the orders were drawn up for a Soviet-backed Communist coup in June or July. It was attended, supposedly, by two Russians, Lomovioff and Tourochoff, the

Catalan poet and politician Ventura Gassol, as a delegate of the Third Communist International, and others.

They prepared detailed instructions for a wave of strikes, bombings and assassinations, giving code words and messages to be broadcast to signal the start of the uprising, listing the members of a new government headed by Francisco Largo Caballero. The Socialist Party leader and trade unionist did in fact become Prime Minister of the Republican government after the Franco coup began. The document explained that the signal for the coup would be the bursting of five small bombs at nightfall in Madrid. A general strike would be declared and hit squads would seize the general post and telegraph office, the Prime Minister's office, and the Ministry of War. A special squad composed solely of machine gunners and bombers would attack the Ministry of the Interior.

Despite Loveday's assertion that the documents were undoubtedly authentic, considerable doubt was expressed at the time and subsequently. As early as 30 May 1936 the pro-Republican Spanish newspaper *Claridad* published the details of two of the documents alongside a story denouncing them as Fascist forgeries.[73]

Loveday claimed to have stolen them from the anarchist headquarters a month later. He did not make them public immediately, although there is reason to think that he submitted them to MI6. In any case, he appears to have given a copy to the Marqués del Moral who posted them on 30 August 1936 from the Belmont Hotel in Sidmouth, Devon, with a personal note, to the head of the Foreign Office, Sir Robert Vansittart. He included photographic copies of the documents, and a translation, and said:

I have secured, after much difficulty, certain secret reports and orders of the Socialist-Communist Headquarters in Spain for the rising projected between 3 May and 29 June but postponed. The document is valuable for the list of Ministers of the National Soviet, the liaison officers and other details of their colleagues of the French Socialist Party. I enclose a photocopy and I shall be glad if you will communicate it to the Foreign Office with my compliments. The man who sent it has risked his life in doing so. Unfortunately I received it only three days ago…

Vansittart's private secretary Clifford Norton wrote on the file:

I should prefer not to put anything in writing to M del Moral. I assume he is on the side of the military party. He does not ask for an answer. If he returns to the charge we could tell him orally that we don't believe them to be genuine.[74]

The Foreign Office was right to be cautious. The documents bore some of the hallmarks of two other notorious forgeries, both of which were suspected to be the work of White Russian propagandists intent on discrediting the Soviet government.

The *Protocols of the Elders of Zion*, supposedly an ancient Jewish conspiracy for world domination, were used by Russian exiles to explain the Bolshevik revolution. A version was published by the *Morning Post* in Britain in 1920 and despite rapidly being shown to be a fabrication the idea took root, usually coupled with similar theories about the freemasonry of the Grand Orient.

The deposed King Alfonso XIII of Spain was apparently convinced by it; Nazi Germany's anti-Semitism thrived on it; and there were many in Britain who subscribed too, not least Captain Archibald Maule Ramsay MP, founder of the secret Fascist-supporting Right Club.

Loveday, who was a member of the Right Club, seems to have been a believer. In his book on the Spanish Civil War he laments what he regards as the one-sided British press and broadcasting coverage favouring the Republicans and concludes that:

A clever, well-organised and wealthy propagandist organisation covers the whole world and floods it with tendentious news, expensive books and one-sided literature. Who is it that directs and finances this organisation? The discovery and exposure of the answer to this question would solve many of the troubles of the world, but that some such organisation exists there can be no doubt.[75]

The second and even more sensitive forgery was the Zinoviev letter for which MI6 has been shown to be the chief culprit. In 1924, just as Britain's first Labour Prime Minister Ramsay MacDonald lost a vote of confidence in the House of Commons and called a general election, MI6's Riga station produced a bombshell: a letter from Grigori Zinoviev, president of the Communist International, containing 'strong incitement to armed revolution and evidence of intention to contaminate the Armed Forces'. According to Desmond Morton of MI6, who later became Winston Churchill's personal security adviser while he was Prime Minister, the letter had been separately authenticated by a member of the Makgill Organisation, an industrial intelligence service backed by British businessmen. This agent, it was claimed, confirmed that the letter had been discussed by the Communist Party of Great Britain.

In the last week of the election campaign, on 24 October, the *Daily Mail* published the letter. It caused uproar. The Labour government was already the butt of criticism that it had been soft on Communist agitators and on the next day the Foreign Office issued a strongly worded protest to the Soviet chargé d'affaires, who dismissed the letter as a gross forgery. Labour lost the election although it is a matter of debate to what extent the letter influenced the outcome.

The incoming Conservative administration conducted its own inquiries and was persuaded that the letter was genuine. Behind the scenes MI6 discovered that its Latvia operation was suspect. The documents had been supplied by unidentifiable sources and had probably originated from White Russian forgers anxious to sabotage the MacDonald government's trade pact with the Soviet Union. And whatever the official position, there were many people who believed that the intelligence services had been behind the leaking of the letter to the *Daily Mail*, and possibly even had a hand in its compilation. In the 1970s the British government conducted a new investigation, whose results were not published, and it was not until 1999 that Gill Bennett, chief historian of the Foreign and Commonwealth Office, was commissioned to write a definitive official account.

She confirmed the forgery theory, dismissed the notion of an MI6 orchestrated campaign to discredit a Labour government, but added:

> Information about the proposed forgery could have reached certain members of British Intelligence Agencies who were on the look-out for opportunities to further the Conservative cause in Britain, and to discredit the Labour Party in the process. Anyone in that position, and with a wide net of contacts in London, was well placed not only to vouch for the authenticity of the Letter but also to encourage its dissemination in quarters where profitable – and mischievous – use might be made of it.[76]

There are parallels between the Zinoviev letter and Loveday's Spanish documents. Their contents are not in themselves hugely surprising. They reflect the international campaign to extend Communist control beyond the Soviet Union. In each case the timing is crucial, with the stated intention to de-stabilise an existing left-leaning government at a moment of crisis.

Loveday's intelligence role is confirmed by MI5's recently released files on Captain Archibald Ramsay MP. He was interned in 1940 after Right Club member Tyler Kent, a cipher clerk at the US embassy in London, was found to have been instrumental in leaking secrets to Hitler. Ramsay kept a red leather-bound membership book, in which Loveday's name appeared.

Maxwell Knight of MI5 used two women agents to infiltrate the Club and report back regularly but in June 1939, well before the scandal broke, a senior member of the Security Service, possibly Knight's superior Guy Liddell, spent a long afternoon at the Carlton Club with Captain Ramsay.

The 'pleasantly spoken and sincere' Captain Ramsay began with

a *tour d'horizon* of the gigantic conspiracy being engineered against
Gentiles worldwide. Stalin and Roosevelt were implicated, as were
Admiral Sinclair, the head of MI6, and Sir Robert Vansittart, chief
diplomatic adviser at the Foreign Office. Admiral Sinclair was guilty
of ignoring a number of significant reports, among them some
from his own agent Mr Arthur Loveday relating to the Spanish
Civil War. The MI5 interviewer firmly resisted Captain Ramsay's
insistence that he should meet Loveday and hear his story at length.
At this point the discussion had been going on so long that staff
at the Carlton were obliged to ask the two gentlemen to adjourn
from the terrace as it was required for a private dinner party. They
retreated to an inner sanctum where Captain Ramsay embarked on
a lengthy assertion of the authenticity of the *Protocols of Zion*. The
interviewer, fearing an all night session, declined an invitation to
dinner, made his excuses and left.

But he reported back to the head of MI5, Sir Vernon Kell, and
then went to see Admiral Sinclair at MI6 where he confirmed,
through Sinclair's deputy Major Valentine Vivian, that Loveday
was indeed an agent and that it was Vivian who had rejected his
reports.[77]

In 1938 Juan March formed a British company to handle
his interests in London. As well as himself, J. March & Co. had
three other directors: Arthur Loveday, José Mayorga and Leopold
Walford. Mayorga had been manager of Kleinwort's Bank in
Fenchurch Street, London and had handled the money March put
up to finance Franco's coup. Walford lived in a mansion opposite
Kensington Palace, in the most expensive street in London, and
owned a shipping line. His wife was the the stepdaughter of March's
oldest business associate, Sir Basil Zaharoff.

Zaharoff is the ghost at the feast as far as this story is concerned.
He died of heart failure in November 1936 aged eighty-seven.
Supposedly his early career was as an arsonist for the Constantinople
firemen, who were paid salvage fees for the fires he started. He was
a bigamist, an embezzler, British intelligence agent and arms dealer
who knew how to play enemies off against each other. He sold

submarines to the Greeks and offered them in equal numbers to the Turks.

Zaharoff's most successful merchandise was the Maxim machine gun. When the British firm Vickers bought the company that made it they began a fifty-year association with him. He opened up a Vickers subsidiary in Spain which ran the nation's shipyards in partnership with the government.[78] Among the directors were senior British military figures.

He was granted an honorary British knighthood, much to the fury of King George V who refused to receive Zaharoff formally at Buckingham Palace to bestow the title. He had granted the honour grudgingly at the insistence of Prime Minister Lloyd George who argued it was an essential reward for acting on Britain's behalf during the First World War. Zaharoff induced neutral Greece to join the Allied cause in 1915 and bribed Enver Pasha and other Turkish leaders to desert Germany and make a separate peace in 1917.

According to Foreign Office files kept secret until 2005, Lloyd George had been prepared to pay $25 million – the equivalent of £200 million in 2010 – if the Turks gave up the fight and allowed the British fleet safe passage through the Dardanelles to attack German warships. Some reports say Zaharoff handed over £10m in gold although the Foreign Office files say the eventual deal was for the much smaller sum of seven million French francs. In return Zaharoff demanded his 'chocolate' – the reward of a knighthood.[79]

Winston Churchill knew all about Zaharoff's Turkish operation. It was the perfect template for the deal he sanctioned and Juan March brokered to keep General Franco's Spain out of the Second World War.

CHAPTER 5: RISING STAR

Alan Hillgarth was born at 121 Harley Street on 7 June 1899. His name was neither Alan nor Hillgarth. He was christened George 'Hugh' Jocelyn Evans. His parents were doctors, Willmott Henderson Evans and his wife Ann. Ann was one of the first qualified female doctors and her husband was a champion of the right of women to be admitted to the Royal College of Physicians. They both practised at the Royal Free Hospital, in Gray's Inn Road, central London, where Willmott Evans was a specialist in skin diseases. Hugh Pollard's father Joseph was also an expert in skin diseases at the Royal Free and it seems inevitable that their paths must have crossed. They lived a five-minute walk apart in the medical enclave north of Oxford Street. Although there is an age difference of eleven years it seems likely that Hugh Pollard and 'Hugh' Evans were acquainted.

Willmott Evans was descended from William Evans, an eighteenth-century Welsh Methodist fire and brimstone preacher, and three generations of Royal Navy surgeons.[80] The young Hugh Evans followed in the naval tradition, attending the Royal Naval College, Osborne in 1911, at the age of twelve, and transferring to the Royal Naval College, Dartmouth in 1913, but his education was interrupted the following year with the outbreak of the First World War.[81]

He joined the cruiser HMS *Bacchante*, flagship of what became known as the Livebait Squadron, as a midshipman. The squadron's first duty was to protect British merchant ships in the North Sea. The ships were slow and virtually obsolete. On 22 September 1914 three ships of the squadron were sunk by a single German submarine, with the loss of 1,459 lives. There was a public outcry and Winston Churchill, as First Lord of the Admiralty, took much of the blame even though he had privately recommended that the elderly ships should be transferred to less dangerous duties. HMS *Bacchante* was posted to the Mediterranean for the Gallipoli landings in 1915 and had to move close inshore to fire on Turkish artillery in an attempt to give some protection to infantry landing at Anzac Cove. Midshipman Evans was wounded but recovered to resume his duties as a sub-lieutenant on the battle-cruiser HMS *Princess Royal* on Atlantic patrol in 1917–1918. Captain John Kelly described him as hardworking and thoroughly reliable with a good power of command. A fellow officer wrote:

> An exceptionally valuable officer. He knows his work thoroughly and has been particularly successful in his way of treating the men and running the internal organisation of the ship. As a mess mate he is a great acquisition owing to his unfailing good temper and charming disposition.

However, he also tried unsuccessfully to get a transfer to the Royal Naval Air Service and then faced a court martial, accused of being asleep while on duty as officer of the watch, from which he was acquitted. He was sent to Cambridge University for a year and then to HMS *Dryad* for a navigation course. In 1920 he applied to be put on half pay so that he could spend several months in Switzerland and France improving his French because he had been turned down for an interpreters' course.[82]

During 1920 he was assigned to 'duties for the Director of Naval Intelligence outside the Admiralty'. He served in the light cruiser HMS *Ceres*, patrolling in the Mediterranean and the Black Sea. In February 1922 the ship was at Port Said, at a time when there was unrest over British proposals to grant Egyptian independence under King Fuad. The ship's captain, John im Thurn, was an expert in wireless and signals. He deputed Lieutenant Evans to assist on the local military wireless board which was attempting to set up a secure transmission system and prevent jamming by rebel factions. Knowledge of wireless transmission systems was to come in handy later when Evans maintained communications between Majorca and British ships in the Mediterranean during the Spanish Civil War. Captain im Thurn's brother Donald had been an MI5 agent in the First World War and had business connections with Russia. In 1928, during a parliamentary inquiry, he admitting passing a copy of the Zinoviev letter to the press. He had been one of the first to know of its existence. Donald im Thurn's closest confidant during the Zinoviev affair had been Major Guy Kindersley MP, sometime director of Eyre and Spottiswoode, and uncle of Hugh Kindersley, a business associate of Juan de la Cierva.

It was while HMS *Ceres* was in port in Gibraltar on 18 October 1921 that Hugh Evans contracted an unlikely and short-lived marriage, in the Rock's register office, to Violet Tapper. He was twenty-three, she was twenty-seven and this was her second marriage.

Her marriage to Hugh Evans was no more successful than her first. After the wedding they had lived together at the Hotel Reina Christina in Algeciras before returning to London and setting up home in St John's Wood. During divorce proceedings in 1924 she accused him of committing adultery with an unknown woman at the Westcliff Hotel, Westcliff-on-Sea in July of that year. He was said to have no job and to be living at Rose Court, Pluckley in Kent.

Evans's naval career came to an end about the same time. He had successfully completed a gunnery course in 1921 but in May 1922 a senior officer's report stated:

> Not likely to go far. Chief defect an irritating and bad manner with subordinates. Has carried out duties satisfactorily as far as ability goes.

He was placed on the retired list at his own request in September 1922, with the rank of lieutenant. In August 1923 he commuted his annual pension of £97 for a one-off lump sum of £1,370. In 1924 he applied successfully to the Board of Trade for a master's certificate, qualifying him to command private vessels, and had to get it replaced a year later after a motor yacht that he was commanding blew up.[83]

This mysterious incident occurred on the night of 8 April 1925 in the Spanish port of Almeria when the 80-foot, twin-engine, wooden motor yacht *Constance*, carrying 100 gallons of fuel, exploded and rapidly burnt out. There was nobody on board and since the *Constance* was moored away from other yachts in the harbour the fire did not spread.

Lloyd's insurance assessors were unable to discover the cause of the explosion and the vessel was written off. The 60-ton yacht, bound for Gibraltar, had only just arrived after cruising down the coast from Monte Carlo via Barcelona and Alicante. She belonged to Sir Cecil Harcourt Smith, recently retired after fifteen years as the first director of the Victoria and Albert Museum and about to take up the position of Surveyor of the King's Works of Art – a post later filled by the KGB agent Sir Anthony Blunt.[84]

Around this time Hugh Evans visited Morocco and witnessed for himself the bloody insurrection led by the Rif leader Abd el-Krim against the Spanish army in Morocco. It was a period when he could indulge his passions for writing, travel and adventure. His life entered a new phase, socially and professionally, and he adopted the pen name Alan Hillgarth. He embarked on a series of popular novels, with an element of autobiography in them, including *The Princess and the Perjurer*, *The Passionate Trail* and *The War Maker*.

The last of these, published in 1926, included a dedication reading:

> Adventure was once a noble appellation, borne proudly by men such as Raleigh and Drake. Unfortunately, like so many fine old words, it has now sunk to a poor use, being reserved for the better-dressed members of the criminal classes. This is so palpably a misnomer that it becomes in itself a crime.[85]

The book's opening scene is set on the terrace of a hotel in Algeciras, and involves the British hero gun-running to the Rif leader Abd el-Krim in a yacht which comes under naval attack.

Hillgarth also began a romance that would lead to a scandalous divorce case in which he was named as the guilty party by the aggrieved husband. On 21 May 1928, in the High Courts of Justice, the President of the Probate, Divorce and Admiralty Division, Lord Merrivale, granted a *decree nisi* to Geoffrey Hope Hope-Morley, son and heir of Lord Hollenden. The court had heard that his wife, Mary Gardner, daughter of Lord Burghclere, had committed adultery with Alan Hillgarth on the 2nd and 3rd of January that year at the Savoy Hotel in The Strand, just a couple of hundred yards from the court, and 'on divers occasions' before and after that date at Hillgarth's home.[86] She and her husband had been living apart for some time.

Hillgarth's relationship with Mary brought about a huge change in his social standing, even though divorce carried a stigma. As a child she had school lessons in Buckingham Palace alongside the young Prince Albert – the future King George VI who acceded to the throne soon after the start of the Spanish Civil War and reigned throughout the Second World War. He knew her affectionately as Lion, because of her mane of golden hair. His parents, King George V and Queen Mary, sent her personal wedding presents.

Mary's mother Winifred was the daughter of the 4th Earl of Carnarvon, one of the great statesmen of the Victorian age, and sister of the fifth Earl, the celebrated Egyptologist who discovered Tutankhamun's tomb in the Valley of the Kings. Mary knew Spain well and was related to Esmé Howard, the former ambassador. Her favourite uncle, Mervyn Herbert, had been First Secretary at the Madrid embassy in the early 1920s. Her aristocratic and diplomatic pedigree played an important and entirely unsung part in Alan Hillgarth's secret work in Spain during the Second World War. She was obliged to be the reluctant hostess to Falangists and Fascists whose beliefs she detested. It contributed to a severe strain on her marriage which eventually jeopardised the covert relationship with Franco's generals.

Hillgarth's relationship with Mary Gardner brought him into contact with the bright young things of the late 1920s. The author

Evelyn Waugh, encountering him at a country house weekend, wrote: 'Very sure of himself, writes shockers, ex-sailor.'[87] Waugh was briefly Hillgarth's brother-in-law after marrying Mary's younger sister, also named Evelyn, in June 1928. By September 1929 he was filing for divorce after his wife admitted adultery.[88]

On 24 February 1928 the *London Gazette* carried a notice that Hugh Evans had changed his name by deed poll to Alan Hugh Hillgarth. He then took off to Bolivia on a gold prospecting trip which brought him no riches but the material for another novel, *The Black Mountain*.[89] He married Mary at Chelsea Register Office on 2 January 1929 and they set off for the Mediterranean and the island of Majorca. Years later, Mary recalled their first years together were spent virtually penniless, living in primitive surroundings.[90]

Their son Jocelyn was born in September 1929 and the family spent most of their time in mainland Spain and Majorca. They planned a round-the-world cruise in a converted Dutch pilot schooner, the *Blue Water*, but shortage of funds meant they opted to stay in Majorca. In 1932 they bought a substantial but semi-derelict property, Son Torella, about fourteen miles from the capital, Palma. At first they could not afford furniture and lived on the boat during the two years it took to make the house habitable. According to Jocelyn, who contributed substantially to his mother's memoirs, there were cows in the stables, donkeys tethered round the patio and contraband tobacco stored in the galleries.[91] This implies an early encounter with Juan March who controlled the illicit tobacco trade.

The restoration, which included a library eventually accommodating 15,000 books, was paid for out of his mother's small private income and a fortuitous half-share in a winning lottery ticket bought with an Austrian barman called Joe in Terreno.

Since Alan Hillgarth had already commuted his navy pension, and had only royalties and film rights from his novels to live on, it is surprising that he took on a virtually full-time, unpaid job as British vice-consul for the island. Interestingly, before the Foreign Office could confirm the appointment, in December 1932, they had to ask the Admiralty's permission, even though Lt Cdr Hillgarth had gone on the Retired List in 1922 yet been promoted to his current rank in 1927. The Foreign Office file noted:

> The Admiralty have no objection to his accepting the appointment … but [they] would continue to have first claim on his services in the event of war or emergency.[92]

This smacks of an unacknowledged intelligence role and certainly his job entailed considerably more than getting drunken British seamen out of Spanish jails. When the full-time diplomat Gerald Meade, vice-consul in Barcelona, went to inspect the island in September 1934 he produced a report on Hillgarth's confidential work which has been excluded from the Foreign Office files.

As well as providing help and advice to British residents and tourists, keeping birth, marriage and death registers, issuing visas and furnishing the office out of his own pocket, Hillgarth was keeping a close watch on the 'many shady characters' suspected of drug running and on the movements of shipping. He recorded the visits of seventy-eight warships during 1933 among them British ships of the Mediterranean and Atlantic squadrons. The Balearic Islands were strategically important because of their proximity to Italy, which coveted them; as a staging post to the Straits of Gibraltar and the main Mediterranean shipping routes; and as a refuelling stop for limited range air transport between Europe and North Africa. Vice-consul Meade reported:

> Lt Cdr Hillgarth is very conscientious with regard to his duties which he performs with efficiency and intelligence. He is fortunate in possessing considerable private means and, ably assisted by his wife … he does a good deal of entertaining. He and his wife are very popular on the island and they are on very friendly terms with the Governor, Captain General, and other high officials, and the Vice-Consul is thus in an excellent position to intercede on behalf of any British subject who finds himself in trouble with the Authorities. It

is fortunate that Lt Cdr Hillgarth has no business activities, as he is obliged to devote several hours a day to consular duties.[93]

The Captain General with whom Lt Cdr Hillgarth was on such friendly terms was General Francisco Franco. Although Franco had refused to join General Sanjurjo's ill-fated coup in August 1932, the Prime Minister Manuel Azaña was not totally convinced of his loyalty. In January 1933 Franco had suffered a personal humiliation when the reorganisation of the military high command relegated him from first to twenty-fourth in the pecking order of brigadier generals. Azaña made a small conciliatory gesture the following month by giving him command of the Balearic Islands, which would normally have gone to someone of higher rank, while privately commenting that 'he will be far from any temptations'. Franco had not been fooled and had made his resentment plain. Nevertheless, he set about improving the island's defences, which would turn out to be a worthwhile exercise during the Civil War, and rebuffed an approach to become a right-wing candidate in Madrid in the elections later that year. He got his reward in March 1934 when a new government made him the youngest Major-General in Spain.[94]

Hillgarth expended a great deal of time and effort in the second half of 1935 trying to obtain the release of Captain Alexander Kane, master of the steam ship *Brompton Manor*. Captain Kane, on his first visit to Spain and speaking not a word of the language, had put into port at Mahon on the island of Menorca in mid-June and spent a day with three of his fellow officers refreshing themselves in the island's bars, ending up at 3am in the *Los Chatos* cabaret where they got into a dispute over a bar bill. Pushing and shoving occurred and Captain Kane found himself arrested at gunpoint.

At a *Tribunal de Urgencia* in Majorca he was sentenced to two years and eleven months in prison for a public order offence of assaulting a policeman. This was a minimum sentence taking into account the mitigating circumstances of Captain Kane's partial inebriation.

Hillgarth drafted a four-page missive to the Justice Minister in Madrid demanding that the three judges of the tribunal be impeached on the grounds that they had been prejudiced against the defendant and failed to listen to the evidence. One judge had read a book throughout the hearing, he claimed.

The ambassador, Sir George Grahame, had no intention of forwarding such an explosive document, judging that it would only inflame the situation. He stuck to the preferred Foreign Office option of quiet diplomacy, which so often appears to the outsider as masterful inactivity.

It did nothing to placate Hillgarth, who raged against the creaking inefficiency of Spanish bureaucracy and implied that the British embassy was equally enervated. This so irritated the counsellor at the embassy, George Ogilvie Forbes, that he suggested to London that Hillgarth should be removed from his post. But in London the Foreign Secretary was facing angry questions in the House of Commons, from Winston Churchill among others, about the disproportionate sentence and the officials had to admit, privately, that Hillgarth had a point. Norman King, the consul in Barcelona who was responsible for Hillgarth, attempted to smooth over the accusation that he had been throwing his weight around by explaining:

> Hillgarth has a very keen sense of the propriety of things and seems liable to forget that he is no longer a naval officer giving orders, and I gather … that the dilatory action, or lack of action, on the part of the local authorities has irritated him now and then.

Captain Kane was eventually released just before Christmas 1935, having served six months, and emerged not much worse for his ordeal into the waiting clutches of a reporter from Lord Beaverbrook's *Daily Express*.[95]

In December 1935 Alan and Mary Hillgarth played host to a disgruntled Winston Churchill, who had just been passed over for a Cabinet position in the new Conservative-led government formed by Stanley Baldwin. Churchill had already been outspoken about the need for re-armament to counterbalance Germany's rapidly increasing military might and had been included by Baldwin, earlier in the year, in a secret sub-committee working on ways to increase aircraft production. Churchill nursed hopes of a Cabinet recall but Baldwin, aware that a by-election result and a Peace Ballot showed the electorate's deep antipathy to re-armament, had aligned his campaign accordingly and did not feel that Churchill's aggressive stance was in keeping with party policy. He later explained:

> One of my biggest problems was whether to include Winston in the Cabinet. We may not get through this business without a war. If we do have a war, Winston must be Prime Minister. If he is in now we shan't be able to engage in that war as a united nation.[96]

Unaware of this backhanded compliment, Churchill and his wife Clementine took an extended family holiday, starting in Majorca. They stayed at the luxurious Hotel Formentor on the northern coast but Churchill spent time at Son Torella relaxing and painting, well supplied with food and drink, and deep in discussion about the political developments in Spain. He formed a strong impression of the merits of the vice-consul, quite probably prompted by a shared delight in adventure.[97]

From there he moved on to Barcelona in the week before Christmas. He recalled:

> Our comfortable Barcelona hotel was the rendezvous of the Spanish Left. In the excellent restaurant where we lunched and dined were always several groups of eager-faced, black-coated young men purring together with glistening eyes about Spanish politics, in which quite soon a million Spaniards were to die.[98]

He stayed on, painting in the sunshine, then cruised to Tangier where he met up with Lord Rothermere, owner of the *Daily Mail*, and went on to Marrakesh to meet the former Prime Minister and Liberal leader Lloyd George. So there was no shortage of powerful men picking up the prevailing currents in Spain. Churchill only returned to Britain on hearing of the sudden death of King George V on 20 January 1936.

This brought to the throne King Edward VIII and for most of the ensuing year Britain was distracted by his desire to wed the double-divorcee Wallis Simpson, with Baldwin upholding parliamentary and constitutional propriety and Churchill seeking to play honest broker to accommodate the King's wishes.

The new King had spoken approvingly in the past of the benefits of dictatorship and had been supportive of the German re-occupation of the Rhineland. The political diarist Chips Channon described him as 'going the dictator way … and … against too much slip-shod democracy'.[99]

In the days before the Abdication, in December 1936, Sir John Reith, director general of the BBC, wrote in his diary:

> I suppose anything might happen in the country now; it might be the end of the monarchy, or we might have the King as a sort of dictator, or with Churchill as PM, which is presumably what that worthy is working for.[100]

The prevailing political mood for many in Britain was that dictatorships were not necessarily a bad thing, especially for foreigners. From those quarters General Franco was assured of a sympathetic reception.

CHAPTER 6: DRAGON RAPIDE

Luis Bolin's original instructions had been to hire a seaplane that could fly direct to the Canaries and then to Morocco without needing clearance to land on an airstrip. Juan de la Cierva realised at once that this was impossible and recommended instead hiring a *Dragon Rapide* DH89 from Olley Air Service at Croydon Aerodrome.

The prototype had first flown in 1934, developed by de Havilland as a twin-engine air taxi with a cruising speed of 132mph and a range of just under 600 miles. The plane Bolin hired was an executive version with room for only six passengers plus the pilot.

Captain Gordon Olley, like many of his contemporaries, had learned his trade during the First World War. He started out as a despatch rider with the Royal Flying Corps before graduating to observer and then pilot. Post-war he was test pilot for Handley Page and then charter flying manager for Imperial Airways who commanded the lion's share of the scheduled traffic.

In the 1920s and 1930s his client list included the Prince of Wales, King Albert of the Belgians, film star Douglas Fairbanks, singer Josephine Baker and leading jockeys Steve Donoghue, Gordon Richards and Harry Wragg. He was personal pilot to wealthy patrons, chief among them Alfred Loewenstein and his business partner Sir James Dunn.[101] They led a flamboyant lifestyle flitting between high society and dubious deals from their base in Biarritz. They had fingers in many pies, among them the Barcelona Traction Company which provided electricity to the whole of Catalonia and would later become the focus of a financial scandal involving MI6.

Alfred Loewenstein died in mysterious circumstances on a flight when Olley was not at the controls. Travelling from Britain to France, he apparently stepped out of the aircraft, fell 4,000 feet into the English Channel and died, not from the fall but through drowning. The incident has never been satisfactorily explained.[102]

Aviation was still a fledgling industry, unfettered by bureaucracy and regulation. It was dangerous and unpredictable but Olley and his airline enjoyed a good reputation. Croydon was London's main airport, handling 132,000 passengers a year. The winged-globe emblem of Imperial Airways greeted passengers as they arrived at the art-deco headquarters. In the radio tower on top of the building, looking out over the grass runways, the first system of air traffic control was developed.

Private charters were the fashionable thing. Captain Olley, diminutive but elegantly dressed in Savile Row suits and habitually with a Craven A cigarette on the go, was a familiar figure in the lobbies of the best London hotels, making sure the doormen, porters and receptionists knew it was worth their while to send potential passengers in his direction. His catchphrase was 'Good Golly, it's Olley.'

At first he was chief salesman, pilot and mechanic, with a local girl, Muriel Rignall, straight from secretarial college, to handle the admin. Business was expanding and in 1935 he took over a small rival firm, run by long distance aviation pioneer Sir Alan Cobham, and in doing so acquired his chief pilot, Cecil Bebb.[103]

Bebb, born in 1905, had served in the RAF from 1921–29 and had been with Cobham Aviation since 1931, touring Africa and barnstorming around the country – stunt flying and offering joyrides.

For Olley and Bebb, each day might herald a different destination in the UK or across Europe. Sightseeing trips over London were a ten shilling treat for the better-off. The casinos at Deauville and Le Touquet paid them to fly high-rollers out from London and in 1937, after King George VI's coronation, they flew the Prime Minister and members of the Cabinet over central London to view the illuminations.[104]

Although the airline bore Olley's name and he acted as its front man he did not actually own the company. The principal shareholder and financial backer was Sir Hugo Cunliffe-Owen, who had his own aircraft factory. Between 1935 and 1937 he loaned Olley nearly £100,000 – equivalent to £3.7m in 2010 – to get started and to finance rapid expansion. Olley had taken over companies running routes to Liverpool, Blackpool, the Isle of Man and Ireland.

Cunliffe-Owen named one of his string of race horses, which included winners of the Derby and the Oaks, FlyOlley. He was a director of the Midland Bank. His sister had married into the Wills tobacco family and he began his career in the family business, making his fortune and eventually becoming chairman of British American Tobacco (BAT). He had been responsible for expanding BAT's interests in China, where one of his representatives was Roger Hollis, a future director of MI5. As one of the leading lights in the international tobacco trade he would have been well acquainted with Juan March who was bankrolling Franco's coup from Biarritz.

In 1933 Cunliffe-Owen set up an investment vehicle, the Tobacco Securities Trust, which organised a buy out of Boots the Chemist from its American owners. His business partner for this enterprise was Sir James Dunn, who was also a minor shareholder in Olley Air Service. Dunn was a friend of fellow Canadian Lord Beaverbrook, proprietor of the *Daily Express* and future Minister of Aircraft Production in Churchill's War Cabinet. Cunliffe-Owen held a senior position at the Ministry of Information under Beaverbrook during the First World War, directing propaganda towards the Far East. His older brother, Frederick, had been a diplomat and was military attaché in Istanbul at the start of the Great War.

In 1938, two years after bringing Franco to power, Olley Air Service was taken over by British and Foreign Aviation, part owned by Harley Drayton, a legendary figure in the City for his discretion in handling large amounts of sensitive investment. He was rumoured to handle investments for the royal family and the Church of England.

It is unlikely that Luis Bolín and Juan de la Cierva simply chanced on Olley Air Service. Cunliffe-Owen's extensive commercial and social connections may well have been known to them. Cobham and Bebb had been making semi-secret flights to Tangier, hoping to use the airport there as a route from London to Gibraltar. Olley's private flight records show that he had provided a plane for a tour of Algeria and Morocco by naval officers and that Bebb and another pilot, Frederick Midgley, spent the first week of June 1936 on a trip that took in Cannes, Marseilles, Barcelona, Seville, Granada, Casablanca, Tangier and Fez. It could almost have been a rehearsal but there is no record of their passengers. June was a time of frenetic activity among the Spanish army officers plotting the coup.

So the proposition that Bolín put to Olley and Bebb may not have been as far fetched as it sounds today. He wanted them to take him and his three guests, Major Pollard and the two young ladies, to the Canaries. They were to fly via Bordeaux, Lisbon and Casablanca but they were on no account to land in Spain. At that stage Bolín's instructions were to wait in Casablanca for a messenger to authorise the next leg of the journey. If no message arrived by 31 July they were to return to London.

Olley, according to Bolín, asked no awkward questions, although he did require an insurance indemnity for the *Dragon Rapide*, G-ACYR, which was to make the trip.[105]

Bebb, according to his later account, was under the impression that they were to collect a rebel leader of the Rif mountain tribesmen who were in revolt against Spanish rule and fly him to northern Morocco. This seems a flimsy cover story but even the plotters may have been uncertain what journey the plane was to undertake. On Saturday 11 July, the day that the flight departed, General Franco was not actually part of the plot.

In February the new Republican government had appointed Franco Commandant General of the Canary Islands, an important position but in his eyes it constituted a demotion and banishment. Before setting off for the islands he discussed the possibility of a coup with a number of his fellow officers, among them General

Emilio Mola. They agreed that if there were to be a rising it should be led by General Sanjurjo who had gone into exile in Portugal after his previous failed attempt.

While Franco smouldered on his far off island, developing an obsession with golf and planning a Scottish holiday in July to improve his game, General Mola was busy organising the coup. Various officers and politicians came and went from his headquarters in Pamplona during May and June. Franco, while aware of what was going on, was not central to the organisation and was less than enthusiastic, doubting the level of support and telling General Orgaz, who had also been banished to the Canaries, that seizing power would be immensely difficult and bloody.

Mola and his supporters wanted Franco on board, not only for his military skills but because his presence would cause others to fall into line. He was still their chosen candidate to lead the Spanish-Moroccan army despite an ambiguous letter he wrote to the Prime Minister. It implied that he was the man to help the Republicans prevent a coup while simultaneously dealing severely with Communist disturbances.

His fellow conspirators derisively nicknamed him 'Miss Canary Islands 1936' but they continued to include him in their plans while he played hard to get. For that reason one of the rebels, Francisco Herrera, flew to Biarritz on 3 July and saw Juan March the next day, persuading him to finance the hiring of a plane to ensure that Franco could get to Morocco if he did decide to take part. Once March agreed, Herrera informed the Marqués de Luca de Tena, editor of the newspaper *ABC*, who issued his instructions to Luis Bolin in London on 5 July. The plane was booked on 6 July in Croydon and the flight paid for in cash on 9 July. But Franco was still refusing to say whether he was in or out and on Sunday 12 July, when the *Dragon Rapide* was already heading for Lisbon, he sent a message to say that did not believe the time was right.

General Mola, who only received the message on 14 July, was furious and decided to manage without Franco. He sent the Spanish aviator Juan Antonio Ansaldo to Portugal to collect General Sanjurjo and take him to Morocco to lead the army instead. Sanjurjo had seen service in Morocco in 1909 and in 1920. His success in quelling the tribal riots had earned him the nickname 'Lion of the Rif' and later the official title Marqués del Rif. Bebb's story of expecting to fly a Rif leader to North Africa may have emanated from that. His Spanish passengers had spent part of 12 July in Lisbon in talks with Sanjurjo. At this point one of the leading figures of right-wing politics, Calvo Sotelo, was assassinated and the conspirators decided the uprising could wait no longer. It was enough to convince Franco, who heard about it on 14 July while on the golf course and and declared to his playing partner: 'This is the last straw.' So Bebb was told to continue his journey from Casablanca. Had he not been there when Franco made his decision he could not have got to the Canaries in time.[106]

CHAPTER 7: THE FLIGHT

According to Hugh Pollard's daughter Diana, in a 1983 interview for the Imperial War Museum, there were six or seven people on the *Dragon Rapide* when it left Croydon – Bebb the pilot, an unnamed radio operator and possibly another man, Luis Bolin, her father, herself and Dorothy. They picked up the Marqués de Merito in Bordeaux and possibly dropped off the man whose name she didn't know. They reached Bordeaux in pouring rain, to be greeted by the Marqués and a group of fellow Spanish conspirators who made it fairly obvious they were up to no good. She went on:

> For the first time one got a picture that perhaps it wasn't just taking a plane to Africa. These Spaniards hitching a lift added a sort of MI5 interest. They wore their usual dark suits and tidy hats and they had more than one passport. They showed us those as if it would comfort one. In fact one was rather surprised. They were clearly nervous men.
>
> Bolin, obviously being secret, went out because they didn't wish to be overheard. They made a little group in the pouring rain. I thought: Well! If that's a conspiracy and anybody is watching what on earth are they going to think?
>
> Bebb was cheeky and professional – didn't drink and when he was worried he sucked oranges. And he had lots of reasons to get worried as time went on. I respected him for being very professional. If there was a matter of skill he wasn't under the weather like the wireless operator who was totally drunk and useless. We can't have given the impression of rich tourists. We took our best clothes, a

hat and gloves and a small suitcase with two cotton dresses. You took as little as you could.

After Bordeaux we got into this spy thing. These Spaniards insisted on flying over the whole of Spain without stopping. They were very excited and nervous. I hadn't seen men on adventures before. I think they showed it more than women.

In Lisbon we were told things were very frightening and the Spanish part of the party couldn't continue. Calvo Sotelo was murdered about that time. It gave them a very bad shock. There was a great deal of murdering going on by the Left of the Right and this was driving them into desperation. The war was really starting quite without Franco.

These men said it was no good going on … but once my father was involved in an adventure he wouldn't stop and he said there was no reason why we shouldn't go on. So Bebb said we would pop down to Casablanca. At Casablanca we asked the consul to send the wireless operator home.

I think I was carrying the papers [my father] had to deliver, wrapped up in a copy of *Vogue*. I didn't see the papers; I wasn't going to ruffle through them. I just clutched them.

Next place was Port Juby. Just after we left Agadir we could see the waves beating on the desert shore, wrecks marking the coast … and Bebb eating oranges. Port Juby was just a couple of tiny sheds and Spanish Moroccan soldiers had to stay there three or four years. Well they had never seen anything like this come out of the sky: two girls with hats and gloves. We had to refuel the aeroplane from the back of a camel. They asked us in for lunch. It was real Sahara. They put on a gramophone and we danced the tango with them, which was rather stupid.

My father was a little bit worried. He hadn't thought we'd end up in a place like this with no way of getting away. The Commandant said he was very sorry but everywhere was closed and all aerodromes shut down and we couldn't continue. My father said there were no facilities for women and he couldn't leave these beautiful ladies in such a situation. And then people had very good manners, even if they were going to kill you they would apologise. We didn't waste one minute. We got on the plane and headed for Gran Canaria. As soon as we left they sent up an army plane to catch us because the message from Gran Canaria was to stop us. But we were faster so we landed in Las Palmas and they impounded the aeroplane.

Now the difficulty was that my father had to deliver these papers to the next island and we were the object of great suspicion. It was a good thing my father was there – I wouldn't have had the nous. We went into this English hotel and put down our cases. We shot out of the back of the hotel and down to the port. We went off to Tenerife and stayed at a small hotel. My father had to take the papers to a local dentist who could get them to General Franco.

The next morning some very fashionable young men arrived with an enormous map and spread it on a table with a great deal of hush hush in the middle of the patio and sat down there … they had to make a plan to get Gen Franco off the island and … back to Africa.

At this point fate intervened. General Amado Balmes, military commander in Gran Canaria, shot himself, apparently accidentally, in the stomach at a shooting range and Franco could legitimately claim his presence was required at the funeral.

Franco and his entourage travelled there on the same boat as Hugh Pollard and the two girls. Diana recalls:

At Gran Canaria Franco was taken somewhere off shore. We went back to the hotel and you could see people shooting each other behind sand dunes. The assistant consul used to come in with stories. It was decided that Dorothy and I and my father would get the boat back and Bebb would fly Franco to Morocco. I think it was about three weeks before we got a boat and then we were given a state room. Shooting and stuff went on for a bit of time. We mostly stayed in the hotel. It was very nasty for those involved. We were offered a decoration by Franco. The Foreign Office were frightfully stuffy. They didn't want us to go over there and have it pinned on our bosoms. They would rather sweep it all under the carpet.[107]

According to shipping records, they arrived at the Port of London on 30 July aboard the Royal Mail Lines ship *Highland Brigade* which had called at the Canaries en route from Argentina and Brazil.

Diana's account is supplemented by letters Dorothy Watson wrote to a couple of friends in a kind of running commentary, although Hugh Pollard seems to have ensured that they did not get posted until the mission was completed. On the night before the flight she wrote excitedly from the Welbeck Hotel, in Welbeck Street, Marylebone:

> We have been in town all day and are staying at a most posh hotel, hence my writing to you as I just had to use their notepaper. I know very little of our movements except that we shall most likely be at Bordeaux for lunch and Lisbon for dinner, stay the night and next day proceed, probably, to Casablanca. I don't know if we go on anywhere from there or proceed slowly back by Algiers and Fez. We will decide everything when we get there. In case of accidents I am insured for £1,000 which I have directed be sent to you, so you can go a bust on the proceeds.

Her next communication was from Oporto, where she reported:

> It is now 9 o'clock and the funniest scene you ever saw is taking place. We landed at the 'drome here, on the beach, and were immediately surrounded by ragged caricatures of gypsies, and two airforce men, one in uniform and one in a clown's get up, sort of mechanic I think – they were thrilled with us, and we can't speak Portuguese and they can't speak French or English so things are definitely amusing. We had a marvellous drive to Oporto from the aerodrome – there was a fiesta in town – the firemen's night out! All the firemen in polished helmets letting off fireworks and generally making whoopee. Suppose I should write to Dad to tell him I'm here – he doesn't know yet – or shall I send him a postcard from Casablanca?

Finally, on Wednesday 15 July she wrote from Hotel Pino de Oro, Santa Cruz, Tenerife describing the rough crossing from Gran Canaria, with passengers being seasick, and the scenery ... flowering trees of all kinds everywhere, and marvellous palms, banana and pepper trees. They feasted on delicious bananas, figs, baby honey apricots and yellow plums. She and Diana were hoping to stop at Casablanca and Marrakesh on the way back to buy souvenirs. She at least was playing the part of the carefree tourist.[108]

While Diana's recording was made long after the event, it is in many ways the most dispassionate and credible. It points up some of the discrepancies that emerge from the earlier descriptions by those concerned to create the mythology of Franco's rise to power. There are question marks over who was on board the plane at different times; how strictly secrecy was maintained; the roles the various individuals played; and the degree to which the Spanish authorities were aware of their mission.

The drunken radio operator, whom she and Dorothy mention, is common to every account yet none mentions his name or explains why it is left to Major Pollard to remove him from the flight at such a crucial juncture when it would appear to be the pilot's responsibility. According to Luis Bolin, no regular Olley Air Service radio operator was available and he was brought in specially.

To further complicate matters, there are two candidates for the role of flight engineer. In some interviews Cecil Bebb identifies him as George Bryers but another possibility is Walter Petre, Olley's chief engineer. They may even have both started the flight and one acted as radio operator. One or other would have had to travel separately from Bordeaux to Casablanca to make way for the Marqués de Merito.

Petre's family believe that he took part in the whole mission and it would seem to make sense that he should. He flew frequently with Bebb, including a trip to Spain in February 1936, and in March accompanied another of Olley's best pilots, Sammy Morton, on a flight to Barcelona, Valencia and Malaga. He and Bebb remained lifelong friends and kept in touch into their nineties. His flight log, still in the family's possession, records that he was in the *Dragon Rapide* with Bebb for the later stages, ferrying the leaders of the coup between Biarritz and Perpignan at the end of July, but contains no entries for mid-July.

He came from a staunch Roman Catholic family descended from the Barons Petre of Essex, one of whom died in the Tower of London, falsely accused of plotting to assassinate King Charles II. Walter Petre's father was a Rear Admiral and several close relatives were aviation pioneers. One founded the Australian Flying Corps; another, Mildred Petre, made an unsuccessful attempt to fly one of La Cierva's *autogiros* from Croydon to the Cape of Good Hope. According to Walter Petre's daughter Geraldine he was on the flight from the beginning to the end:

> It was a charter out of Croydon. They were told where to go but not why. There was a radio operator whose name he couldn't remember. They got as far as North Africa and the radio operator got drunk in the souk so they flew on without him. They were just told to pick up some passengers. There were three or four of them. They got on in civilian clothes. My father turned round to say they were landing in a couple of minutes and recognised Franco who had changed into his uniform. I think they were pretty horrified when they realised who they had on board. There was nothing much they could do about it and anyway they had reached their destination.[109]

George Ovey Bryers was a complete contrast to Petre. He was a proper Cockney, born and brought up within the sound of Bow bells in East London. His father, William, a journeyman scalemaker, died of peritonitis in 1903, when George was six. His mother, Elizabeth, was too poor to support the family and a series of increasingly desperate letters show how she pleaded for George and his younger brother and sister to be taken into an orphanage. The two boys went to George Müller's Orphan House, a great grey brick building at Ashley Down on the outskirts of Bristol. It had a reputation for providing boys with a good education. Their records show that in

1911 George, aged fourteen, was sent to Thomas Osbourne's Supply Stores, at Nancledra, a small village in tin mining country south of St Ives in Cornwall. He was indentured for five years and then served with the Royal Welsh Fusiliers in the First World War. In the 1920s he worked as a ground engineer in Egypt, probably for the RAF or for the new Imperial Airways service to India, returning to Britain in 1930. In 1935 he was flight engineer on an Olley *Dragon Rapide* chartered by Lord Beaverbrook for a European tour.

It is possible that George Bryers began to get cold feet as the operation dragged on and the likelihood of getting shot or imprisoned loomed larger. Bryers, a 39-year-old bachelor, was engaged to be married and he made sure he kept his date with Maisie Simmonds, twenty-eight, a local shop assistant, at the altar of St Peter's Church, West Crawley on Saturday 5 September 1936.

Bebb was the first to give his version of events, in a world exclusive for the *News Chronicle* on Saturday 7 November 1936 in which he revealed that Juan March was bankrolling the coup. He repeated the story a number of times subsequently, including a detailed account for *Aeroplane Monthly* in August 1986.

On that occasion he described how the party had gone through the normal formalities with customs and immigration by 8.15am on Saturday 11 July and been led out to their plane by Captain Olley in brilliant sunshine. By 8.30am they were airborne.

When they made their first stop, at Bordeaux, he found a familiar face among the group of Spanish conspirators awaiting them. Amazingly, the Marqués de Merito had come to his aid a year earlier when he got into trouble with the authorities at Madrid airport for landing there while it was closed because of a Communist insurrection. Quite why the Marqués should have been at Madrid airport, let alone interceding on behalf of a complete stranger, was not explained. However the Marqués intended to join Bebb's flight and had to be told there was no room unless he sat on the lavatory. It was then that the engineer was despatched to find his own way to Casablanca. Apparently he succeeded because he and Bebb spent a day preparing the plane for its onward journey to Las Palmas.

Bebb's flight from Bordeaux was anything but straightforward. They encountered bad weather over the Pyrenees and had to turn back to Biarritz. At the second attempt they got lost and were not helped by the radio operator's incoherent and insecure attempts to make contact with someone on the ground. Bebb made the decision to land at Espinho, just outside Oporto, because he hadn't enough fuel to reach their intended destination of Braganza.

From there they flew to Lisbon, where the two Spaniards went off for a conference with Sanjurjo, before they hastened on to Casablanca. The two Spaniards now left the plane and sent Bebb and Pollard on with the girls. They reached Las Palmas at 2pm on the fourteenth and Pollard, Diana and Dorothy headed for Tenerife while Bebb relaxed in a hotel. Then the cloak and dagger stuff began. Pollard had told him that he should go nowhere unless an agent arrived bearing a message, hidden in the secret compartment of a signet ring, saying: 'Take these two fellows to Mutt and Jeff.'

Mutt and Jeff were characters from an American cartoon strip, and Cockney rhyming slang for deaf, but on this occasion it was intended to convey to Bebb that these were the passengers he was to transport to Bolin and Merito in Casablanca. In the meantime an army officer arrived at the hotel, demanded to know why he had landed without a permit, and then insisted that they should rendezvous in the cathedral square at 4pm. From there, Bebb was driven to a villa in the hills to meet General Orgaz. Sticking to his cover story, Bebb claimed that he had flown a wealthy horticulturalist to the island and was awaiting his return from Tenerife, where he was collecting specimens. The next day, the army officer appeared again, this time equipped with signet ring and message but no passengers for Bebb's plane. Pollard and the girls returned and in the early hours of the next morning, 18 July, Bebb was whisked away to a barracks to await his passenger.

At this point, the British consul appeared, asked if he could do anything to help and passed favourable comments on Bebb's mission. In his 1986 interview, Bebb admitted: 'Our spirits rose at the thought of the British government being involved.'

The hours ticked by and it was not until early afternoon that

Bebb was taken back to his plane and saw his passenger being carried shoulder-high to the shore from a small boat. It was then that he was introduced to General Franco as the man who would save Spain from Communism. Bebb's first words to the future dictator were to say that there was no time to lose if they were to get to Casablanca in daylight and that if he wanted to change out of his uniform he would have to do it on the plane.[110]

Pollard's version of events was reported in the *Sunday Dispatch* of 8 November. He said he had warned the two girls beforehand of the danger they faced:

> I put the facts to them plainly. I told them that if we were caught we should probably be shot out of hand; that the fact that they were women would certainly not save them from the Reds. They were not in the least shaken; they insisted on going.

This rather gives the lie to the idea that Pollard did not know the purpose of the mission before they set off. He claims to have been amused by the reception committee of Spanish conspirators at Bordeaux, not least because eight of them were wearing Eton ties – a testament to Pollard's capacity for hyperbole.

He described how, when they reached Tenerife, he had to pass messages to Franco using various intermediaries with passwords and codes. He went to the *Clinica Costa*, at *Viera y Clavijo 52*, where he gave the password 'Galicia Saluda a Francia' – Galicia salutes, or greets, France – and as a result spoke to Dr Luis Gabarda, a major in the army medical service who was able to see Franco without arousing suspicion.[111]

Dr Gabarda, in a separate account, says he had been summoned to see Franco on the afternoon of 13 July, told the password and to expect an airman to arrive at the clinic. He was telephoned from Madrid three times on the fourteenth, asking whether the plane had arrived. Pollard duly turned up at 7.30am on the fifteenth and introduced himself, in bad Spanish. He passed Pollard on to Franco's cousin Francisco Franco Salgado. The arrival of the English party attracted a brief mention in the society notes column of that afternoon's local paper.[112]

It is unclear why Bebb did not simply fly to Tenerife in the first place, but it may have been because there was a safer landing strip at Las Palmas, or that it was within easier flying range. Tenerife was also liable to be shrouded in cloud and mist. However, Franco needed an excuse to explain to the authorities in Madrid, without raising their suspicions, why he was leaving his post in Tenerife to visit the neighbouring island. With uncannily good timing for Franco, and greater misfortune for himself, General Amado Balmes, managed to shoot himself.

Franco set off in the early hours of Friday 17 July on the mail ferry accompanied by his wife and daughter, who were booked on a German liner to take them to safety in France, and an escort of fellow officers, with Pollard and the two girls discreetly in attendance. According to Pollard:

> Every deck was packed with picturesque but sinister-looking gentlemen in raincoats, their pockets bulging with revolvers. It was rather like a tough scene in any gangster film.[113]

They arrived in Gran Canaria at about 8.30am and Franco attended the funeral as announced. During that afternoon Pollard and Bebb made the final arrangements with General Orgaz.

The rising was scheduled to begin the next day but in Morocco, fearing that their leaders were about to be arrested, they jumped the gun and seized the garrisons at Melilla, Ceuta and Tetuan in Franco's name on the evening of the seventeenth. He heard of this in the early hours of Saturday and while one of his officers roused Bebb from his bed, others seized key facilities and he sent a declaration of revolt to the local radio station. This was a trifle premature, since it alerted supporters of the Republican Popular Front on the island who broke out their weapons and sporadic shooting began. Hence Franco's rather undignified arrival at the airport by tugboat – the roads were not safe to travel by car. [114]

On board the plane, bound for Casablanca, were Bebb and the engineer, Franco and his cousin Salgado, and possibly a Spanish air force officer as a reserve pilot. They travelled without incident to Agadir where Bebb had some difficulty persuading the local Shell staff to refuel the plane until they got higher authority. He also sent a telegram to Luis Bolin in Casablanca saying 'Father left Agadir 1915hr,' Father being the codename for Franco. They arrived at Casablanca to find the airport in darkness but as Bebb rather desperately buzzed the airfield the runway lights came on. On the ground Bolin had persuaded the solitary airport manager to turn them on but at the first attempt they had blown a fuse. Bebb having decided it was too dangerous to fly on to Tetuan that night, they bribed the airport manager handsomely not to inform the authorities and grabbed a few hours' sleep in a nearby hotel. In the hotel Franco shaved off his trademark moustache. This led to later comment by one of his detractors, General Queipo de Llano, that it was the only thing he ever sacrificed for Spain.

At 4am they were airborne once more to be greeted rapturously at Tetuan by the Spanish Foreign Legion.

According to Bolin, five Spaniards awaited them at Bordeaux, including the Marqués de Luca de Tena. Bolin sent a cable to his wife saying: 'South American buying tangerines,' which she would understand to mean that Merito had joined them. Why she needed to receive this coded message is a mystery unless, of course, she was reporting to higher authority in London.

In view of the drunken radio operator's failings as a navigator, Merito took over giving directions from a map purchased in Biarritz. When they got to Lisbon they had to find Sanjurjo to tell him what was happening but managed only a brief conversation in an alleyway. Sanjurjo, showing no ambition for leadership, stressed the importance of Franco's presence at the head of the revolt.

At the Carlton Hotel, Casablanca, Bolin registered as an Englishman, Tony Bidwell. Pollard announced that he was arranging with the British consul to send the radio operator home on a tramp steamer. It is unclear why the consul would do this, or indeed that he ever did. They discovered from the newspapers that Calvo Sotelo had been murdered, convincing Bolín that the coup was about to start and he must send the plane on to collect Franco without waiting for further instructions.

He decided to stay in Casablanca. Merito went to Tangier to find another plane. Pollard was sent on ahead with instructions to find Dr Gabarda in Tenerife and give the password. According to Bolín, Pollard could not speak enough Spanish to master the password and had to write it down and practise saying it phonetically. With that sketchy briefing Pollard was to be the sole protagonist upon whom the whole success of the revolution rested. It had the merit, Bolín argued, that a purely British flight with no Spaniards on board was less suspicious. To some extent that was borne out when they made the refuelling stop at Port Juby and the commandant informed Madrid of the unauthorised arrival of the British plane. Bebb was told in Casablanca, supposedly for the first time, that he was going to the Canaries and cheerfully replied 'Right-o.'

Bolín says that he received a telegram at Casablanca airport on the evening of 17 July sent from London by his wife and Juan de la Cierva, reading 'Father leaving tomorrow,' a coded message to tell him that Bebb would be setting off from the Canaries the next day with Franco. They had learned this from Captain Olley. This is curious since Bebb, in his account, claims only to have found out in the early hours of the eighteenth that Franco was to be his passenger and was ready to leave. And since Olley was supposedly completely in the dark as to what was going on, it was clever of him to pass on the news.

In any case, Bebb duly arrived with his illustrious passenger. General Franco, in a dark suit and a hat with the brim pulled down over his eyes to prevent recognition, sat in the empty airport bar with his two travelling companions drinking beer and eating ham sandwiches. Bebb sat at the next table with the mechanic.[115]

Bolín's vital liaison role in Casablanca seems to have involved wandering aimlessly around the town, shaking off imagined Republican agents who were shadowing him, keeping the airport manager sweet, and exchanging passwords and tell-tale coded messages on insecure telephone lines with co-conspirators. Merito in Tangier seems to have had even less to do, other than warn the others not to follow him because there were armed assassins lying in wait. Would they really have entrusted Pollard with the absolutely vital job of delivering Franco if he was merely an innocent front man? Words and deeds suggest that he was fully briefed from the start and playing an active and commanding role.

During his last days in Tenerife, General Franco was noticed to have been behaving out of character. On the morning of 18 July he skipped his one-hour English lesson. His teacher, Dora Lennard, had never known this happen, as she explained a year later in an admiring article for the pro-Nationalist *Morning Post* – a title subsequently taken over by the *Daily Telegraph*.

Under a headline promising a study of the mind and nature of the junta leader, she began:

Not many Latins, probably, are heroes to those who undertake to drum the vagaries of English grammar into their bewildered heads. But one of them at least earned his teacher's wholehearted admiration and affection. I was that lucky teacher. My pupil was General Franco.

Three times a week, he spent the hour between breakfast and office duties, 9.30–10.30, being coached by Dora. He wrote compositions for her, not about arms or politics but about his new found obsession with golf. She had known nothing about him previously, other than recognising him from a magazine photograph leading the Spanish Foreign Legion in Morocco, but quickly realised she was in the presence of a great man. She marvelled, she said, at the breadth of his knowledge of the world, his love for Spain and his family. She also taught the General's five-year-old daughter and knew that his enemies had threatened to kidnap her. The little girl played happily, oblivious to the death threats accompanied by a hammer and sickle in red chalk on the walls of surrounding buildings.

Dora had seen a changed man when Franco appeared for
his lesson on 16 July, after news of Calvo Sotelo's murder had
reached them. There had been shooting in the vicinity overnight;
he appeared to have had no sleep and to have aged ten years.
By coincidence they had talked that morning about a passage
of English describing Abraham Lincoln and the start of the
American Civil War. It read:

> He did not make war on the South until he was forced to do
> so. His big heart recoiled from bloodshed. His heart was wrung
> with anguish on account of the sufferings he was forced to inflict
> upon his brothers in the South in order to ensure future peace and
> prosperity to the country.[116]

How prophetic! What an inspiring choice of text. How disingenuous!
Dora Lennard was no parochial English schoolmarm. She was the
wife of Antonio Alonso Fernandez. The pair were correspondents
of the American news agency Associated Press, on the Nationalist
side and broadcasters of 'reliable' radio reports from Tenerife. Their
contribution to the Francoist cause did not end there. On the night
that his eventual triumph was broadcast by radio in Madrid, 1 May
1939, Dora and Antonio were there to make the announcements in
Spanish, French and English.[117]

Despite the supposed secrecy of the journey, Cecil Bebb seems
to have kept in regular contact with the Olley Air Service office at
Croydon. Olley's secretary, Muriel Rignall, used to record each day's
flying in her Letts Young Airman's Diary.[118] It is impossible to say
when she made the entries but from the way they are interspersed
with details of other flights and occasional errors where the
route was changed at the last moment, it appears she was told
in advance.

She tracked their progress from Croydon to Espinho, on to
Casablanca and Las Palmas and back. The later entries show Bebb
flitting between Toulouse, Biarritz, Marseilles and Nice. From being
a willing but supposedly ill-informed man with a single mission,

Bebb had become the chief courier pilot of the leaders of the coup as they dashed hither and thither seeking allies and arms.

According to Bebb, Franco's first instinct was to send him to bomb Madrid. This, he pointed out, was all very well – he could get there but he wouldn't have enough fuel to get back. Dropping bombs, he told an interviewer later, was not for him. Instead he flew Luis Bolin to Lisbon to report to General Sanjurjo, who was still the nominal leader of the coup.

There is some suggestion that Bebb was asked to fly Sanjurjo to join Mola in Pamplona and declined to do so on the grounds that the landing facilities there were inadequate for the *Dragon Rapide*.[119] Sanjurjo then opted to fly in a smaller Puss Moth aircraft, piloted by Juan Ansaldo, with fatal consequences. The Portuguese authorities, anxious not to be seen to be actively promoting the coup, would not allow them to take off from a major airport. Ansaldo was weighed down by his quite bulky passenger and an excessive amount of baggage including the General's full dress uniform that he expected to wear as the new head of state. He attempted to take off from a small airfield and crashed into the surrounding trees. He survived. Sanjurjo did not.[120]

Bolin carried a letter of authorisation from Franco, endorsed by Sanjurjo, to negotiate urgently in England, Germany or Italy for the purchase of aircraft and supplies. Bebb and Bolin flew on to Biarritz and then to Marseilles, from where Bolin flew to Rome to ask for twelve bombers, three fighters and a supply of bombs. Mussolini rejected the approach and was only persuaded after further representations from General Mola and a phone call from King Alfonso.

Franco made similar requests to Hitler, who was attending the Wagner festival in Bayreuth. The rebel air force commander General Kindelan was allowed to use British telephone links via Gibraltar because the Republicans had cut his phone line. Three of Franco's personal emissaries flew to Berlin in a Lufthansa aircraft which had been 'commandeered' – just as Bebb's *Dragon Rapide* had been – in Gran Canaria on 19 July to take General Orgaz to join

Franco in Morocco. The aircraft they procured enabled Franco to transfer 12,000 men from Africa to Spain in the first two months of the war.[121]

Bebb says that after dropping Bolin in Marseille he returned to Biarritz, collected more passengers who were bound for Berlin and Rome and ferried them to Marseille and Nice to join connecting flights. He tried to take Juan March from Biarritz to Majorca but their progress was halted in Perpignan by the French authorities. While March made other arrangements, Bebb returned to Biarritz where he was arrested and his plane impounded. He managed to get rid of secret documents he was carrying on the Nationalists' behalf before he was detained. He and the plane were eventually released, on condition that they went straight back to Britain

Bebb suggests, in his first newspaper interview, that he had also flown General Mola to Burgos. This seems unlikely yet the claim is repeated by Captain Olley in an official report he wrote for the British government in 1939. Mola arrived in Burgos from Pamplona on 21 July. It seems doubtful that Bebb could have fitted the journey into his schedule but it is clear that Captain Olley considered his contribution to the revolution as something for which he could expect the British government's admiration. His report was written as a preliminary to him taking over the direction of all civilian aviation, including the airlifting of vital supplies, during the Second World War.[122]

Bebb and Pollard's progress in North Africa was monitored by the Foreign Office. On 16 July, the day that Pollard made contact with Franco in Tenerife, the British ambassador in Spain, Sir Henry Chilton, sent a despatch to London about their activities. That report, although referred to in subsequent correspondence, is missing from the official records and it is not clear how Chilton or the Spanish government could have known about the flight at that early stage. Certainly the Foreign Office did nothing to stop it.

Harold Patteson, the consul in Tenerife, tried on 18 July to warn London that the coup was taking place but his telegram was blocked in Madrid. He did get through on 20 July and followed up with a detailed account on 23 July in which he referred to Bebb and his plane having been 'commandeered' by Franco after it had been detained at Gando airport on Gran Canaria for having no permit to land or fly over Spanish territory. He reported that both Bebb and the mechanic, George Bryers, had left with Franco while their passengers, Major Pollard and the two girls, would depart from Gran Canaria on 24 July on the *Highland Brigade*. One Foreign Office diplomat in London rather gave the game away by noting on the cover of Patteson's report:

> It is interesting and strange that the Spanish Govt's suspicions about Major Pollard's aeroplane date from 16 July, 2 days <u>before</u> Gen Franco commandeered it. Possibly there was some pre-arrangement. Gen Franco must have made sure of getting quickly to Spanish Morocco.[123]

CHAPTER 8: COUP

The Cabinet first discussed the coup on 22 July. The Foreign Secretary, Anthony Eden, revealed that his information was 'somewhat fragmentary' as a result of the Spanish Republican government preventing telegrams getting through from Madrid. The Admiralty had dispatched ships to the main Spanish ports to protect British citizens and find out what was going on.

There was no embargo on the Republican government making commercial arrangements to re-fuel its fleet from Gibraltar, except that the Spanish navy was stranded in Tangier and no British merchant ship was likely to risk being bombed by Franco's forces while conveying oil there. On that basis the Cabinet decided no action was necessary.[124]

Four days later Prime Minister Stanley Baldwin noted: 'I told Eden yesterday that on no account, French or other, must he bring us into the fight on the side of the Russians.'[125]

When the Cabinet met again on 29 July it was told that British Airways was trying to sell four aircraft to Franco. It decided not to interfere in a civil, commercial transaction. It would not prevent Spanish government arms purchases from Britain either but all current production was probably required for Britain's own use. That same morning, the Cabinet's Committee of Imperial Defence met to consider a quite alarming assessment of Britain's military capability in the Mediterranean, written by the Navy's director of planning, Rear Admiral Tom Phillips, and others. It concluded that as a result of Italy's growing naval and air power Britain could not be certain to fulfil its defence commitments in Egypt or the eastern Mediterranean by sending reinforcements and equipment via Gibraltar. Nor was Malta adequately defended against air attack. The Committee concluded that no new defence commitments should be entered into in the area, since it would take years to regain supremacy, and in the meantime nothing should be done to alienate Italy.

Whatever the Foreign Office knew in advance, the coup came as no surprise to Winston Churchill after his December visit to Alan Hillgarth in Majorca and New Year holiday in Spain and Morocco.

He wrote:

At the end of July 1936 the increasing degeneration of the Parliamentary régime in Spain, and the growing strength of the movements for a Communist, or alternatively an anarchist revolution, led to a military revolt which had long been preparing. It is part of the Communist doctrine and drill-book, laid down by Lenin himself, that Communists should aid all movements towards the Left and help into office weak Constitutional, Radical, or Socialist Governments. These they should undermine, and from their falling hands snatch absolute power, and found the Marxist State. In fact, a perfect reproduction of the Kerensky period in Russia was taking place in Spain. But the strength of Spain had not been shattered by foreign war. The Army still maintained a measure of cohesion. Side by side with the Communist conspiracy there was elaborated in secret a deep military counterplot. Neither side could claim with justice the title-deeds of legality... Bitter civil war now began. Wholesale cold-blooded massacres of their political opponents, and of the well-to-do, were perpetrated by the Communists who had seized power. These were repaid with interest by the forces under Franco.

In this quarrel I was neutral. Naturally I was not in favour of the Communists. How could I be, when if I had been a Spaniard they would have murdered me and my family and friends? I was sure however that with all the rest they had on their hands the British Government were right to keep out of Spain.[126]

Having initially allowed military supplies to reach the Republican government, while blocking arms for Franco, France decided on 8 August, under pressure from Britain, to promote an international policy of non-intervention.[127]

By then a steady stream of pro-Franco lobbyists was arriving at the Foreign Office. David Eccles, chairman of the Anglo-Spanish Construction Company, called on Sir George Mounsey on 6 August after a visit to Spain. Sir George wrote:

> Mr Eccles ... was clearly so entirely prejudiced in favour of the rebels and determined to help them individually and collectively that I felt bound to give him a word of warning and explain the Government's attitude in regard to the Spanish trouble. A point of interest he mentioned was that it was generally known that the Communists were preparing an uprising for August 2. The Spanish government was so perturbed over this prospect that they moved numbers of troops out of the towns to the centres where they expected trouble, with the result that the towns fell prey to the Communist elements thus freed from any control. The military rebels were still unready for their movement and their plans were thus upset.

Sir George thought this lent credence to a remark made by an Italian diplomat that there was not one revolution going on in Spain but two and the feeble Spanish government was powerless to cope with either.[128]

Eccles had a sound reason to favour the rebels. Workers on his company's Santander–Mediterraneo railway were not receiving their wages because of a communications breakdown between Burgos and London. General Mola, who had led the coup from Pamplona only ten days earlier, had provided the money for the wages but wanted repayment in sterling in London. The Foreign Office advised against.[129]

Britain's ambassador in Russia, Viscount Chilston, took a different view. On 10 August he told the Foreign Secretary in a long despatch from Moscow:

Although the war seems likely to end in the establishment of a Communist regime in Spain, I do not think that the news of its outbreak can have been received with any enthusiasm by the Soviet government. Señor Quiroga's government was probably quite good enough for the Kremlin in present circumstances, and no troubling of the European waters which gives Germany a chance to fish can be very welcome here… This correct and neutral attitude might have been maintained but for the growing weight of evidence that the two principal 'Fascist' states were actively assisting the insurgents.

As a result the Soviets had raised £500,000 by public subscription to send to Spain, rather in the same way that collections had been organised in Russia to support the trades unions during the 1926 General Strike in Britain.[130]

Britain suspected Germany and Italy of conspiracy with the rebels. By 8 August George Monck Mason was reporting from Tetuan that he had a brief meeting at the aerodrome with Franco, who was departing for Spain, and was introduced to General Orgaz. There were up to thirty large Italian and German aircraft with pilots kitted out in Spanish Legionnaires' uniforms.[131]

When Cabinet met again on 2 September they were presented with a new assessment by Eden and a compelling warning by the Chiefs of Staff. They said, even at this early stage, that Britain's objective should be:

The maintenance of such relations with any Spanish Government which may emerge from this conflict as will ensure benevolent neutrality in the event of our being engaged in a European war.

They considered that open intervention by Italy in support of the Nationalists would precipitate a major international crisis; Italian occupation of anywhere on the Spanish mainland or Morocco would be detrimental or a threat to British interests; but, amazingly, occupation of the Balearics or the Canaries, while undesirable, could not be regarded as a vital menace. Yet again, they were anxious to do nothing to alienate Italy.[132]

Eden for his part took the view that Italy would regard the disturbances in Spain not only as a struggle between Fascism and Communism but as an opportunity to strengthen her own influence and weaken British sea power. He foresaw that a Communist victory in Spain might be used by Mussolini as a source of grievances that would justify his occupation of the Balearics, whereas if Franco triumphed, or even held on only to Spanish Morocco, he might be so weak as to accept Mussolini's support at any price.

Eden reminded the Cabinet that Britain had been accused of not making it abundantly clear to Mussolini that they opposed his Abyssinian conquest. They should not make the same mistake now. He found it difficult to suggest any useful action they could take, other than a discreetly worded statement by him or the Prime Minister which would be universally understood as a warning that Britain would not remain indifferent to any alteration in the balance of power. If Italy would agree to join the non-intervention agreement the warning could be given in comparatively gentle terms because of the necessity of avoiding antagonising Italy or Germany.

He favoured a simple and vague formula:

Any alteration of the *status quo* in the Western Mediterranean must be a matter of the closest concern to His Majesty's Government.[133]

The Cabinet also received 'formal and categorical assurances' from the Italian Foreign Minister Count Ciano that neither the Italian government nor any Italian had done any deals with Franco.

Of course the Foreign Office was well aware from Monck Mason's reports in Tetuan and Hillgarth's despatches from Majorca that Ciano's statement was a blatant deception but there is nothing in the Cabinet record to suggest that this was drawn to their attention. Instead they decided that if the Foreign Secretary saw fit he could pass on his 'simple and vague formula' while thanking Count Ciano for his assurances.[134]

On the day of the Cabinet meeting, Juan de la Cierva, who

had been at the lunch at Simpson's in July, called by invitation at
the Foreign Office and had a long conversation with Sir Robert
Vansittart's private secretary, Sir George Mounsey. The Prime
Minister's office had felt it was inappropriate for someone connected
to the rebels to be seen in 10 Downing Street but they were anxious
that La Cierva should be shown every consideration, as he had been
introduced by his business associate, the Air Ministry adviser Lord
Weir. Mounsey's handwritten account of the meeting, made the
same day, explains that La Cierva:

> …is purely a private person, neither a politician nor a diplomat.
> His concern is for the welfare of Spain, his leanings are towards
> monarchy but of a liberal type and that he is convinced of the
> necessity of good relations between Spain and this country.

He had gone to Spain a couple of weeks earlier to explain British
feelings about the uprising to Franco, whom he already knew, and
General Mola.

> He says that General Franco, who is perfectly straight forward and
> certainly would not have deceived him, stated categorically that not
> only has he never made any offer of any kind to Italy or Germany
> in return for their help, but their assistance had been given quite
> spontaneously and without any suggestions of conditions being
> attached. This attitude he could not of course but contrast with that
> of other countries.

Franco had gone on to complain that Tangier had not remained
neutral; the British port of Gibraltar had initially been made
available to ships of the Spanish Navy which had remained loyal
to the Republican government; a blockade of Nationalist-held
Morocco had been accepted; telegraph communications had been
cut between the Canaries, Cadiz, Vigo and the UK; foreign exchange
restrictions prevented exports of farm produce from Nationalist
areas; and that the British press, including *The Times* and the *Daily*

Telegraph, had lumped the Communists and the rebels together in the matter of atrocities. Mounsey added:

> Though the rebels did admit taking and shooting a number of prisoners, on entry into towns etc., this was only done under the momentary provocation of witnessing the tortures, burnings and other savageries which the communists had been perpetrating without any provocation. He thought no soldiers in any country would have been able to refrain from immediate retaliation on the perpetrators of the horrible cruelties which they encountered in every town and village.

Before leaving, La Cierva had thanked the Foreign Office for the efforts it had made to ensure the safety of members of his family still in Spain. Mounsey in turn thanked him for the information, and declined his offer to act as an emissary on his return to Spain in a few days. The Foreign Secretary, Anthony Eden, sent a copy of Mounsey's report to Sir Henry Chilton.[135] Britain's ambassador to Madrid had based himself in Hendaye, just along the north-western coast from San Sebastian, on the French side of the border. He had more contact with the Nationalists, even though they were not recognised diplomatically, than with the Republican government in Madrid where the chargé d'affaires George Ogilvie Forbes was left in charge.

Whatever help the Foreign Office gave to Juan de la Cierva's family, it was not enough. His father and relatives sought refuge in the British embassy and were refused. He turned instead to the Norwegian consul Felix Schlayer who took him in and arranged for his other son, Ricardo, to be flown to France with members of his family. At the last moment Ricardo was recognised by a Republican militiaman and dragged off the plane, despite Schlayer's protests. He was taken to Madrid prison and later executed during the notorious massacre of prisoners at Paracuellos del Jarama.[136]

Four days after his meeting with Mounsey La Cierva left Croydon for Paris in an Olley *Dragon Rapide*, G-ACTT, chartered at an hour's notice. Sergeant William Rogers, the airport's Special

Branch officer, was unable to discover the purpose of the trip but La Cierva's subsequent correspondence with General Mola suggests that he was heading straight for Berlin.

On the day before La Cierva's visit another of Vansittart's assistants, Horace Seymour, wrote an assessment of the state of the Civil War for Anthony Eden, who had spent the early part of August on holiday.

> It is difficult to express an opinion whether the victory of the Right or of the Left in Spain would be the more undesirable from the point of view of British interests. On the whole it can be assumed that an extremist government of either complexion would be a serious embarrassment to us. A Communist Spain would mean the loss of the whole of the British invested capital in Spain and the end of British capitalist enterprise in the Peninsular, and it might also favour the spreading of Communism into France. On the other hand, it is unlikely that an extreme right Government, on Fascist or closely similar lines, could establish itself on a lasting basis without some kind of foreign support, financial or other. Such a Government would naturally tend to look for support to Italy and Germany ... We have no information enabling us to conclude which side is likely to win.

The insurgents had consolidated their forces ready to attack Madrid, San Sebastian and Irun but their preliminary attacks had not been conspicuously successful and although their troops were better disciplined their leaders showed few signs of any strategic skill. Morale of the government supporters in Madrid was high, but diminished nearer to the fighting and certain militiamen preferred to remain near the capital murdering suspect civilians rather than joining the battle front. Seymour concluded:

> The factor which may, of course, be decisive in the issue will be the extent to which the various countries will evade the obligations of the non-intervention pact, and this adds to the difficulty of forecasting the result.[137]

Italy, Germany and Russia paid lip service to the non-intervention agreement while more or less openly disregarding it. The international committee set up to oversee the pact did not hold its first meeting until 9 September and was, in any case, largely ineffectual except in depriving the legitimate Republican government of supplies, military or otherwise. It was what the Labour peer Lord Strabolgi described as 'malevolent neutrality'.

La Cierva did not make a direct request to the British government for arms supplies but comments he made later imply that he was also having talks with more clandestine contacts. It can hardly have escaped the attention of MI6 that La Cierva was more than 'a respected and well-known private citizen'. Along with Luis Bolin, he was one of the Nationalists' chief arms procurers. He was running his operation from London and the Metropolitan Police Special Branch were filing regular reports to MI5 and the Foreign Office.

A procession of aircraft was leaving airports in the south-east to join the Nationalist forces, organised by La Cierva, Bolin and the celebrated British aviator Tom Campbell-Black, whose career began with the Royal Air Force and Royal Naval Air Service in the First World War and continued with pioneering flights across Africa. He won the London to Melbourne air race in 1934 in record time and had been personal pilot to the Prince of Wales – the future Edward VIII – when he visited Kenya.[138] In early August he had been reported to be in Pamplona training pilots for the Nationalist forces.[139]

On 1 August 1936 *Dragon Rapide* G-ADCL, similar to the one which carried Franco from the Canaries to Morocco, had left Croydon for the Nationalist headquarters at Burgos. It had been bought from Airwork Ltd of Heston Aerodrome, the forerunner of Heathrow, by La Cierva and Tom Campbell-Black for use as a fighter/bomber. The pilot was Lord Malcolm Douglas-Hamilton, another aviation fanatic who had been in the RAF in the early 1930s. He had connections to Kenneth de Courcy and the Imperial Policy Group. After the Second World War, in which he re-joined the RAF, he was the founding co-chairman of Common Cause, an organisation devoted to countering the threat of Communist subversion in Britain. His American wife Natalie Paine ran a sister organisation in the United States which had close links to the CIA.[140]

Lord Malcolm's flight came to the attention of MI5 according to a report which was kept secret until 2005. The director, Vernon Kell, forwarded it to Vansittart's private secretary Clifford Norton on 6 August 1936.

On 2 August another plane left Heston for Burgos, supplied by Dick Seaton, Britain's leading racing driver. Seaton went on to race for the Mercedes team, culminating in a famous victory at the 1938 German Grand Prix in the Nürburgring where he gave a Nazi salute from the podium. When he died racing for Mercedes in 1939 Adolf Hitler sent a huge ostentatious wreath to the funeral.[141]

Vernon Kell's Special Branch informant reported from Heston:

> It is common knowledge here that these two aircraft have been sold through a secret negotiator to the anti-government forces in Spain. From conversations overheard I have come to the conclusion that it is intended by interested parties to use this airport as a sort of clearing house for aircraft … being sold to the anti-government forces and although the names of the intermediaries do not seem to be generally known, I have come to the conclusion that Thomas Campbell Black and Señor Juan de la Cierva are the two persons in question.
>
> …I have good grounds to suspect that Campbell Black's role in this matter is to accompany the sold aircraft in his own machine and then fly the pilot or pilots back out of Spanish territory… A great deal of secrecy is being observed at the moment by the chiefs of Messrs Airworks Ltd regarding their transactions with aircraft.[142]

As early as the third week in June, long before Bolin received the instructions that set the coup in motion, La Cierva had initiated

Operation Faubourg to buy arms from the Germans. La Cierva was taking his orders from General Mola who did all the groundwork for the revolt while Franco wavered on the sidelines.

According to Mola's private secretary, Felix Maiz, La Cierva wrote to the General in September:

> I hope the time will soon come when I can tell you in detail about my latest journeys, both to our English friends and the conversations in Berlin with Admiral Canaris.

He had met the head of German military intelligence at his home in Berlin and his weekend villa at Schachtensee. As a result, a shipload of arms and ammunition were sent from Germany to Vigo, in Nationalist Spain. The letter announcing the success of the mission was delivered to Burgos by a British airman, a friend of La Cierva, flying from London on 19 September. La Cierva arrived two days later for a late night briefing with Mola. His colleagues in London were still searching everywhere for supplies.[143]

At around the same time, Special Branch in London observed La Cierva's car being used to ferry General Eoin O'Duffy around. O'Duffy was a former IRA chief of staff who became the first commissioner of the Garda Síochána – Irish police – when the de Valera government was formed in 1922 in the newly created Irish Free State. O'Duffy, who had turned to Fascist politics, took 500 of his Irish Blueshirts to fight for Franco in Spain.[144] MI6 considered planting someone in O'Duffy's entourage to keep them informed about the Civil War's progress, although as it turned out the Blueshirts saw little action and returned home in 1937.[145]

At his meeting with Mola, La Cierva brushed aside warnings about his personal safety but on the morning of 9 December he died when a KLM scheduled flight taking off from Croydon Airport for Amsterdam in heavy fog crashed into a house and exploded, killing fifteen of the seventeen on board. The pilot had no radar to guide him, only a white line painted on the grass airstrip, and was assumed to have lost his bearings. There was no suggestion of sabotage but

Nationalists nevertheless recorded that their hero had 'died in the service of his country'.

Two days after La Cierva's visit to the Foreign Office, the Marqués de Merry del Val wrote from the Stafford Hotel in St James's to Vansittart, describing himself as the representative of the Spanish provisional government at Burgos and seeking a meeting. The Marqués had been Spanish ambassador in London from 1913 to 1931 and his father had been secretary of the Spanish Legation in London before him; his younger brother had once been tipped as a future Pope. They were an Anglophile family with Scottish and Irish ancestry. His cousin Francis Zulueta changed his nationality to British in 1914 in order to fight on the Allied side in the First World War; Zulueta's son Philip was private secretary to three successive British Prime Ministers – Eden, Macmillan and Douglas-Home – in the 1950s and 1960s.[146]

So while Vansittart observed diplomatic propriety by not entertaining Merry del Val at the Foreign Office, he sent his private secretary Clifford Norton round to the hotel to convey his apologies and of course Norton stayed to chat. The Marqués assured him that the provisional government was not Fascist and was not under any obligation to any foreign power. It was determined to restore Spain to her former glory, even though it might take fifty years, and had no intention of giving up any of her territory. They hoped for good relations with Britain and France but might find themselves driven to favour those who offered them greatest support.

Vansittart's response, written on 18 September, was to say:

> We shall have henceforth to bear in mind the possibility at least of the Burgos government winning; and we should take any reasonable care not to antagonise them, with an eye to the future. We can, however, only await developments now and observe our neutrality strictly and properly.[147]

There was big money to be made selling aircraft to either side in Spain and plenty of aviation entrepreneurs were quick to cash in.

Nevil Shute, who later found fame as the author of *A Town Like Alice* and *The Far Country*, was running an aviation business in the Midlands. He sold most of his fleet including an ancient wooden Airspeed Envoy trainer which alone went for £6,000 cash. It became personal transport for Franco's main rival for leadership of the coup, General Mola. He died when it crashed into a hillside near Burgos on 3 June 1937.[148] Crilly Air Transport was on charter to the Nationalists, ferrying emissaries and messages between Portugal and the parts of Spain controlled by Franco and Mola. Its founder, Irishman Frederick Crilly, tried to sell four second-hand Fokker F.XII aircraft to the Nationalists for £60,000, using British Airways as an intermediary.[149]

The deal was negotiated by British Airways' star pilot Robert 'All Weather Mac' McIntosh who had been chartered by a party of journalists to fly to Burgos three days after the coup was launched. McIntosh spent the first few days running news reports back to the nearest reliable telephone lines in Biarritz, where the journalists could also evade the Nationalists' strict censorship. Towards the end of July he was summoned by Mola and asked to undertake a special mission to Lisbon. He flew General Miguel Ponte, one of the seven-man junta of national defence, to Portugal to secure the support of the Portuguese government.

On 9 August 1936 Air Force Captain Alberto Bayo, leading Republican troops in a passenger ship, two destroyers, a submarine and six aeroplanes, quickly overwhelmed the Nationalist garrison of fifty on the island of Ibiza.

At dawn on 16 August Bayo's force of 8,000 invaded Majorca, landing on a beach on the east coast near the small town of Porto Cristo. They were driven out again by a force of Italian Blackshirts, led by Arconovaldo Bonaccorsi, better known as Count Rossi, who drove around the island in a red sports car terrorising the inhabitants. He was backed up by Savoia bombers and Fiat fighter planes and a force of Falangists. Republican wounded, sheltering in a convent, were murdered. The Italian reinforcements were paid for by Juan March.[150]

The Nationalists had seized Majorca from the start but not the neighbouring island of Menorca with its naval base. British warships were sent to stand by, among them the battle cruiser HMS *Repulse*, commanded by John Godfrey, later appointed head of naval intelligence. By 30 July he had taken on board more than 500 refugees from Majorca, 209 of them British.[151]

Alan Hillgarth was on leave when the coup began and only managed to return from Marseilles to Majorca on the morning of 10 August aboard the newly launched destroyer HMS *Gipsy*. On this occasion the Foreign Office were more appreciative of his naval propensity for swift response and peremptory orders, describing his immediate action as invaluable.

Within hours of his arrival he was forwarding intelligence gathered by HMS *Granville* from Menorca about the size of Bayo's forces and his likely method of attack. He reported that the people of Majorca were solidly in favour of the coup and in the control of the right-wing forces who could muster 8,000 troops plus 2,000 Falangists and militiamen. There were 600 Leftists in gaol or aboard prison ships but 'only fifteen' had been executed in the first days of the uprising. His immediate concern was to persuade about seventy British inhabitants to leave, and then to safeguard their property.[152]

Over the next two weeks he filed a series of detailed reports on the attempted invasion by Captain Bayo, the response of the island's Nationalist defenders and the support provided by the Italians, including the arrival of armed seaplanes and the building of an underground hangar for land-based aircraft. Juan March's son, also named Juan, was commuting between Palma and Rome organising the delivery of ammunition. Hillgarth estimated Republican casualties at around 1,000, three times that of the Nationalists, and in addition Majorcan left-wing sympathisers were being executed at the rate of fifteen per night, although that could not continue much longer as there were not many left to shoot.[153]

Towards the end of August, Hillgarth reported the arrival of an Italian destroyer escorting a merchant ship which secretly unloaded aeroplanes and armaments on the quayside at Palma overnight. The following day, 28 August, Count Rossi assumed command of the forces defending the island against the Republican attack, and the Italian planes, with Italian pilots in Spanish Foreign Legion uniform, began bombing and machine gunning the opposing forces. Italian naval officers and crew were much in evidence in Palma but the Germans, who had also been giving assistance, were far more reticent. Hillgarth concluded, on the basis of conversations with local authorities, that the Italians' motives went beyond mere assistance. While the islanders remained strongly nationalistic, they would be liable to accept an Italian protectorate as an alternative to Communism.[154]

This view coincided with fears expressed by the French Admiral Darlan but the First Lord of the Admiralty, Sir Samuel Hoare, dismissed them as panic and refused to believe that the Italians would contemplate any kind of coup in the Balearic Islands.[155]

A month later, Sir Robert Vansittart declined a French request to raise this with the non-intervention committee, arguing that the French were simply trying to manoeuvre Britain into taking the lead in antagonising Italy.

But by December 1936 Hillgarth's intelligence left the Foreign Office in no doubt of the danger of an Italian takeover of the island. He reported that the general population was weary of war and feared being recruited to fight on the mainland. They were liable to opt for Italian occupation in preference. At the same time Sir Eric Drummond, ambassador in Rome, reported that 40,000 Blackshirts – Fascist militia – were being recruited to send to Majorca.

This was sufficiently alarming for the Foreign Secretary, Anthony Eden, to complain that the situation was becoming more and more important and was being accepted far too easily. He wanted urgent action including increased naval presence, active support from the French and an immediate visit by Drummond to the Italian Foreign Minister Count Ciano to demand an end to Count Rossi's provocative behaviour on the island. Ciano simply laughed off the protest, saying that Rossi was acting quite independently of the Italian government. While this angered Eden, warning voices pointed out how difficult it would be for Britain to thwart Italian ambition on the island. Against that Sir Robert Vansittart remarked:

> If we allow the Italians to take over Majorca we can wave goodbye to any remnants of prestige in the Mediterranean.[156]

He complained again of the 'tepid' Chiefs of Staff and Eden encouraged him by noting that Britain's forces in the Mediterranean were more than powerful enough to show their teeth if the Italians would not back down. The Foreign Office contemplated giving the League of Nations a mandate to take control of the Balearics and deny their use to either side in the conflict. In mid-December 1936 Eden presented an appraisal to Cabinet of Count Rossi's 'sinister presence' and Mussolini's intentions. In January 1937 the Chiefs of Staff reiterated their view that Italian occupation of the Balearics was not a vital strategic issue, even if it would involve some loss of prestige. Since Eden was not present Cabinet decided not to discuss it.[157] The Italians, meanwhile, had withdrawn Count Rossi, and replaced him with an official military mission which, they made clear, would leave if Franco were victorious – and by implication would stay if he were not.

Italian and German aircraft continued to be based at Majorca and, according to a report to the Committee of Imperial Defence, primed by intelligence supplied by Hillgarth, they were responsible for the majority of attacks on Republican-held ports on the Mediterranean coast of Spain, the Republican navy and on merchant vessels suspected of supplying the Republicans. The Committee was given detailed accounts of the types of aircraft used, tactics including high and low level and dive bombing, and the use of high explosive and incendiary devices. Hillgarth kept up a constant flow of such reports.[158]

In October 1937 the Cabinet was given further evidence of Italian duplicity. Their Foreign Minister, Count Ciano, had assured the British chargé d'affaires in Rome that no further support would be sent to Franco. The Nationalists had been bombing Republican ports where food supplies were being unloaded. Simultaneously, Hillgarth warned that more aeroplanes had arrived from Italy and that an increase in bombing must be expected. There were more than 140 planes in Majorca. Italian troops and arms were being landed at Cadiz and twenty of Mussolini's air aces, with their planes, had left Sardinia for Spain within the last two days.[159]

Rear Admiral Godfrey in the *Repulse* returned to Majorca in 1938 and commented that the non-intervention policy meant that Britain intervened on either side in pursuit of her own objectives, which were to exert a stabilising influence and to protect distressed British subjects. He took more refugees on board and then headed for Barcelona and Valencia which were still in Republican hands. It was then that Alan Hillgarth was able to use his influence with the pro-Franco Captain General of Majorca and the commander of the Italian bomber force to call a halt to their assaults while the *Repulse* visited the hostile territory. Godfrey thought this a remarkable achievement and therefore had no hesitation, when he became director of naval intelligence, in nominating Hillgarth as naval attaché in Madrid.[160]

Hillgarth's final contribution in the Civil War demonstrates his capacity for decisive action, the strength of his relationship with Franco and his confidence in shaping Britain's foreign policy while leaving his superiors in London to fall into line. He had already made frequent efforts to reduce the bloodshed and arrange prisoner exchanges. In January 1939, when it was clear that victory for Franco was imminent, the local Nationalist air force commander, the Count of San Luis, secretly briefed Hillgarth on plans to bombard Republican positions on the neighbouring island of Menorca prior to an invasion. The Count was opposed to the action, believing it would lead to needless slaughter by the Italian bomber crews, and was suggesting that the two of them should travel to the island on a British warship to negotiate surrender. Hillgarth agreed to do it, on the condition that Franco personally approved.

The Foreign Office suspected the Nationalists might be bluffing about the invasion, using a British warship to induce the Republicans to give in under duress. By the time San Luis returned with Franco's agreement the Germans and Italians had brought in more aircraft. Reporting this to the FO, Hillgarth pointedly reminded them that General Franco was an old friend who had no intention of allowing the Germans and Italians to claim the final victory or of involving British officers in mediation. The warship would simply provide the neutral territory on which the Nationalists and Republicans could talk.

The Foreign Office accepted that it would be better if a Spanish official could agree terms without the need for military intervention by the two Fascist powers. They vetoed Hillgarth's plan to travel with San Luis on HMS *Devonshire*, fearing that it would be interpreted as direct British involvement in the negotiations. This, as it turned out, was a wise precaution. San Luis successfully negotiated the surrender and the safe passage from the island of Republicans whose lives might have been at risk. The whole exercise was almost scuppered by Italian bombers after their commanding officer, in defiance of his instructions, ordered an attack on Menorca while the talks were proceeding. The *Devonshire* was only able to demand a halt to the attacks because Hillgarth had stayed behind and was in radio contact with the ship. In London the Foreign Secretary, Lord Halifax, was outraged by the deplorable behaviour but attempts to get Franco to confirm in writing the assurances he had given to San Luis and Hillgarth were repeatedly rebuffed and eventually abandoned.[161]

Hillgarth's work for the Admiralty during the Civil War led the Royal Navy's Commander in Chief in the Mediterranean, Sir Dudley Pound, to recommend him for promotion to the rank of Commander even though he was still technically on the retired list and did not have enough active service to qualify.[162]

Britain's self-interest was clearly served by the non-intervention policy. Prime Minister Stanley Baldwin's first reaction to the military coup had been to warn his Foreign Secretary on no account to allow France to drag them into a fight on the side of the Russians by supporting the Spanish Republicans. His foreign policy was dictated by a determination to avoid war with Germany or Italy.

A thick file of Foreign Office correspondence from the period, kept secret until February 2011, reveals how great was the danger that Britain would be inveigled into such a conflict.[163]

It deals initially with the secret fortification of Gibraltar, blasting siege tunnels into the rock on which the fortress stands and using the debris to create a landing strip on the racecourse, extending into the Bay of Gibraltar from the isthmus that connects the Rock to mainland Spain.

Britain's occupation of Gibraltar remains to this day a subject of dispute between the two countries and before the file was released, as a result of a Freedom of Information request, a substantial part of it was removed or obliterated as too damaging to Britain's international interests to be made public.

The plans were already at an advanced stage in 1937, by which time Franco's troops controlled the surrounding area of Spain, including Algeciras across the bay, the north Moroccan coast and the Spanish enclave of Ceuta. They occupied commanding positions on either side of the Straits of Gibraltar which are only nine miles wide at their narrowest point. When Franco began building new coastal fortifications, under German supervision, there was great alarm, not least from Winston Churchill who began asking awkward questions in the House of Commons.

The questions threatened to reveal technicalities of the Treaty of Utrecht of 1713, by which Britain acquired Gibraltar from Spain, and a secret defence treaty between the two countries drawn up in 1898. The Treaty of Utrecht brought to an end the War of the Spanish Succession, which had seen the zenith of the military career of Winston Churchill's ancestor John Churchill, 1st Duke of Marlborough, with victories over the French at Blenheim, Ramillies, Oudenarde and Malplaquet. It confirmed Philip V as King of Spain but led to the break-up of Spain's European empire. Gibraltar had been captured in 1704 by Admiral Sir George Rooke and the treaty stated that 'the town, castle and fortifications were to be held and enjoyed [by Britain] absolutely with all manner of right for ever without any exceptions or impediment whatever'.

The 1898 treaty had come about because Spain started building coastal gun batteries to defend herself against the United States navy when the two countries were at war. Britain objected that the guns were a threat to Gibraltar and to resolve the situation made a promise that they would not allow the United States navy to mount an attack through Gibraltar's territorial waters. They also offered to protect the Canary and Balearic Islands against foreign attack.

Any protest against the guns Franco was building might lead to those treaties being invoked. The Foreign Office legal adviser in 1937, Sir William Malkin, did not believe the Treaty of Utrecht gave Britain the right to prevent Spain building coastal defences. Sir William drily pointed out: '… the fact that General Franco is not in our eyes the Spanish Government would have to be borne in mind.'

A Foreign Office official, Evelyn Shuckburgh, made a similar point, saying that to argue that Franco was bound by the treaty would be tantamount to recognition of his legitimate status. But the documents that have been released do not explain what would have happened if the Republican government had raised the issue.

The 1898 treaty offered to protect Algeciras, the Canaries and the Balearics against foreign invasion. It might not apply to Franco landing troops from Morocco at Algeciras, even though he had done so using aircraft supplied by Italy, but it would certainly have a significant bearing on the presence of Italian naval vessels off the coast of Majorca and Italian troops, led by Count Rossi, effectively occupying the island.

Not surprisingly, the Foreign Secretary, Anthony Eden, did not relish the prospect of facing questions from Winston Churchill, or anyone else, on the floor of the House of Commons.

On Thursday 15 July 1937 Eden spoke to Churchill on the telephone and followed up with a letter about the debate scheduled for the following Monday. Eden explained that the provisions of the Treaty of Utrecht were far weaker than Churchill might imagine and that the Spanish guns did not, in any case, constitute a threat to

Gibraltar. He asked Churchill not to mention the treaty, or at least not to ask his opinion of it, since any answer he might give would be unsatisfactory and only serve to expose Britain's weakness. He added a handwritten plea:

> This question may well have to be taken up again with the Spaniards but I am by no means convinced, for reasons I had rather not put into a letter, that the moment is now.[164]

Churchill chose substantially to disregard the request, telling the House:

> Under the Treaty of Utrecht, I believe, we have legal rights to the immunity of the Bay of Algeciras, provided we also forbid any enemy of Spain access to that Bay ... But surely, we should not regard the mounting of these enormous guns, to menace Gibraltar or to obstruct the Straits, as dependent upon the interpretation of ancient treaties.

He suggested that Franco might be constructing these gun emplacements as the price to be paid for military help from a foreign power and argued that the issue could best be dealt with by an official representative of the British government attached to the Franco headquarters at Salamanca expressing Britain's anxiety directly.

The reply to the debate came from the Minister of State, Lord Cranborne, rather than the Foreign Secretary. He made no mention of the Treaty of Utrecht but was at pains to remind the House that it was a civil war that they were discussing and that it was not unnatural that General Franco should seek to defend himself from assault by the Spanish government forces. Lord Cranborne was satisfied that Franco's guns were inferior to those on the Rock and did not constitute a menace. It would not be in the public interest to say more, he added.

CHAPTER 9: CIVIL WAR

While Britain and France tried to portray the Civil War as an internal conflict, justifying their policy of non-intervention, Italy, Germany and Russia made a mockery of it. So did tens of thousands of individuals who sympathised with the legal Republican government, and a much smaller, but proportionately more influential number, whose allegiance was to Franco.

For Germany, the Condor Legion comprised around 6,500 flyers and technicians whose expertise and modern equipment wielded military might that far outweighed their numbers. Since the personnel were rotated, as many as 19,000 were able to hone their fighter and bombing skills prior to the greater conflict that lay ahead. The devastation of the Basque town of Guernica and its civilian population was testament to that. Italy accounted for 80,000 men over the course of the war, more than half from her regular army and around 30,000 Blackshirt militia.

On the Republican side, supplementing those elements of the military that remained loyal and the political militias were around 40,000 members of the International Brigades from around fifty countries. By contrast Franco had the benefit of about 1,500 foreign volunteers – British, Irish, and Portuguese among others. It suited him to play down the foreign support and portray himself as a purely Spanish bastion against international Communism.[165]

But the help he received from Germany came at a very high price. According to an assessment drawn up by the British embassy in Madrid in July 1940 the Germans had taken 10,000 million pesetas worth of goods – roughly £500 million – from Spain and Spanish Guinea in return for the supply of men, munitions, aircraft and machinery for the Civil War. When the Second World War began the Germans tried to reinforce their iron grip on the Spanish economy, through the Falange, by blocking loans and trade deals with the United States and Britain. Franco resented the intense pressure.[166]

Neither the Foreign Secretary, Anthony Eden, nor his senior officials set any great store by the international non-intervention committee they had helped to establish. In December 1936 Evelyn Shuckburgh at the Foreign Office complained that the other Powers did not believe in the committee and it would be better to institute control by force rather than pessimistically putting forward ineffective bluffs or imagining that the committee 'could save Europe from committing suicide on this Spanish pyre'. He advocated a powerful naval blockade with powers to stop and search all ships, including Spanish ones from either side, to prevent arms or volunteers getting to the battleground. Eden agreed, saying Germany and Italy did not want to go to war over Spain and that if Britain was timorous now it would have to face war at a later date. His views did not convince the Cabinet.

Probably the best known of Franco's British fighting men was Peter Kemp, the well-connected son of a retired chief judge of the Bombay High Court, who had just completed his degree in classics and law at Cambridge. By his own account, he wanted to go to war to fight *against* Communism rather than *for* Fascism. Kemp travelled with journalistic accreditation provided by the *Sunday Dispatch*, a Rothermere paper. While his only previous military experience was in the Officer Training Corps at Cambridge, Kemp initially served in a cavalry unit of the Carlist *Requetes* but switched to the Spanish Foreign Legion in search of serious action.

Kemp encountered a number of other British volunteers, among them James Walford, son of Juan March's friend Leopold Walford and his wife Christina, stepdaughter of Sir Basil Zaharoff.

Kemp was injured twice, first in the throat and arm and then, in May 1938, his jaw was shattered when his dugout took a direct hit during a mortar attack. He returned to Britain to convalesce but went back to Spain in 1939 to receive a personal award from Franco and was astonished to hear the dictator express his admiration for Britain. It was during his time in Spain that he met Douglas Dodds-Parker, a founder member of the secret military intelligence unit MI-R which became part of the Special Operations Executive. Dodds-Parker recruited Kemp to SOE who sent him back to Spain in the Second World War.[167]

Apart from men who would fight and journalists who would report favourably, the Nationalists were keen to recruit opinion formers from Britain who would influence attitudes towards the regime, particularly once the tide of the Civil War began to turn in Franco's favour. Luis Bolin hit on the idea of battlefield tours, earning £8 a head in valuable foreign currency, and taking the eager holidaymakers to see the sights of Nationalist triumph and hear the tales of Republican terror. One frequent admiring visitor was Arnold Lunn, who had done much to popularise skiing and introduced the downhill slalom event to the 1936 Winter Olympics in Bavaria.[168] Arnold Lunn had links to the intelligence service and his son Peter, a member of the Olympic skiing team, was with MI6 during the Second World War and went on to be head of station in Vienna and Berlin in the 1950s.[169] Sir Arnold's father, the travel agent Sir Henry Lunn, founded one half of what was to become the Lunn Poly travel agency. In the 1950s they pioneered package holidays to the Costa del Sol and Majorca, encouraged by Spain's director of tourism – Luis Bolin.

Among Arnold Lunn's travelling companions was Winston Churchill's son Randolph. Douglas Jerrold also made the trip in 1937, in company with Francis Yeats-Brown and Major-General John 'Boney' Fuller, a military theorist and expert on tank warfare. They travelled all over the Nationalist part of the country, coming under sniper fire, and meeting General Franco.

Yeats-Brown told the ambassador, Sir Henry Chilton, that Franco, who had seen the film of his book *Bengal Lancer*, starring Gary Cooper, was familiar with General Fuller's military strategies and grateful for the help Jerrold had given in arranging for the

plane that picked him up from the Canaries. Sir Henry was keen
for more gentlemen of this calibre to visit 'His Excellency' General
Franco but when his report reached the Foreign Office it fell into
the hands of John Cairncross, who went on to wartime service
with MI6 and later admitted to being a KGB agent. His only
comment was: 'It may be mentioned that Major Yeats-Brown is
a Fascist.'[170]

Only two British women had volunteered to help on the Franco
side during the Civil War. Gabriel Herbert, a cousin of Alan
Hillgarth's wife Mary, and Evelyn Waugh's sister-in-law, drove an
ambulance. Pip Scott-Ellis, daughter of Lord Howard de Walden
and friend of the Spanish royal family, was a nurse. She became
close to Peter Kemp and they met up in Madrid at the end of the
Civil War. She had spent the day with Prince Ali, her childhood
friend and relative of King Alfonso, who took her for a joy-ride in
his Italian-made Savoia bomber and, knowing that she was a keen
pilot, allowed her to take over the controls. She joined Kemp for
dinner at the Ritz and later recalled:

> I found him there talking to an Englishman and a Spaniard. The
> Englishman was oldish, grey-haired, Major Pollard, a spirited man
> who used to be in the Secret Service. He produced the aeroplane
> for Franco to fly from the Canaries to Spain to start the revolution.
> He also dealt with Porfirio Diaz in Mexico and various other
> revolutions, knows all about efficient tortures, and would use them
> without a qualm, etc. He accompanied Peter and me to dinner.[171]

So it would appear that not only was Pollard active in Spain during
the Civil War, he was given to boasting over dinner that he had
been in the Secret Service and helped launch Franco's coup. He also,
apparently, made advances to Pip, unabashed by the fact that she
was twenty and he forty-eight and despite her obvious friendship
with Kemp, who soon blotted his copybook by trying to wheedle
military secrets out of her highly placed Spanish friends to pass on
to the British military attaché.[172]

From the start the Catholic Church in Britain, unsurprisingly, offered active support to the Nationalists. The Archbishop of Westminster, Cardinal Hinsley, saw the Spanish dispute as 'in essence a contest between Christ and Antichrist'. In March 1939, the day after the Nationalist capture of Madrid, Hinsley wrote to the dictator:

> My dear Generalissimo,
>   Your most kind action in sending to me, through Mrs Herbert, a signed photograph of yourself calls for my heartfelt thanks. I shall value this likeness as a treasure, for I look upon you as the great defender of the true Spain, the country of Catholic principles where Catholic social justice and charity will be applied for the common good under a firm peace-loving government.

He kept the photograph on his desk.[173]

Hinsley set up the committee for the Relief of Spanish Distress. Its chairman was Lord Howard of Penrith, the former ambassador to Spain. While officially intended for the relief of the sick, wounded, refugees and destitute children, the committee was anti-Communist and maintained close links with the Friends of Nationalist Spain. The Friends were also allied to the United Christian Front, formed by Captain Archibald Ramsay MP 'to prove the real fact, that General Franco was fighting the cause of Christianity against anti-Christ.'

One of the earliest backers of the United Christian Front was Viscount Wolmer, Conservative MP for Aldershot and a director of the National Provincial Bank – now part of NatWest.[174]

Viscount Wolmer had an impeccable political pedigree. His father had been First Lord of the Admiralty and High Commissioner for South Africa. Wolmer's maternal grandfather was Lord Salisbury, three times Conservative Prime Minister towards the end of the nineteenth century. He was a Conservative MP for nearly thirty years, from 1910, and a friend of Winston Churchill.

In the space of a week in 1942 two dramatic changes took place. He inherited the title Earl of Selborne on the death of his father, and Churchill made him Minister for Economic Warfare. Among his new responsibilities, he became the political head of the Special Operations Executive, the sabotage unit established by Churchill with the remit to 'set Europe ablaze'.[175]

The new Lord Selborne thus became the minister most directly involved in sending agents behind enemy lines, supporting Resistance movements and generally subverting Hitler's regime. In that capacity he had under his command some of the agents directly involved in bringing Franco to power and persuading him to stay out of the Second World War, among them Hugh Pollard and Alan Hillgarth. Hillgarth was naval attaché and SOE representative in Madrid and, like Selborne, a close friend of Churchill.

Viscount Wolmer also had a family business interest in Spain through his nephew, Viscount Ridley. Britain was Spain's most important trading partner, taking 21.8 per cent of Spanish exports in 1935 and supplying 10.5 per cent of imports. British investment in Spain was far greater than any other country's and concentrated in the mining industry.[176]

Rio Tinto owned 32,000 acres of freehold copper and sulphur mining property at Huelva in southern Spain. In Basque territory two British companies had an 80 per cent holding in the Orconera mining company which produced roughly half of Spain's iron ore. They were Guest, Keen & Nettlefold – whose directors included the Tory MP Col Henry Guest – and the Consett Spanish Ore Company, where Viscount Ridley was a director.[177]

These companies had suffered at the hands of the Republican government. In 1936 it issued a decree requiring all employers to reinstate workers previously sacked on political grounds. This was interpreted to mean not only anyone who had been on strike but those who committed political murder or sabotage. Rio Tinto was one of the first to be affected and the ambassador, Sir Henry Chilton, predicted the decree would have a disastrous effect on economic life. He considered that the new Prime Minister, Manuel Azaña, had made promises during the election that he never expected to have to keep because he did not expect to win.[178]

A new threat to the investments emerged with German backing for Franco in the territories the Nationalists controlled. Hitler needed raw materials for re-armament and regarded them as a reasonable price to extract in return for supplying aircraft, munitions and men for the Nationalist war effort. Rio Tinto found their minerals output being diverted to Germany while they were prevented from taking currency out of Spain and effectively forced to wait for payments totalling £2m.[179] In 1937 the British Chamber of Commerce for Spain – vice-chairman David Eccles – filed claims on behalf of twenty-seven British companies similarly affected, totalling £7m.[180]

The oil industry was vital to General Franco's success. In 1935, Spain imported all of its petroleum products through two state-regulated monopolies: Campsa on the mainland and Cepsa on the Canary Islands and in Morocco. British Shell was one of Cepsa's suppliers; Juan March held 75 per cent of the shares.[181]

British companies were also approached by Franco supporters with demands that they contribute to his war chest. Rio Tinto and the other mining firms, sherry shippers and the boilermakers Babcock and Wilcox all paid up.[182]

Babcock and Wilcox's Bilbao factory was run by a former British military intelligence officer, Francis Cowlrick, who continued to supply information through his intelligence colleague Leslie Burgin, a government minister. The Spanish company, 20 per cent British owned, had built railway locomotives but switched to armaments and by the end of the Civil War had a testimonial from Franco congratulating them on making more ammunition than all his other suppliers put together. They were turning out 3,000 shells a day and Burgin suggested to the Foreign Secretary in April 1939 that Britain might benefit from their output.[183]

Cowlrick carried on working there during the Second World War and died on 1 June 1943 when the Luftwaffe shot down a commercial KLM flight from Lisbon to Bristol. Among the other passengers was the British film star Leslie Howard, who played Ashley Wilkes in *Gone With the Wind*. There has long been speculation that he was the target because he was on a secret mission to Spain and Portugal under cover of a goodwill visit organised by the British Council. Alternatively, the Luftwaffe might have thought that Churchill was on the flight, returning from a visit to Algiers. Howard's agent, Alfred Chenhalls, bore a passing resemblance to the Prime Minister.

Rio Tinto led the campaign to protect British mining interests and made sure they kept the British Foreign Office and Board of Trade onside. They installed their political adviser, Captain Ulick de Burgh Charles, at the Nationalist headquarters in Burgos.

Captain Charles had been commercial secretary at the Madrid embassy for seven years in the 1920s and he now became a source of intelligence for the British government, via Rio Tinto in London. Sir Auckland Geddes, chairman of Rio Tinto, dealt directly with Robert Vansittart, permanent under secretary at the Foreign Office. He warned Vansittart:

> The economic and strategic importance of these British-owned mines in Spain ... has not escaped the attention of the Spanish Insurgents or their masters – Germany and Italy – all of whom are using every means to exploit and consolidate their present situation in a manner most detrimental to Great Britain ... all our researches in Spain and Germany give credibility to the reports that a bargain was struck between the Insurgents and the aggressive elements directing German foreign policy ... together with those directing the Goering Plan for economic self-sufficiency.[184]

Geddes had been director of recruiting at the War Office from 1916–1918, then President of the Board of Trade followed by a spell as ambassador to Washington. He knew the Prime Minister, Stanley Baldwin, and at his instigation had set up a company to harvest the mineral wealth of southern Africa for British interests.[185] Now he began to lobby for diplomatic and naval intervention to protect Rio Tinto's output in Spain from German seizure.

He found a sympathetic ear in Vansittart, who was deeply distrustful of Germany but not averse to seeing Franco triumph. Sir

John Reith, director general of the BBC, recorded in his diary in March 1937 that he had discussed the Corporation's coverage of the Spanish Civil War with Vansittart who was:

> very apprehensive lest Franco (owing to *The Times* and the BBC) feels unfriendly to this country and so is dominated by Italy and Germany... He would like us to get pro-Franco in our news and even stop using the word insurgents.[186]

Nevertheless Vansittart persuaded the Foreign Secretary, Anthony Eden, that Geddes was right to propose naval intervention to stop ships sailing from Spain with commandeered British cargoes. On 3 March 1937, Eden initiated an emergency discussion in Cabinet, explaining that Rio Tinto and other British companies were being forced to divert up to 100,000 tons a month of pyrites – a source of copper, iron and sulphur – to Germany. As a result Rio Tinto's copper plant at Port Talbot in South Wales was standing idle and forced to lay off workers. The companies were being paid in pesetas at an artificially low exchange rate and being forced to deposit sterling in Spain to pay their costs. It was clear that Germany was stockpiling these raw materials for a war economy and once Franco captured northern Spain they would treat the British owners of the iron and steel works in the same way.

The First Sea Lord, Sir Ernle Chatfield, persuaded the Cabinet that while the Navy might be entitled to stop British or Spanish ships it was doubtful whether they would be justified in international law in stopping German ships carrying the cargo. They might provoke war with Germany and find themselves cast as the aggressors. Neville Chamberlain, as Chancellor of the Exchequer, argued that they should not threaten Franco but simply make strong representations that British firms should be properly compensated.

Against that background, the Board of Trade sent a delegation to Burgos to discuss with Franco's brother Nicolás better trade and currency arrangements. On 17 March, despite an unsatisfactory initial response from Franco on the mines issue, the Cabinet

considered whether to appoint an official agent to the Franco
headquarters. The Army and Air Force had realised they were
getting no intelligence back on the military capabilities of the
Italian and German forces supporting the Nationalists and needed
to appoint military observers. Cabinet approved the appointment
but insisted strict secrecy must be observed during negotiations,
fearful of the storm it would provoke in the House of Commons
since it gave legitimacy to the Franco rebellion.[187] By September
1937 the Nationalists controlled the northern territory where the
Orconera mines were situated and immediately ore shipments
began to be diverted to Germany. This added new urgency and Sir
Robert Hodgson was sent to Burgos as official agent of the British
government. Sir Robert's Spanish counterpart in London was that
familiar figure to the British government and to the Friends of
Nationalist Spain, the Duke of Alba.

While civil war raged in Spain significant changes were taking
place in the British government. The undercurrents that flowed
inexorably towards the Second World War also eroded what
resistance there might have been to Franco's brutal progression
to victory.

Anthony Eden, as Foreign Secretary, had been ready to confront
the Italians over their invasion of Abyssinia and support for
Franco in defiance of the non-intervention pact. The new Prime
Minister, Neville Chamberlain, went behind his back to maintain
friendly relations with Mussolini in pursuit of appeasement.
Sir Joseph Ball, former MI5 agent and head of the Conservative
Research Department, was conducting clandestine talks through an
intermediary with the Italian Foreign Minister. Chamberlain was
convinced they were about to bear fruit and engineered a meeting
between himself, Eden and the Italian ambassador, Count Grandi,
during which he openly overruled his Foreign Secretary.

Eden felt insulted and compromised. He resigned, to be replaced
by Lord Halifax, and Grandi, having achieved a diplomatic
objective in the departure of the obstructive Foreign Secretary,
then gratuitously promised the Prime Minister that Italian

Raring to go: Hugh and Diana Pollard on either side of Dorothy
Watson at a Sussex hunt meeting in the 1930s.

Hugh Pollard: Small wars
and revolutions a speciality.

Diana Pollard: No one
would call her a coward.

RIGHT: Dorothy Watson, happy to play the role of carefree tourist.

BELOW: The Spread Eagle pub at Fernhurst where the conspirators recruited Dorothy.

ABOVE: Douglas Jerrold in his publishing office in 1947 with author and former MI6 agent Graham Greene (left).

OPPOSITE TOP LEFT: Juan March in 1948, the year he captured control of the Barcelona Traction company.

OPPOSITE TOP RIGHT: Captain Alan Hillgarth, naval attaché and head of espionage in Madrid.

OPPOSITE BOTTOM LEFT: Luis Bolín, Franco's man in London who hired the *Dragon Rapide*.

OPPOSITE BOTTOM RIGHT: Aviation pioneer and arms dealer Juan de la Cierva.

ABOVE: George Bryers (right) and Walter Petre (at the rear) wheeling out a refuelling bowser.

BELOW: Dapper as ever, Captain Gordon Olley in his office beneath the control tower.

OPPOSITE ABOVE: *Dragon Rapide* G-ACYR on display outside the Aerodrome Hotel.

OPPOSITE BELOW: Franco's pilot Cecil Bebb (left) greeting passengers for a trip from Croydon.

General Franciso Franco salutes his troops during the Civil War.

troops would be withdrawn from Spain. This spared Chamberlain the embarrassment of a Cabinet revolt and further ministerial resignations in sympathy with Eden.[188]

It did not prevent Italian bombers, under Franco's control, attacking British merchant shipping a week later. It took six months for Italy to withdraw 10,000 troops – less than half the total. Pilots, tank corps and 12,000 of their best troops remained and by the time the war ended that figure had grown again to 20,000.[189]

A month before Eden resigned the hawkish and outspokenly anti-German Sir Robert Vansittart had been elevated to the grand but hollow position of chief diplomatic adviser and replaced as permanent under secretary at the Foreign Office by Sir Alexander Cadogan.

An appreciation of the prevailing attitude can be gained from the reaction to a document sent in June 1938 to the new Foreign Secretary, Lord Halifax, by the Labour MP and pacifist Ellen Wilkinson. It was a copy of a lecture delivered by one of Hitler's favourite generals, Walter von Reichenau, in which he echoed all the warnings Rear Admiral Phillips had given the Committee for Imperial Defence two years earlier. He had told his National Socialist audience at a meeting in Leipzig that Italy had demonstrated, by sheer boldness in the Mediterranean, how easy it was to intimidate England and France. Boldness had been a feature of both sides in the Spanish Civil War but with good leadership and well-trained troops it could alter the whole character of military operations in a way that suited German tradition and spirit.

Their presence on Franco's side had shown them new ways of gathering intelligence and the advantages of using sympathetic Spaniards to infiltrate their fellow countrymen rather than transplanting outsiders. Two years of hard military experience were more use than ten on the training ground. Britain's vital lifeline through the Mediterranean to the Suez Canal and thence to its empire in the Far East was now under threat. Italy had more naval bases astride the route. Germany had the opportunity to install long range artillery either side of the straits of Gibraltar, at Algeciras in Spain and Ceuta in Spanish North Africa. More importantly, British shipping was vulnerable to air attack. He went on:

> Generally speaking, no big troop transport and no systematic trade in raw materials would be possible in the Mediterranean unless the hostile air force had previously been greatly reduced. England has definitely lost her monopoly of the Mediterranean. That sea has become a No Man's Land in which no fleet may operate in security and for the possession of which a stiff fight is being waged… The riparian peoples of the Mediterranean basin are looking on while the prestige of England and France crumbles away with every new success of General Franco. Since everyone knows that these successes are due in very large part to German arms, it follows that our prestige as well as our actual military strength have risen considerably.

The document, of which several copies were in circulation, was passed to Gladwyn Jebb, who had been private secretary to Sir Robert Vansittart and now held the same position with Sir Alexander Cadogan. Part of his duties was to liaise with MI6. Jebb, having satisfied himself that the document was probably genuine, took a remarkably relaxed view of its contents. It was, he said, a piece of internal propaganda designed to persuade doubters that Germany's intervention in Spain had been justified. It should not worry them very much because it dwelt on factors favourable to Germany and omitted those that were not.

He accepted that Germany had been able to gain valuable military experience and potential bases in Spain but thought that von Reichenau was entirely mistaken in supposing that Spain and Portugal might form an alliance or that Franco might annexe his Iberian neighbour. Nor would Italy acquiesce in the formation of a rival Mediterranean power.

Jebb believed that in victory Franco would seek 'to free himself from the grip of his totalitarian friends'. This should not be difficult since neither Germany nor Italy was in a position to occupy or physically dominate Spain, nor did they have sufficient economic influence to bring Franco to heel. He recommended that the economic, strategic and diplomatic aspects should be discussed with the newly appointed representative to Franco's Burgos headquarters, Sir Robert Hodgson. Jebb concluded:

> If we really feel, on the basis of such a technical investigation, that there is a definite prospect of 'the Dictators' being able to make good use of a Franco Spain in the event of a European War, then clearly we should revise our whole Spanish and Mediterranean policy. If we do not, then, equally clearly, it would be advisable for us to continue our present policy and endeavour to be on good terms with the victor at the end of the Spanish War.

Alongside Jebb's remark about a complete change of policy his new boss, Alexander Cadogan, wrote: 'How?'

Jebb made a sarcastic note in pencil at the foot of the page referring to Cadogan's belligerent predecessor Sir Robert Vansittart:

> By charging about, encouraging the French to open their frontier, picking a quarrel with Franco over the bombing of ships, and generally 'standing up' to Mussolini – in fact the policy of Sir R.V.!¹⁹⁰

In June 1938 Franco sent a message to the Prime Minister thanking him for his friendship towards Spain and assuring him that they were both defending the same ideals and principles. Embarrassed, Chamberlain and his Foreign Secretary agreed that there must be no publicity for the greeting.[191]

Around the same time, Sir Auckland Geddes at Rio Tinto was trying to persuade Franco to stop extorting money from his company. He pointed out that they had already handed over to the Nationalists £2m in sterling, cash and goods, just to keep the business going. They were subsidising it from their Rhodesian profits. When he got no response he suggested to the new Foreign Secretary, Lord Halifax, that the way to put a stop to the conflict was by a direct bribe of £1m to Franco to agree a ceasefire and the return of the monarchy under Prince Juan. Geddes recognised that the British government could not pay the bribe directly and therefore suggested that the money should be handed over to Rio Tinto 'to make use of as the occasion offered'. He argued that unless some kind of truce could be negotiated, either Russia or Germany would seize control of Spain's raw materials. The loss of Rio Tinto's iron pyrites imports was already jeopardising Britain's re-armament programme.

Lord Halifax was sufficiently interested in the idea to ask one of his senior officials, Sir George Mounsey, to investigate. He in turn took soundings from the Duke of Alba on Franco's behalf, Spanish Republicans and recent British visitors to Spain, before concluding that Franco would never agree to a truce with Republicans whom he regarded as murderers and assassins. He advised Halifax:

> Sir Auckland Geddes' scheme of bribing Spain indirectly through General Franco in order to re-establish the monarchy has no prospect of a successful issue. There would be no guarantee that the money so used would in effect induce General Franco to adopt this solution... The only real result would be that the Rio Tinto company would be provided with funds by His Majesty's Government which would enable them to maintain better relations with General Franco and possibly secure more facilities for shipping pyrites to this country.

This idea that Franco or his followers could be bribed seems to have gained wide currency. A Left Book Club publication, *Tory M.P.*, published in 1939 under the pseudonym Simon Haxey, commented:

> Certain Conservative circles believe that Franco-Spain can be bought, but the realities of the situation show that this is nothing but a pious hope, dictated perhaps by the feeling that they must indicate a way out of the serious situation created by their betrayal of Spanish democracy. The Italian press confidently jeers at the ineffective British suggestions of bribery.

This was a response to a report in *The Times* of 16 February that year quoting an Italian newspaper as saying:

> Ah, yes! There is always a condition attached. On condition that the blood shed by the noble youth of Italy be bartered for a sack of gold…
>
> We are delighted to inform you, gentlemen of the democracies, that we shall make you pay even for this last attempt at bribery. For we hold the knife by the handle. The victory of Spain is a Fascist victory, and you have got to reckon with it.[192]

By February 1939, the British government felt able to accept the Duke of Alba's request for formal recognition of the Franco regime as a legitimate government in Spain. The Duke visited Lord Halifax to stress that Spain had joined the Anti-Comintern pact solely because they opposed Communism and not because they were committed to the policies of the other pact members, Germany, Italy and Japan. He felt that Britain did not appreciate the sacrifices the Spanish people had made to keep the Bolsheviks at bay. He went on to dismiss rumours that Spain planned a military attack on Gibraltar. Halifax concluded that they were not as closely bound to the Germans and Italians as was frequently suggested and fully intended to pursue an independent line.[193]

Sir George Mounsey, through whose hands most reports on the war seem to have passed, made his feelings clear after reading an account of the fall of Madrid. He wrote:

> The strength of the Communist element right up to the last is shown in this account. Despite all the stories we have heard as to their suppression … it is quite clear that General Franco has in fact been fighting Communism in Spain and it is a great pity that our own reports and press accounts have done so much to obscure this fact and present us with an unbalanced picture. Those who have suffered under this anarchical rule and are now discovering the extent of the damage done will insist on some form of retaliation

and we must expect to see General Franco yielding to a considerable extent to those demands.[194]

With recognition of the regime, thoughts immediately turned to safeguarding Britain's commercial interests. With his experience as chairman of the British company that built and operated the Santander–Mediterraneo railway in northern Spain, David Eccles was on speaking terms with most of Franco's chief advisers. The line's principal station was at Burgos, which had been the Nationalist HQ, and Franco had used it to move men and matériel from Castile to the battlefront in Catalonia.

In March and April 1939 Eccles and a Board of Trade official spent several weeks in Spain discussing a long-term economic treaty and the possibility of reconstruction credits. They were followed by a German delegation with similar ideas. The stumbling block was past debts. Hitler demanded a $215m return as the price of the military spearhead provided by the Condor Legion and other support.[195]

By August the pendulum was swinging back towards France and Britain. The head of the Foreign Office economic department, Frank Ashton-Gwatkin, went to Paris for talks with Colonel José Ungriá, chief of the Spanish secret police.

MI6's formal presence in Spain was pretty thin on the ground. Its main representative was Colonel Edward de Renzy Martin, a former Inspector of the Albanian gendarmerie. When allegations surfaced in Spain that Britain had been running a pro-Republican espionage operation, Gladwyn Jebb, responsible for liaison with the intelligence service at the Foreign Office, recorded: 'My Friends have at present no organisation in Madrid and nothing is known of this matter.'[196]

David Eccles, however, was ranging well beyond his commercial brief. In mid-August he told Sir George Mounsey that he had a very reliable informant who had been close to Franco while the dictator was appointing his first Cabinet. His view was that the new Foreign Minister, Colonel Juan Beigbeder, was a man of quite exceptional ability. He was an isolationist in favour of 'Spain for the Spaniards'. Half the Cabinet were military men who owed Franco personal loyalty and the more extreme elements of the Falange had been excluded. Franco favoured Don Juan over King Alfonso but in any case was not prepared to contemplate a restoration of the monarchy in the immediate future.

This report found greater favour in London than a similar assessment by the ambassador, Sir Maurice Peterson. It seems that Sir Rex Benson, the merchant banker with MI6 connections, echoed Eccles's view. No report of his appears in the Foreign Office file but one diplomat commented:

> We are still in the same difficulty as we have been for months – namely how to approach Franco successfully and what to offer if we do get his ear – hard cash being out of the question. Let us hope that Col Beigbeder will in fact prove as much of a realist as Mr Rex Benson's recent memo would make him appear.[197]

Never one to miss a financial opportunity, Juan March was acting as intermediary to arrange a £20m loan for the new Spanish government through a group of Continental banks. Sir Robert Kindersley, a director of the Bank of England, was asked by the Foreign Office to stall the deal. If Señor March was going to be pulling the purse strings they wanted a hand in it.[198]

CHAPTER 10: MONARCHY

A t the start of the Second World War, the position of the Spanish royal family began to loom large in the thoughts of the Foreign Office. If Franco showed signs of throwing in his lot with Hitler there was an argument that it would be best to overthrow him and restore the monarchy to unite the Spanish people against Nazi-ism. Even if Franco remained neutral, it was vital not to allow King Alfonso, or his son Juan, to become figureheads of a German invasion. When war with Germany was declared King Alfonso was in Italy, where Mussolini had yet to commit himself to the Axis; Queen Ena, from whom he was effectively separated, divided her time between London and Rome but was later persuaded to move to neutral Switzerland. Alfonso and Juan's allegiance was uncertain.[199]

Behind the scenes the Foreign Office and Buckingham Palace had been quietly looking after Queen Ena, and to a lesser extent King Alfonso, ever since the fall of the monarchy in Spain in 1931. Queen Ena was born at Balmoral. Her mother, Princess Beatrice, was Queen Victoria's youngest daughter and constant companion even after her marriage to Prince Henry of Battenberg. Ena grew up in the royal court and spent her teenage years at Kensington Palace. Her first encounter with Alfonso was a State Banquet at Buckingham Palace. Their eventual estrangement followed the discovery that she carried the strain of haemophilia which debilitated many of Victoria's offspring. It had passed to several of Ena and Alfonso's seven children and only one of her five sons, Prince Juan, was healthy enough to ensure the succession.

He had been attending a Spanish naval college when Alfonso relinquished the throne in 1931. When the family went into exile he transferred to the British Royal Naval College at Dartmouth, spending five years in the Navy and rising to the rank of lieutenant. The King and Queen initially settled in France but soon led separate lives. Queen Ena moved to London. Alfonso settled in Rome.

The Queen maintained good relations with the British Prime Minister Stanley Baldwin, passing on messages from the Duke of Alba and interceding to obtain the release of a prisoner in a Republican jail.[200]

The British embassy in Madrid spent four years negotiating the removal of truckloads of Queen Ena's possessions from royal palaces in Spain. King George V's keeper of the privy purse, Sir Frederick Ponsonby, kept the embassy up to date with the Queen's requirements and King George picked up the bill. The diplomats had to be circumspect because they needed the co-operation of the Spanish Republican government without alerting the wilder elements of the left wing who might be tempted to loot the palaces for their treasures.[201]

The Metropolitan Police commissioner, Sir Philip Game, tried to withdraw a police protection patrol from outside Queen Ena's London home in Porchester Terrace, Bayswater in April 1938 on the grounds that he was short of manpower and there had never been any threat to her majesty's safety. He backed down immediately after a letter from King George VI's private secretary, Sir Alec Hardinge, saying that the King did not think it would be right, particularly as it appeared that Franco would win the Civil War and might then re-instate the monarchy in the form of Prince Juan, Ena's son.[202]

Arthur Yencken, soon to be minister at the British embassy in Spain, had reported in March 1939 from his previous posting in Rome that Prince Juan was the most suitable candidate for a restoration. Yencken had met him on a number of occasions, invited him to dinner and played golf with him. He considered him 'an excellent fellow'.[203]

The following month a diplomatic exchange took place between Frank Ashton-Gwatkin, chief economic adviser at the Foreign Office, and Prince Max von Hohenlohe, an Anglophile German prince who had a home in Spain and was close to King Alfonso. Ashton-Gwatkin had met the Prince in August 1938 during an ill-fated mission to find a peaceful solution to the Sudetenland dispute which paved the way for the Munich agreement. But in April 1939 they were discussing Spain's economic situation and the attempt by Franco to raise a £20m loan to get the country back on its feet.

In a 'Very Secret' addendum to his report, Ashton-Gwatkin revealed that Prince Max had met King Alfonso only two days previously. The King, whom Prince Max considered 'a clever man but a poor character', had said that he was too old to contemplate a return to the throne and was doing everything in his power to promote his son's prospects. He had stopped short, however, of actually transferring the rights to the throne until Juan's acceptance in Madrid was assured.

Sticking to his economic brief, Ashton-Gwatkin suggested that in these circumstances the British government, which was extremely doubtful about supporting the £20m loan in any case, might do better to wait and see whether it was to be given 'to our friends or our enemies'.[204]

There were strategic implications in von Hohenlohe's relations with the Spanish royal family. Anglophile he might be, but he was still German and a close confidant of Walter Schellenberg, who became Hitler's intelligence chief. If Hitler saw any mileage in Spanish royal support for a Fascist alliance between Germany and Spain then von Hohenlohe would have been the man to achieve it.

The British Foreign Office view was that the Spanish royal family would be safer on neutral territory. As war loomed the former Foreign Secretary, Anthony Eden, visited Queen Ena at Porchester Terrace to advise her that the government could not guarantee her safety. She was persuaded to go to Lausanne, staying at the home of the Marchioness of Craymayel, daughter of a Scottish shipping magnate. It was there that King George VI wrote to her, a week before war was declared, signing himself with his family name 'Bertie' and telling her that he still entertained hopes that with God's will war might yet be avoided. He added that he hoped she would not be away for long and that a visit to Balmoral might still be possible.[205]

In September 1939 the Foreign Office began diplomatic manoeuvres to safeguard Alfonso, while Hugh Pollard, who had been building up his contacts in Spain during the Civil War, began to dabble in various monarchist plots which varied from moderately practical to quite fantastic. He was working under the instructions of Lt Col Lawrence Grand, a dapper Royal Engineer sporting a carnation in his buttonhole, who had been appointed in April 1938 to run MI6's newly formed Section D, for destruction, and told to plan sabotage and stay-behind operations in the event of war with Germany. Alan Hillgarth got involved. He was newly promoted to naval attaché in Madrid, considerably above his previous status, on the recommendation of the director of naval intelligence, Admiral John Godfrey, who had been so impressed by his undercover work in Majorca. Their activities quickly revealed the underlying tensions and jealousies within the various branches of the intelligence services.

The Foreign Office had never been Pollard's biggest fan and they were even more damning of his boss Lawrence Grand. Gladwyn Jebb, private secretary to the permanent secretary Sir Alexander Cadogan, was especially scathing. He told an inquiry into the running of the intelligence services:

> Grand's judgment is almost always wrong, his knowledge wide but alarmingly superficial, his organisation in many respects a laughing stock, and he is a consistent and fluent liar. To pit such a man against the German General Staff and the German Military Intelligence Service is like arranging an attack on a Panzer Division by an actor mounted on a donkey.[206]

Jebb had a special interest. He was the Foreign Office liaison point with MI6 and was about to be transferred to be chief executive of the newly formed Special Operations Executive, which replaced Section D.

Grand's department occupied the top three floors of St Ermin's hotel in Caxton Street, just round the corner from New Scotland Yard. From there he plotted to deny German access to Romania's oilfields by sinking barges full of concrete at the Iron Gates, where the Danube cut through the Carpathian Mountains. The project was botched. An attempt to disrupt Swedish supplies of iron ore was similarly unsuccessful. The furore over Grand's plan to bring the monarchy back to Spain probably hastened his departure, to spend the rest of the war on engineering duties in India.

Grand's nemesis was a chain-smoking fellow Royal Engineer, Lt Col 'Jo' Holland, who, without his colleague's knowledge, had been appointed head of a guerrilla warfare unit at the War Office codenamed MI R. Holland was bald, burly and short-tempered. He had won the Distinguished Flying Cross during the First World War, served in Ireland and with Lawrence of Arabia in the Middle East. He considered Grand rash and careless. Grand considered Holland a stick-in-the-mud. When their departments were merged, inevitably they did not get on.[207]

Rumours abounded in Spain of a return of the King. In late November 1939 David Eccles wrote home from Madrid:

> The more I see of the situation here the less I like it. The poverty, misery and inefficiency are heart-breaking. No administrative competence anywhere and no leadership. Franco really has failed, and I always heard that if he did fail the only course would be to have the King back. And this is what is happening, a huge reaction in favour of Alfonso; of Alfonso and not of his son because the poor people want to get their friends – 800,000 – out of prison and they think Alfonso could impose an amnesty much better than his son, and he would stand no nonsense with the Falange but Juan might. Rumours fly, such as that Alfonso is here already, that five persons saw him praying at the tomb of his father in the Escorial, that someone else has received orders to brush up the Palace, that he visited Franco by night and is now in La Granja [the royal summer palace near Segovia] …[208]

At the beginning of May 1940, ten days before Churchill was appointed Prime Minister and just over a month before Italy declared war, Grand and the director of MI6, Sir Stewart Menzies, had meetings with Alan Hillgarth and Sir Percy Loraine, Britain's ambassador to Rome. Grand also sent briefing papers to Pollard.[209]

Hillgarth told Grand and Menzies that if Spain came into the war on the Nazi side or if Italy tried to seize part of Spain – such as the Balearic Islands – it might be possible to stage a revolution. He suggested using Francisco Herrera as an intermediary. It had been Herrera who acted as the go-between for General Mola, arranging to charter a plane in London to collect Franco from the Canaries to join the uprising.[210] Hillgarth offered to arrange a meeting with Herrera at San Sebastian, just inside the Spanish border with south-western France. He predicted that disaffected generals would welcome a return of the monarchy. The Army, the Church, industrialists and the rest of the country would fall in behind them if the monarchy promised a neutral Spain and political reorganisation.

Pollard, using the codename Don, was enthusiastic and wrote to Grand on 3 May:

> I do not think it would be necessary to stage a war or rebellion in order to effect the restoration, for the generals are, and always have been, predominantly monarchist. General Orgaz … is a fairly good organiser and it was with him that I worked when getting Franco from the Canaries. I am of the opinion that most of this stuff is being arranged in Paris… I think I can run our immediate needs for material, contact with Juan March, and a general browse around the situation all into one thing. I might like to go down to Spain itself later. I have no doubt that it will all prove to be very intricate and difficult, because a Spanish conspiracy always has to be far more complicated than we should consider desirable. Every Spaniard is jealous of every other Spaniard.

He claimed to know representatives of all the parties on the winning side in the Civil War – Carlists, *Requetes*, Catholics and Monarchists

– and suggested that they would favour the return of Alfonso's son, Don Juan. He added in a separate note that the people of Spain were fed up with Reds and Falangists, having tried both. Pollard had a dig at the Foreign Office, suggesting that 'it would not be inconsistent with actual history for the last four years if the FO were wrong in their opinion about Spain'.

He arranged to meet Juan March in Paris the following Wednesday, 8 May, even though he was still waiting for the War Office to confirm details of separate discussions he was to have on their behalf. He told Grand that he needed a diplomatic passport adding:

> I had better be as luxuriously equipped as possible. I attach considerable importance to this, as I must have not only company manners designed to impress, but a fairly substantial 'build-up' behind them, to meet, as tactfully as possible, those far reaching powers the Spaniards will assume I have at my back.

Someone, presumably Grand, wrote on his memo 'Good' and noted that the documents he asked for should be couriered to Spain. These were to form part of his *bona fides* for a separate and ultimately more significant mission.

The evidence of a serious rift in MI6 thinking came on 5 May when the Service's newly appointed head of station in Madrid, Leonard Hamilton-Stokes, sent a memo to Grand, a large chunk of which remains secret more than sixty years later. He began by complaining that Hillgarth was 'not generally regarded as an authority on Spain', having recently been rapidly promoted from his position as a retired lieutenant-commander and vice-consul in Majorca. He agreed that there was great unrest in Spain, which might easily flare up, but doubted whether Herrera was a reliable link. He went on:

> I do not believe that there is any popular strength behind a movement for the Monarchy ... [Next three paragraphs remain secret] ... In my view, a Republic has very much more hope of success and I believe that one formed along the democratic lines

we propose, uniting most of the many dissident parties in the old Republic, would pull the country together, allow them to get on with their trade and reconstruction, and keep them benevolently neutral in the war. I disagree with Don's views of this matter and do not believe he is *au fait* with current opinion among the general population of Spain.

Grand had noted, in his report on the meeting with Hillgarth, that restoration of the monarchy might fit in very well with Hamilton-Stokes's idea of a 'Democratic Alliance' in Spain which would include some monarchists. It was imperative to get the King out of Italy before the Italians realised he was their strongest trump card. If Franco were willing to remain neutral, they could use the King to upset him; if Franco were deposed by revolutionary elements (of the Left) the King could be a rallying point for a counter coup of the Right. He stressed also the need for utmost secrecy.

Sir Stewart Menzies had asked Sir Percy Loraine to speak to King Alfonso about the possibility of returning to Spain to command a neutral government but on 6 May Sir Alec Cadogan, the FO permanent under secretary, warned Sir Percy against the idea that Britain should play the monarchist card in self defence. He had no evidence that Spain would rise up in support of King Alfonso or Don Juan. On the contrary, he thought there was little demand for their return and monarchist influence was diminishing. The most likely outcome would be that Franco would remain in control or be ousted by an extremist pro-Nazi coup.

Cadogan advised Sir Percy to approach King Alfonso about his welfare in Italy and possible residence in a neutral country but not to link it to a potential uprising. His letter was marked 'Most Secret' and 'Burn after reading'. Sir Percy replied a week later that the King was confident that if the Germans or Italians attempted to seize Spanish territory his people would rise against them and he would raise his voice in their support.

Meanwhile in London disquiet over Grand's scheme was spelled out in three memos, unsigned but apparently written by Jo Holland, using the code-sign R, either to his opposite number Lawrence Grand or to higher authority. He began by telling Grand that the overwhelming need for secrecy had already been compromised – although he did not specify how – and that the plan was therefore 'foredoomed to failure'. He attacked Hillgarth, saying:

> What slight information I have of this officer and his former experience suggest that he is unfitted to reach a valuable conclusion upon such an extremely delicate and highly technical matter.

'R' went on to say that the 'Democratic Alliance', which Hamilton-Stokes was in the process of creating, appeared to offer a much greater chance of eventual success, which should not be jeopardised by this 'rather hare-brained scheme' to restore the monarchy. He then added a direct admonition to Grand himself:

> I think it is imperative that if any further action in the matter should be taken, it should at least be delayed until you have informed yourself fully in every respect regarding all action which may have been taken by Don.

In a separate memo, he spelled out further his concern that Grand had gone a long way to allowing Don (i.e. Pollard) to try his hand in the matter, even to the extent of possibly seeing his friend Franco, presumably to get him to acquiesce to a return of the monarchy. The memo continued:

> This intervention of Don scared me a great deal. He is most indiscreet, quite out of date in his information and a dyed-in-the-wool Franco-ite … I told D [Grand] it would be fatal to let Don touch the matter in any way at all politically and he was finally convinced of this.

In the meantime Hillgarth had been arranging the suggested meeting with Herrera at San Sebastian. The third memo, also assumed to be from Holland, complains that Hillgarth had exceeded his brief but culminates in Holland deciding that he should go to Bordeaux, just the other side of the French border from San Sebastian, to confer with two MI6 agents in Spain about the attitude of the generals and the chances of getting the monarchists to combine forces with the 'Democratic Alliance'. Holland was concerned that the meeting with Herrera was a 'frame up' and the spectre of Venlo was raised. Consequently, on 18 May, Hillgarth was told that MI6 would not send an emissary to Spain and that, unless Herrera was prepared to go to Biarritz, in French territory, the proposed meeting would be dropped.[211]

The Venlo incident was probably the nadir of MI6's fortunes. At the start of the Second World War two teams of agents had been running in Europe quite separately from each other. The first, long established, operated under the cover of consulate Passport Control Officers but was feared to have been at least partially penetrated and compromised. The second was deputy director Claude Dansey's Z Organisation, based on his widespread business contacts.

Although these two outfits were supposed to be insulated from each other, in Holland they were run in tandem by Richard Stevens, MI6's representative in The Hague, and Sigismund Payne Best, Dansey's man. The pair got sucked in to what they believed was an anti-Nazi network in the German army, supposedly including such senior figures as General von Runstedt. At the beginning of November 1939, the Prime Minister Neville Chamberlain approved further discussions with the German contacts and on 9 November both Payne and Best went to a rendezvous at Venlo on the Dutch–German border. It was a sting, orchestrated by the SS intelligence officer Walter Schellenberg, and the two British spies were captured, imprisoned and interrogated. It was a huge propaganda coup for Germany and, worse, it betrayed MI6's entire Dutch network. Best was actually carrying a list of his agents' names and addresses when he was caught. Needless to say, this disaster coloured the attitude of the new director of MI6, Stewart Menzies, and the rest of the service towards talk of dissident revolutions generally and army-led ones particularly.[212]

It appears that the idea of a monarchist coup in Spain was dropped at this stage although the outcome is not clear because parts of the National Archives files remain secret. However, Hillgarth was warned that the monarchist scheme risked compromising the security services with General Franco and this theme was taken up immediately by the new ambassador, Sir Samuel Hoare, when he arrived in Madrid in June 1940.

Hamilton-Stokes, like Hillgarth a retired lieutenant-commander, had previously been based in Gibraltar and had not won many plaudits for his intelligence on the Civil War. His plans for a 'Democratic Alliance' necessitated conspiring with trades unionists, some of them Communists, the very people who had just been defeated in a bloody civil war. This most definitely did not find favour with Sir Samuel. He foresaw that the minute Franco got wind of such interference in Spain's internal affairs he would close down the operation and, quite likely, be driven into Hitler's arms. Hoare demanded that Hamilton-Stokes be removed and all MI6 activity in Madrid should cease.[213]

This tension between those who saw Franco's continued ascendancy as the safest route to neutrality and those who hankered for a return to Republican government continued throughout the war. It is apparent in the MI5 files on Tom Burns, the press attaché at the Madrid embassy for most of the war, which cast a rare spotlight on arguments that went on behind the scenes.

Burns was a right-wing, Franco-supporting Catholic whose background, like Douglas Jerrold's, was in publishing. He fitted in well alongside Alan Hillgarth and mixed secret operations with his official duties. But part of his role involved trying to get the British point of view across in the pro-German, state-censored, Spanish press. Like Eccles and Hillgarth he had a slush fund to win over agents of influence and to publish and distribute a propaganda bulletin.[214] He consistently supported the accreditation of Spanish journalists to London whose background, when they were vetted by MI5, invariably and justifiably aroused suspicion. Burns believed that was a risk worth taking. Others disagreed.

His case was not helped by the political beliefs of those doing the vetting – Tomás Harris and Anthony Blunt at MI5, Kim Philby and his sympathetic boss Dick Brooman-White at MI6. Two of them were later unmasked as Soviet agents, Harris suspected of at least being a fellow-traveller, and Brooman-White gulled by Philby's undoubted abilities into supporting him almost to the last. Between them they composed a letter to Sir Alexander Cadogan, demanding Burns be dismissed, and tried to get the head of MI5, Sir David Petrie, to sign it. Petrie decided to hold fire, possibly because he was conscious of the direct link from Hillgarth to Sir Stewart Menzies and Churchill.[215]

Sir Samuel had an equally negative reaction when he discovered that Jo Holland's team from MI R were preparing a stay-behind Resistance movement in case Germany invaded. In July 1940 he told Lord Halifax:

> I have just heard to my surprise that there is some secret organisation of a section of the War Office, I think called MI R, at work in Spain. If my reports are correct it is spending considerable sums of money in circles of the Left with a view to stirring up internal trouble. I hope that these reports are untrue for I cannot imagine anything more dangerous and objectionable. There are only two possible policies here at present: the first to support a government that wishes to keep Spain out of the war, the second to stimulate a revolutionary movement against it. The immediate result of the second policy would be the entry of the Germans and Italians into Spain. I should be very glad to hear that either my reports are incorrect or that the organisation has been definitely suppressed. From what I hear the Spaniards already have some suspicion as to what is supposed to be happening.[216]

Churchill's friend Hillgarth, on the other hand, he was prepared to countenance. He wrote to the Prime Minister in June 1940:

> I am finding Hillgarth a great prop. Our minds work quickly and closely together and I have already given him a number of jobs to

do including a whole series of security measures for the Embassy and the staff.[217]

Hillgarth had greeted Hoare's arrival with a nine-page memo spelling out everything he thought was wrong with the embassy's operations and attitude. It was defeatist and lacking urgency, infested by the dilatory malaise of the Foreign Office; without even a 24-hour switchboard; lacking in expertise to present their case to the Spanish people with clarity and forcefulness; understaffed in vital areas like encryption and security. He recommended lending Spain economic assistance, without fanfare, while making clear that Britain would not be bullied by the Axis and its sympathisers into unacceptable concessions like the ceding of Gibraltar.[218]

Hoare took the message to heart. He quickly asked for a senior figure to come out and advise on press relations, leading to the appointment of Tom Burns, and suggested that Britain's leading film-maker, Alexander Korda, should be sent on a brief mission to recommend ways of spreading the British viewpoint. Korda, who had links with MI6, had already made a propaganda movie, *The Lion Has Wings*, starring his wife, Merle Oberon, and Ralph Richardson.

Hillgarth followed up his report to Hoare with a four-page memo which was broadly approved by the Chiefs of Staff and sent to the War Cabinet in January 1941. He argued that he already had Spanish support for a Resistance movement should Hitler invade and what was needed was a team of around forty specially trained British officers who could be sent in to provide leadership, expertise and military hardware. This became Operation Relator based in Gibraltar. Fighters, bombers and ships needed to be on standby for rapid deployment and Spain needed tangible evidence of British intentions in the form of immediate food supplies, starting with 100,000 tons of wheat.

Hoare was sympathetic to the monarchist scheme, albeit doubtful of its chances of success, and contacts were maintained throughout the war with members of the Spanish royal family and their representatives.

On the death of King Alfonso in February 1941 Hoare reported on a resurgence of monarchist feeling in Spain, brought about, he said, by the fact that the country was in the worst condition it had ever been: a miserable government, no food, 500,000 people in prison and an enemy on the frontier. He added:

> This terrible state of affairs makes people spend their whole time morbidly reflecting on their misfortunes and prevents them taking actions and decisions. The only way to dissipate this deadening atmosphere is to explode something into it. I believe that a monarchist restoration would be just the kind of explosion that is needed. It would give the Spaniards something else to think about and particularly give them the chance of believing that they were starting upon a new chapter.[219]

Queen Ena had rejoined her husband King Alfonso in Rome after the outbreak of war and remained there after he died but a channel of communication was kept open between her and Buckingham Palace, via her brother, Lord Carisbrooke, using diplomatic channels with the Vatican. When Lord Carisbrooke warned the Foreign Office that Queen Ena was short of money they tried to arrange for the Treasury to transfer her sterling and dollar income to Italy via Switzerland, in contravention of regulations prohibiting currency exchange with enemy territory. They wanted her to stay in Italy to stop her son falling under Mussolini's influence. Messages were relayed to her by Wing Commander Archie James, an honorary First Secretary in the embassy in Madrid, through Spanish monarchists who were able to visit her in Italy.[220] In due course she and Juan moved to neutral Switzerland. Ena kept Buckingham Palace aware of her situation through letters to George VI's mother, Queen Mary.

She returned to London after the war but eventually settled in Switzerland using a £30,000 legacy from the society hostess Mrs Ronnie Greville, who also lavished money and jewellery on Queen Elizabeth II and Princess Margaret.

Queen Ena was by no means the only royal whose wanderings around Europe concerned the British government. Far more problematic were the Duke of Windsor – the former Edward VIII – and his wife, Wallis Simpson, who had retreated, in the face of the German advance, from exile in Paris to Cap d'Antibes and then, in June 1940, to Madrid. Sir Samuel Hoare had the job of simultaneously entertaining and insulating them from German enticements. They were persuaded to move on to Portugal where David Eccles and Tom Burns were responsible for protecting them and countering the insinuation, planted by a Falange emissary of Walter Schellenberg, that the couple would be safer under Nazi protection in Spain. Franco's brother Nicolás, Spain's ambassador in Lisbon, tipped off Eccles who countered with Winston Churchill's telegram appointing the reluctant Duke governor of the Bahamas. This was reinforced by the arrival of Walter Monckton, who had been the Duke's lawyer during the abdication crisis and was now deputy director of the Ministry of Information, bearing a letter from the Prime Minister encouraging him to do his patriotic duty and warning him that he already knew, through intelligence sources, of the German blandishments.[221]

Hugh Pollard meanwhile submitted a report in December 1940 claiming there was support for a combined kingdom of Spain and Vichy France. This cannot have done much for his credibility in the Foreign Office. His self-confessed right-wing politics had already jeopardised his undercover operations. MI5 began to receive reports of his friendship with known Fascists, and Jane Archer, a senior record keeper at MI5 headquarters, had to warn her local officers in Kent and Sussex to 'lay off' after confirming with Valentine Vivian at MI6 that Pollard was working for them.[222]

There were other mysterious rumours about Pollard's activities. In March 1940 Dr Gerald Roche Lynch, director of chemical pathology at St Mary's Hospital, Paddington, and nicknamed 'The King's Poisoner' because of his role as a toxicologist for the Home Office, wrote to the security services asking for official sanction to divulge secret information to Pollard. They were old acquaintances through their work for Scotland Yard and Pollard had approached him about new developments in poisons.[223]

It was not Roche Lynch's most sensitive wartime inquiry. He was later called in to ensure that a consignment of cigars sent to Winston Churchill by the Cuban government was not booby trapped or poisoned. By the time he finished his tests Churchill had already smoked a batch of them and handed them round to the Cabinet.[224]

Pollard's last hurrah was an MI6 dirty tricks operation which began with the assignation he made with Juan March in Paris. Pollard's original requirement was for Italian ammunition and weapons to be obtained secretly by MI6 for use by Italian Resistance fighters opposing Mussolini's support for Hitler.

In pursuing this objective he got drawn in to a much larger opportunity to obtain 70,000 rifles and 80 million rounds of ammunition, plus 700 machine guns, with a price tag of just over $4m in US dollars payable to Juan March's Swiss bank account.

On 21 June 1940 the ambassador in Madrid, Sir Samuel Hoare, sent a telegram to London with the details, explaining that the arms belonged to the Spanish government and needed to be purchased secretly and urgently to ensure that they could not be used against the Allies by invading German forces or Spanish Fascists. Over the course of the next fortnight the scale of the deal grew to $10.5m dollars and included several thousand machine guns, and mortars with shells.

Hugh Pollard had been flitting between Madrid and Lisbon, involving himself in various schemes and making Sir Samuel Hoare, among others, distinctly nervous. The War Office welcomed his attempt to obtain the larger amount of arms but refused to take any responsibility for his MI6 activities or the tactics he employed. The Foreign Office likewise denied any responsibility while the Treasury was more concerned that some of the arms came courtesy of untrustworthy Middle Eastern arms dealers based in New York. Major Kenyon of MI R summed up:

> Our position *a propos* of the Secret Service is not very strictly defined and ... the War Office cannot undertake any responsibility

for the methods employed by SIS agents, even when the object for which the particular agent may be working is one in which the War Office may be particularly interested. I have made it quite clear throughout this deal that we are solely concerned with 'getting the goods'. I myself was unwilling in any way to become involved in the methods employed by Pollard who, as an agent of the SIS, is really responsible ultimately to the Foreign Office (or somebody in the Foreign Office) if the methods he employs, either at this end or the other, lead to trouble.[225]

The Foreign Office response to this was to adopt its traditional arms-length approach to the Secret Intelligence Service – to pretend they did not exist and simply refer to them as 'The Friends'. Sir Samuel Hoare and the embassy were advised to give Pollard discreet assistance but no official support. It fell to Captain Hillgarth to walk this particular tightrope.

It appears that the mission was aborted but it had established the important precedent of a willingness to channel large amounts of money into Juan March's Swiss bank accounts for nefarious purposes. Pollard began to fade from the scene and by July 1941 a decision had been taken to allow him to return to civilian life. A letter to Colonel William Jeffries, head of military intelligence in Ireland in the early 1920s when Pollard was working there as an agent, explained that: 'Certain jobs Pollard could apparently do well, but he was definitely unreliable where money and drink was concerned.'[226]

CHAPTER 11: DEALS

The Luftwaffe began the invasion of Poland at 4.45am on 1 September 1939. At 11.15am on Tuesday 3 September the Prime Minister, Neville Chamberlain, announced on BBC Radio that Britain was at war with Germany. Nineteen days later, Sir George Mounsey, newly transferred from the Foreign Office to the Ministry of Economic Warfare, received a visit from Juan March, who wanted to tell him how he could help the war effort. March was accompanied by his London banker, José Mayorga of Kleinwort's, and Arthur Loveday, the MI6 agent. His companions were both directors of March's London company.

March opened the conversation by telling Mounsey that 'he desired to offer his services ... without any remuneration' to Britain and France. He was chief shareholder of Spain's biggest shipping line, Trans-Mediterranean, which was subsidised by Franco. The General was a personal and intimate friend and had given tacit approval to what March was about to propose. Spain's greatest need was more ships to bring in the raw materials that were vital to rebuild her shattered economy after the Civil War. March wanted British sanction to buy fifty-five German merchant vessels blockaded in neutral Spain at the start of the war. He would re-flag them, and as neutral ships they could be used to supply not only Spain but the Allies. Naturally General Franco was in a difficult position with the Germans, who had assisted his victory, and could not be seen to be involved in such a transaction.

Mounsey reported next day to Admiral John Godfrey, director of naval intelligence, and that same evening Godfrey also met March. He found the Spaniard had a couple more aces to play.

March reminded him of his services to naval intelligence in the First World War. He was prepared to repeat the performance. He controlled oil supplies in Morocco and the Canary Islands. Soon he would do the same in Spain and would be in a position to deny German U-boats re-fuelling facilities in Spanish waters. His extensive contacts in shipping and ports would notify him of any U-boats putting in for supplies. Godfrey was dubious about the practicalities of buying the German ships but he was satisfied that March was genuine in his desire to help England, as by doing so he would benefit himself.

March added, almost as an afterthought, that he was in the process of selling a large quantity of Spanish armaments to the Yugoslavs. Godfrey reported to his political master, the newly appointed First Lord of the Admiralty, Winston Churchill, and added some explanatory notes saying:

> He [March] owns more than half of Majorca and is unquestionably the richest man in Spain. He financed Franco at the beginning of the Spanish Civil War. He was supposed, at one time, to be extremely pro-Nazi and pro-Italian, as against Spain, but this attitude is said to have changed… He is definitely a scoundrel of the deepest dye, but was one of the first Spaniards to try to convince Franco of the necessity for reopening trade with England, and from his commercial interests in this country his sympathies are believed to lie with the Democracies at this time. It is quite possible that his knowledge of the re-fuelling bases for German submarines is due to the fact that he is suspected of having arranged for them during the Great War.

This was just the kind of risky act of derring-do that would appeal to Churchill and he wrote back on 26 September:

> This man is most important and may be able to render the greatest services in bringing about friendly relations with Spain, in acquiring for us German merchant shipping … and in procuring

us, or our allies, munitions. We might even get torpedo boats from Spain through him. The fact that during the last war, when Spain was neutral, and somewhat pro-German, he made money by devious means, in no way affects his value to us at the present time or his reputation as a Spanish patriot. He risked everything for General Franco at the outset of the struggle against Bolshevism in Spain, and financed the Rebel Government to the extent of his whole private fortune. I have no doubt that he hates the Nazi regime as much as the Bolsheviks, both being equally inimical to capital.

Churchill could scarcely contain his enthusiasm and the next day fired off another memo to Admiral Godfrey, saying:

It is most important to buy Spanish destroyers and, through the Spaniards, German interned merchant men. How will the communication be made to him [March]? How long will it take to reach him? I am very sorry I did not see him myself, and I shall be glad to know if he is likely to return here. Supposing his talks with the naval attaché show any substantial promise, it would be well that Senor Marche [sic] should come over here again, when I would see him personally.[227]

The naval attaché in Madrid, Alan Hillgarth, who already knew March well from his time in Majorca, was quickly on to him about the ships and the arms deals but, with the Foreign Office and the Treasury dithering, both deals became locked in a limbo of indecision and conflicting departmental priorities.

On the same day that Churchill was demanding action, government lawyers were explaining that for a neutral country to supply a belligerent country with warships, ammunition or any other form of war material was illegal under the Hague Convention. In other words Spain would cease to be neutral and become a participant, on the Allied side. While this might seem superficially attractive, it would increase the risk of Hitler invading Spain and put the Allies under an obligation to defend her territory. It would also run counter to Franco's intentions.

A background note revealed that Spain had thirteen modern destroyers, built under the supervision of the British firm Vickers in its Spanish naval yards. But if Spain sold Britain its destroyers there was nothing to stop other neutral countries selling their warships to Germany. As for the German merchant vessels, Britain had already issued an international edict that any neutral country re-flagging German ships for their own use would be liable to have them seized by the Royal Navy. By March 1940 a British naval blockade had trapped 222 German merchant ships of more than a million tons around the world. Moreover, although Juan March might claim he would pay the Germans nothing until after the war, simply lodging the purchase price in a Spanish bank, it was doubtful whether that would actually happen. Even if it did, Germany could borrow money from third parties using Juan March's pesetas as security.

In the face of opposition, Churchill paused to take advice and then raged because it was slow in coming and contradicted his wishes. By November 1939 he returned to the charge, claiming that even if Germany did get its hands on some foreign currency, Britain's need for merchant shipping was so great that it would be worth it. Hillgarth had been back in London for consultations and returned to Madrid, with his wife and small son, to conduct further negotiations with March.[228]

Typical of the opposition was Sir Andrew Duncan at the Board of Trade whose views of March were contradicted, word by word and line by line, by Churchill in a memo. Duncan wrote (with Churchill's later red-ink comments in brackets):

> Juan March was pro-German (why should not he be?) and later pro-Nazi (why not?) and he is a clever self-seeking rogue (both ticked). He would certainly double cross us if he could (not certain). He has made a lot of money (why not?) and money-making is his main interest (quite untrue, he was ready to sacrifice everything for Franco).[229]

Churchill sent word via Hillgarth to David Eccles, now based at the Madrid Ritz as a representative of the Ministry of Economic Warfare, that he should draw up a workable scheme for the merchant ships. This, Eccles confided in a letter to his wife via the diplomatic bag, had been 'a devil of a job' both because it was extremely difficult in itself and because he knew his proposals would go straight to the War Cabinet.[230] He suggested a more complicated formula, the effect of which would be for Britain to acquire some of March's existing merchant fleet while he acquired the German vessels. The War Cabinet considered the situation but decided to take no immediate action. In January 1940 Hillgarth wrote personally to Churchill, warning him that there were rival elements in the Spanish government willing to do a deal direct with the Germans.[231]

Juan March's throwaway line to Godfrey about an arms deal between Spain and Yugoslavia got to the ears of the Cabinet Secretary, Lord Hankey, whose mind was turning over how Britain could get out of an awkward defence agreement with Turkey. The country had declared its neutrality but its borders were menaced by Germany and Russia.

A Turkish general, Kâzim Orbay, was in London in October 1939 negotiating arms supplies and met Churchill, who promised him naval protection in the Black Sea, if required, and agreed on anti-submarine measures in the Dardanelles and the Bosphorus.[232] Orbay's priority was to arrange delivery of tanks, light artillery, trucks, anti-tank weapons and anti-aircraft guns with a £25m credit provided by Britain and France. The problem was that Britain needed all the armaments she could lay hands on for her own defence. Hankey hoped that Spain might be persuaded to make a barter deal, taking a Commonwealth export such as jute, rather than hard currency, in exchange for the arms that the Turks needed.

Alan Hillgarth had already confirmed with the Spanish government towards the end of September that Juan March was acting in a quasi-official capacity in arms deals. The Foreign Office tried to override that with a formal arrangement made by the ambassador Sir Maurice Peterson and Vickers Armstrong in

Madrid. In the ensuing muddle the Turks tried to do a deal behind Britain's back and the whole scheme collapsed. The lesson, not lost on Churchill and Hillgarth, was that the way to get results was to deal direct with the man who pulled the strings – Juan March.

By 17 February 1940 Admiral Godfrey's personal assistant Ian Fleming was becoming increasingly exasperated about the shipping issue and wrote:

> I think we should quickly get this matter out of the docket stage and see if it will walk, otherwise let it die. It is already half-throttled with paper. If kept on the present interdepartmental level there will be opposition all along the line. The problem should, therefore, reassume the cloak of brigandage under which it started.[233]

He proposed that it should be handled by himself, Godfrey, Churchill's principal private secretary and a 'sharp financier' from MI6. In April Hillgarth came up with a new proposal from March. He would buy the German ships through his company Trans-Mediterranean for a price to be agreed but not paid until after the war. March would be obliged to stop any of his fleet trading direct with Britain or France. Instead, Spain could divert other shipping lines to Allied trade and March could continue to trade with British colonies. An unofficial British manager would oversee the arrangements and if they did not work to her advantage the Royal Navy could seize the German ships. It was not enough to satisfy the doubters but Hillgarth's negotiations did eventually bear some fruit. In 1942 the Special Operations Executive in Gibraltar handed over £1m to March in exchange for six ships which could be used for attacks on enemy forces in North Africa. March's tobacco smugglers were also active running escape routes for Allied airmen.[234]

While delving into the intricacies of shipping finance and international law, Ian Fleming discovered that March, despite being the richest man in Spain, had got himself in difficulty over a large loan in Britain. March had borrowed more than £1m from Kleinwort's, who had asked for it back at the start of the war.

Baring's bank, with encouragement from the Bank of England and the Treasury, had come to the rescue and now held the debt. Fleming proposed that Baring's chairman, Sir Edward Peacock, should drop a heavy hint to March that if there were problems over the shipping deal, arms purchases or espionage generally, the loan would be called in. Fleming explained:

> A vague hint that it might be called in again would certainly bring M to his senses and get him down to brass tacks. This would involve him in a difficult feat of acrobatics, in view of his various relations with Foreign Powers, but we must bind him body and (if any) soul to the Allied cause … Once we have ensured a firm grip of him through his pocket, I suggest we should get him over here to see the First Lord [Churchill], and that all cards should then be placed on the table and the whole Spanish position thrashed out.

Admiral Godfrey agreed and a week later Fleming reported that Sir Edward Peacock had spoken about it to Arthur Loveday and was sending a message to March via an English sherry producer suggesting that March should come to see Churchill.[235]

A separate report to Admiral Godfrey revealed that March, acting on behalf of the Spanish government, had a £1.8m loan through the private bank Robert Benson & Co., whose chairman Sir Reginald 'Rex' Benson had long association with the intelligence services. The head of MI6, Stewart Menzies, was his cousin.

The loan was covered by £2m of British gilt-edged securities (equivalent to £57m in 2010) but the Bank of England was refusing to take it over. March's banker, Jose Mayorga, appealed to the Foreign Secretary, Lord Halifax, for help and he agreed to take it up with the Chancellor of the Exchequer.[236]

March would have been familiar to Baring's bank. A member of the Baring family had been an intelligence officer in Gibraltar when March was tipping them off about U-boats in the First World War. Sir Edward Peacock's clients had included Alfred Loewenstein and the Barcelona Traction company whose tortuous finances were to

lead Juan March to his greatest financial coup, aided and abetted by
the British Treasury and banking establishment.

With the outbreak of war, new efforts had been made to secure a
trade agreement with Spain. The outstanding pre-war debts became
less of an obstacle. Three pro-Franco MPs, Sir Ralph Glyn, Victor
Cazalet and Wing Commander Archibald James. urged the Prime
Minister to act.[237] Glyn had worked for MI6, was close to its director
Sir Stewart Menzies and went on to work for the Special Operations
Executive; Cazalet was a vociferous supporter of the Friends of
Nationalist Spain and became liaison officer to the Polish wartime
leader General Sikorski; and Wing Commander James became First
Secretary at the Madrid embassy from 1940–41 and closely involved
in setting up the secret operation that kept Spain neutral.

During the summer of 1939 Frank Ashton-Gwatkin from the
Treasury had been making unofficial contacts. In August, on the
brink of war, he was approached by a British businessman, A. E.
Minchin, to conduct secret talks in Paris about £10m worth of
export credits for business with Spain.

This was authorised by Sir George Mounsey at the Foreign Office
after discussions with David Eccles, who convinced him that a more
imaginative and up-to-date method of conducting commercial affairs
unofficially in Spain was called for. Eccles told him that the Bank of
South America in Madrid could bring British and Spanish commercial
interests together without exciting undesirable public notice.

Minchin's contacts in Paris included the Spanish Finance
Minister José Larraz and Colonel Ungriá, head of the secret police.
Minchin explained that Ungriá had a financial interest in the deal,
which therefore had to be conducted in the greatest secrecy, but
could help to wean the Franco administration away from the Nazis.
Ashton-Gwatkin told them that he could not offer gold or cash but
thought an export credit was the next best thing. On 24 August he
reported to London:

> It seems to me that the importance of taking this opportunity
> can hardly be exaggerated and that no time should be lost. If

we can secure the friendly neutrality of Spain at one end of the Mediterranean, and the active help of Turkey at the other, then we have got Italy at our mercy. And it is through Italy that we can defeat the Axis.

He got the wholehearted support of Sir George Mounsey, who regarded the prospect of securing Spanish neutrality as 'absolutely essential'.[238] Less than two weeks later, war intervened and David Eccles took over the negotiations. Eccles, now a counsellor in the diplomatic service, had been recruited early in 1939 to the skeleton staff of the Ministry of Economic Warfare which only officially came into being at the outbreak of war.

During the summer he had prepared a trade brief to give to the Duke of Alba. By September he was billeted with his team at the Madrid Ritz, which was so full he had to share a room with the Treasury official Sir Edward Playfair. Eccles regarded himself as suspended between the Ministry of Economic Warfare and the Foreign Office: 'An amateur surrounded by sharp-witted professionals.'

He was more in sympathy with the Foreign Office than his new Ministry, whose job it was to enforce a blockade that would prevent vital supplies reaching Germany via sympathetic neutral countries. They assumed that Franco would repay his debt to the Axis powers that had helped him win the Civil War. In particular, Eccles did not see eye to eye with his Minister, Hugh Dalton, whose Labour Party background naturally inclined him to regard Franco as Hitler's pawn. Dalton took the view that he would rather have Spain as an enemy now 'naked and starving' than buy her off with supplies and then find she was an enemy still.

Eccles argued strongly that it was in Britain's interests to supply Spain with food and raw materials and by doing so suborn Franco from his Fascist-leaning supporters and, equally, to stop the Fascist supporters replacing him with someone worse.

All Spaniards were sick of bloodshed and would turn against Franco if he led them into another war. As for Franco himself, he cared only for Spain, for the Catholic Church and for shooting rabbits. If one looked at Spain as a whole what did one see? Starving cities with industries at a standstill for want of imported raw materials. Franco would soon learn that Germany could not offer him wheat, oil and cotton whereas the British Commonwealth could … what sense could there be in imposing a blockade on Spain so severe that Franco would be deprived of the most popular reason for remaining neutral, and be in a position to fix the blame on us for the resulting food shortage and unemployment? Even supposing some supplies had been allowed through the Blockade, and then the Germans persuaded Franco to declare war on the Allies, the common people would know where their bread had come from and be on our side, as they were in 1808 when Napoleon invaded.[239]

In their early negotiations, they were helped by the fact that Franco's Foreign Minister, Col Juan Beigbeder, initially pro-Germany, soon transferred his sympathies to Britain. In August 1940 Sir Samuel Hoare wrote to Churchill:

A situation has been created by which nobody could be more surprised than myself. Beigbeder is an emotional romantic who has made a fine reputation in Morocco and a Spaniard in the tradition of Don Quixote. The very opposite, in fact, to my humble self. Nonetheless he seems to have taken a great liking for me and appears at any rate to tell me all his innermost thoughts.[240]

Hoare had access to £500,000 in 'special funds' to ensure that a safe means of approach to Beigbeder was available.[241] Beigbeder had a British mistress, Rosalinda Powell Fox, whom he had first met, by chance, at the Hotel Adlon in Berlin in March 1936. He had been military attaché in the German capital from 1926 to 1935 and had returned with General José Sanjurjo on what is thought to have been an arms buying mission for the forthcoming coup.

Mrs Fox, estranged from her husband, an official of the British Raj, had met Sanjurjo in Portugal while convalescing after a serious illness. She moved to Tangier during the Spanish Civil War and re-introduced herself to Beigbeder, who was Moroccan High Commissioner, in Tetuan. They spent a romantic afternoon on the beach and the affair blossomed. Conscious of Beigbeder's Anglophile sympathies she resolved to bring them to the attention of the British government:

> I could see that it would be tragic that if on the final victory of the Nationalists, Britain were to be regarded as an unfriendly power and Germany as an ally. This would bode ill for Spain, I felt, and above even that, no good at all for my own country, who relied upon Gibraltar and the Mediterranean for its lifeline to the Empire and the dominions in the east. I resolved, a mere woman that I was, with no official capacity, to do what I could to remedy the situation and to strive to enable the British government to see the folly of their present attitude and the need to adopt a far more flexible policy toward the Spanish situation.[242]

Her friend Colonel Henry 'Hal' Durand, who lived in Tangier and was the son of a diplomat, passed on the message to the Foreign Secretary, Lord Halifax, on a trip to Britain. After the outbreak of the Second World War she followed Beigbeder to Madrid where he had become Minister of Foreign Affairs. She was cold-shouldered by the British ambassador, Sir Maurice Peterson, but became socially acceptable when Sir Samuel Hoare replaced him in June 1940.

During the summer of 1940, in San Sebastian, she teamed up with Peter Kemp of the Special Operations Executive to help three Scottish airmen, fleeing the Nazis from France after being shot down, to escape. Beigbeder, she claims, loaned her an official car to get them to a boat in Bilbao.[243]

As pressure on Beigbeder grew, and German antagonism to him became more pronounced, she relocated to Lisbon once more and the affair became a long distance relationship conducted through smuggled correspondence. She opened a nightclub, El Galgo, which became a favourite haunt of spies and diplomats.

The British team were making heavy weather of the trade talks. After months of stonewalling it took a personal meeting between Eccles and Beigbeder at a private party to unlock the deal that would enable Spain to sell goods to Britain and use the proceeds to buy Commonwealth food and raw materials. The deal was signed in March 1940.

It granted Spain £5.5 million in credits on condition that Spain did not re-export to Germany the vital supplies of oil, coal, rubber, cotton and tin supplied by the British Empire. According to a later American analysis:

> One of the major factors which kept Franco neutral during the days of Nazi military victories in 1940 and 1941 was Spain's dependence on the Anglo-American markets for oil, cotton, rubber, tin, and wheat. Anglo-American sea power and control of chartered tankers, coupled with the destruction of the civil war, meant that any Falangist dreams of joining the Axis were more a dream than a reality. Perhaps Franco's sphinx-like stance at his first and only meeting with Hitler – at Hendaye in October 1940 – was forced upon him by economic circumstance; perhaps it was the fruit of an over-narrow nationalist vision.[244]

Churchill's view was that Franco's policy throughout the war was entirely selfish and cold-blooded – dictated solely by Spanish interests. The meeting at Hendaye, on the French-Spanish border where German troops had been gathering since the collapse of France in June 1940, showed Franco at his most crafty. Far from manifesting gratitude for Hitler's help in the Civil War he now asked for the right to redraw the Spanish boundary at the Pyrenees to include part of France and to seize French possessions in North Africa. He showed no willingness to admit the German army to Spain. Churchill commented:

> This narrow-minded tyrant only thought about keeping his blood-drained people out of another war. They had had enough of war. A

million men had been slaughtered by their brothers' hands. Poverty, high prices, and hard times froze the stony peninsula. No more war for Spain and no more war for Franco![245]

Franco dismissed Beigbeder as Foreign Minister a week before the meeting with Hitler and replaced him with his Falangist brother-in-law Serrano Suñer, who paid a return visit to Hitler in November 1940. The Fuhrer's intelligence chief, Admiral Canaris, followed this up in Madrid seeking to arrange the passage of German troops through Spain to capture Gibraltar. Franco expressed willingness, but subject to conditions that he knew to be impossible: only after Germany invaded Britain; only when Germany captured the Suez Canal; only if the capture of Gibraltar could be accomplished by Spanish troops with German equipment.

Beigbeder gave Sir Samuel Hoare a secret briefing about the discussions between Hitler and Franco and then pledged himself to the Allied cause, promising to lead armed resistance if Hitler marched into Spain and tried to capture Portugal and Gibraltar. He intended to bring troops from Morocco to stem the German advance and asked for British air support if the need arose and stockpiles of arms and supplies to be ready in Gibraltar. He planned to declare the restoration of the monarchy and act as Regent, from a base in Madeira. 'Let the lines of Torres Vedras be ready by December 15,' he concluded – a reference to the Duke of Wellington's defensive positions to protect Spain and Portugal from invasion during the Napoleonic Wars.[246]

In an urgent despatch to London, Hoare insisted that any prospect of Britain mounting a resistance action to a German incursion in Spain would depend on support from the Spanish army, rather than the remnants of the leftist opposition movement, and he repeated previous warnings that the presence in London of the former Republican Civil War leader Juan Negrín was a sore point with Franco and his supporters. Foreign Office under secretary Roger Makins minuted:

General Beigbeder's advice is sound but his admonition not to flirt with the Republicans will be most unpalatable to those in MEW

[Ministry of Economic Warfare], MofI [Ministry of Information], the BBC and other places where it is thought that foreign policy should be coloured by political prejudices and not based on realities.[247]

Through the spring of 1941 Beigbeder was warming to his plans for resistance to Hitler. Although he was confined to his home near Ronda, in southern Spain, he managed to have clandestine meetings in April 1941 with Vice-Admiral James Somerville, commander of the naval H Force based in Gibraltar, and with Wing Commander Archie James and Bernard Malley from the Madrid embassy. Beigbeder was dreaming of a Moorish uprising in Morocco uniting the Spanish and French administered territories under a pro-Allied sultan. The Foreign Office in London feared that he might take some precipitate action and 'upset the apple cart'.

However, Sir Samuel Hoare visited Gibraltar and reassured London that these schemes would only come to fruition if the Germans tried to occupy the Spanish mainland. A record of his visit, withheld until the year 2003, also reveals that he had talks with Alvary Gascoigne, consul general for Tangier and Spanish Morocco, about 'certain payments to individuals in Morocco' which he was to make out of funds specially provided from London. Hoare gave Gascoigne a list of Moorish and Jewish activists provided by Beigbeder as useful contacts. He also got approval for the scheme from the head of SOE operations in Gibraltar, Hugh Quennell.

The mention of what was obviously yet another bribery scheme came as a surprise even to senior figures in the Foreign Office who began to ask Alan Hillgarth what was going on. He professed ignorance while urging them to disregard it and certainly not disclose it to anybody else.[248]

By this time Eccles had achieved a second agreement, after intensive personal negotiations with the Portuguese Prime Minister, Dr António de Oliveira Salazar, through which Britain financed Spanish imports from Portuguese colonies and allowed them through the blockade. While in Lisbon, Eccles also negotiated directly with Franco's brother Nicolás who was Spanish ambassador.

These clandestine trade deals needed to be conducted by front companies. One such was the Columba Corporation, run by Sir John Wardlaw-Milne, banker, businessman, MP and wartime chairman of the Conservative foreign affairs committee.

In December 1939 he helped Michael de Tchihatcheff apply for an exit permit to go to Estoril in Portugal, on behalf of the Columba Corporation, to boost Britain's export trade. Tchihatcheff was a personal friend, who was well known in the government's Export Credits Guarantee Department, which understood the importance of the mission. The application was supported by Lt Col Keith Menzies, older brother of the director of MI6, who gave his address as White's Club. Tchihatcheff was also a member and Stewart Menzies often used the billiard room as an auxiliary office of the Secret Intelligence Service. Tchihatcheff had been responsible for introducing Ashton-Gwatkin to Colonel Ungriá of the Spanish secret police the previous April yet he was under long term surveillance by MI5 as a suspected member of OGPU – the forerunner of the Russian KGB. Among his business associates was a former Vickers agent and gun runner, Brigadier Guy Livingstone, who had been involved in the prospective arms deal with Turkey that Hugh Pollard and Juan March tried to set up.

On the plus side, Tchihatcheff, an aristocratic Russian exiled after the Bolshevik Revolution, had been on the staff of the British Military Mission in Petrograd in 1918 and served in the British army in the Baltic under the pseudonym Michael Foster. He also employed Gaspard Ponsonby, son of one of King George V's senior courtiers, as his secretary.

MI5 only found out about Tchihatcheff's mission to Spain in February 1941 when they were tipped off by Eugene Sabline, who had been chargé d'affaires in London for the Tsarist regime and maintained a semi-official role as representative of the Russian community in exile. The deputy director of MI5, Guy Liddell, warned MI6 and SOE that Tchihatcheff was not to be relied upon and they denied employing him, although they plainly knew of his presence in Spain. In June 1941 Harry Hunter, head of MI5's watchers, reported:

> My informant states that Michael de Tchihatcheff was a sympathiser with the General Franco party during the Spanish civil war, and knows that he is making every effort at the present time to keep Spain from entering this war on the side of the Axis Powers. He has written to her to the effect that the great body of opinion in Spain is on the side of Great Britain and that he is doing all he can to foster this feeling. His actual address in Spain is not known to her as he writes through a firm of solicitors in Lisbon.[249]

The Columba Corporation was specially set up in 1939 and although it continued to exist until 1965 all Companies House records have since been destroyed.

Eccles and Hillgarth became involved with events in North Africa. The action being taken to keep Spain out of the war, and the Straits of Gibraltar open, would be worth little if Germany could occupy the opposite shore. The Moroccan coastline was a Spanish protectorate, with Tangier as an internationally administered port. On the Mediterranean side of the straits, Algeria and inland Morocco were under the control of Vichy France and therefore vulnerable to German influence.

Throughout the second half of 1940 Churchill was nagging away at the idea of a military adventure in North Africa which would secure the Allied position. He had proposed an attack on French Morocco in July 1940 – codenamed Operation Susan – at the same time as the French fleet was destroyed in port in Oran to keep it out of German hands. He argued that occupying Morocco would give a much needed boost to General Charles de Gaulle and the Free French and added:

> The attempt to set up a French government in Morocco, and to open up a campaign in Morocco, with a base in the Atlantic, is

in my view vital. It was most cordially adopted by the Cabinet in principle. I should find very great difficulty on becoming a party to its abandonment, and to our consequent relegation to the negative defensive (tactic) which has so long proved ruinous to our interests.

The Chiefs of Staff pointed out that they would need 25,000 troops and the only ones available were raw recruits in the UK who would be vital to the country's defence if Hitler invaded. Churchill raised the issue again in August, and was rebuffed once more by the Chiefs of Staff.[250]

As early as June 1940 Sir Samuel Hoare was offering contrary advice, based on his perception that Franco and Beigbeder were determined to keep Spain out of the war but needed something to boost their military prestige. Morocco, to which both men had a strong emotional attachment, seemed the best outlet. Hoare suggested that they should be allowed Tangier as a trophy and as a counterbalance to German and Italian influence in Vichy-controlled French Morocco. In July Sir Alec Cadogan also suggested to Lord Halifax that Spain should be allowed to encroach into French Morocco unless General de Gaulle could reorganise French Resistance there.[251]

Hillgarth then wrote a report that went to the War Cabinet on 20 September in which he said the Spanish people were impressed by Britain's fighting qualities and that Franco was losing all prestige. The country was not being properly governed and – he added with no apparent irony – 'peculation and bribery are worse than at any time in the past century'.

Hillgarth estimated that the motorised divisions of the German army could storm across Spain in a week and be in a position to attack Gibraltar. But they could not subdue the country in that time and they would be confronted with resistance from the army and the population who would harass their extended supply lines. The danger of Allied action in French Morocco would be that Spain, which did not recognise de Gaulle, would retaliate to protect her own interests and be dragged into the war on the side of Vichy France, Germany and Italy.[252]

Churchill had been won over. A week after the War Cabinet discussion he wrote to Lord Halifax:

> I entirely agree ... that we should delegate authority to our embassy at Madrid to smooth the economic path, and settle minor blockade points out of hand ... I would far rather we should pay our way with Spain by economic favours, and other favours, than by promises of giving up Gibraltar after we have won the war. I do not mind if the Spaniards go into French Morocco ... I would far rather see the Spaniards in Morocco than the Germans, and if the French have to pay for their abject attitude, it is better that they pay in Africa to Spain than in Europe to either of the guilty Powers. Indeed I think you should let them know that we shall be no obstacle to their Moroccan ambitions, provided they preserve their neutrality in the war.[253]

In November the Spanish Foreign Minister Serrano Suñer authorised Spanish troops to take control of Tangier.

Eccles, the master of the bribe and the commercial bait, was sent to Tangier to assess the situation and then, without full authorisation, began exploratory talks, in co-operation with the US consul general in Algiers, Robert Murphy, to see whether General Maxime Weygand, the Vichy commander in North Africa, could be induced to favour the Allies in return for a trade deal for essential supplies similar to that already agreed with Spain. Eccles argued that it would demonstrate to French colonies that friendship with England was possible and valuable, with very little risk of goods being diverted to the enemy, prepare Morocco for an Allied occupation and guard against the Spaniards or the Germans entering Morocco on a pretext of quelling trouble.

Early in November Roger Makins, at the Foreign Office, told Eccles that £1m of the money allocated to the United Kingdom Commercial Corporation, set up to trade with neutral countries, was being 'lost' to make food purchases for Spain and added: 'There are two questions, is the bribe big enough? And will the Americans play?' Despite that encouragement, Eccles was still in pessimistic mood. In a letter to his wife Sybil he talked about the 'demoralisation by corruption' at work in Spanish ministries and wrote:

> I think we are all to blame, but especially the Service Departments who ought to have made their voice heard, and swept aside the hesitations of the civilians in offering the inducements which would have kept Spain neutral. How important to the conduct of the war is the neutrality of Spain? I can't say with any expert knowledge, but I know that if I were fighting in the Eastern Mediterranean my heart would sink if I heard the Western door shut with a clang. And not only my heart, but the hearts of all the French, who put their rising hopes in our cause. How will they feel, trapped and surrounded like Czechoslovakia? For all these reasons we should have gone straight ahead, generously and boldly, buying the neutrality, yes, and the goodwill, of the Peninsula. I never doubted it could be done, I never wavered in my advice or in my efforts, but we are beaten by the old gentlemen and the modern ideologists, who place personal fears and fancies before the King's interest. God forgive them, they lay upon us and upon millions of Spaniards an appalling burden.[254]

His efforts in North Africa did not bear fruit, even though he spent three months early in 1941 in Washington pursuing them. US president Franklin D. Roosevelt was well-disposed towards Weygand but others in the US administration were not. Equally importantly, there were strong objections in London, not least from the leader of the Free French, General Charles de Gaulle. However, Eccles was not wasting his time in Washington. In collaboration with Rex Benson of MI6 and William Stephenson, director of British Security Coordination in America, he helped William 'Wild Bill' Donovan draw up a report for President Roosevelt on the theory and practice of clandestine operations. Donovan became head of the OSS – Office of Strategic Services – forerunner of the CIA.[255]

In a New Year message to his Chiefs of Staff on 6 January 1941, Churchill predicted:

> To invade and force a way through Spain to the Straits of Gibraltar against the will of Spanish people and government, especially at this season, is a most dangerous and questionable enterprise for Germany to undertake, and it is no wonder that Hitler, with so many sullen populations to hold down, has so far shrunk from it. According to Alan Hillgarth … it is becoming increasingly unlikely that the Spanish government will give Hitler passage or join the war against us.

As it later transpired, Hitler had reached the same conclusion, expressed in a New Year message to Mussolini on 31 December 1940:

> Spain has refused to collaborate with the Axis Powers. I fear that Franco may be about to make the biggest mistake of his life. I think that his idea of receiving from the democracies raw materials and wheat as a sort of recompense for his abstention from the conflict is extremely naïve … I deplore all this for from our side we had completed our preparations for crossing the Spanish frontier on January 10, and to attack Gibraltar at the beginning of February. I think success would have been relatively rapid. The troops picked for this operation had been specially chosen and trained. The moment that the Straits of Gibraltar fell into our hands the danger of a French change-over in North and West Africa would definitely be eliminated.[256]

David Eccles's next objective was to keep Spanish mineral supplies and Portuguese wolfram, an ingredient in steel making, out of German hands. He freely acknowledged that his successes, quite apart from any diplomatic skill, were accomplished by extensive bribery.[257]

He remained firmly of the opinion that Franco's 'outrageous' public pronouncements of sympathy to the Nazi cause he had a genuine desire to remain neutral. Franco judged that Hitler would not invade Spain and he had no intention of inviting him in. He could mollify his Falangist supporters with fighting talk while taking British economic aid, ungraciously and without public acknowledgement. He was playing a sly waiting game to see which side would emerge victorious from the war.

CHAPTER 12: BRIBERY

The pattern and principle of covert payments via Juan March to members of the Spanish government and its military hierarchy were well established and had set the scene for Hillgarth's most extraordinary deal of all.

Churchill was acutely conscious of the damage a Nazi occupation of Spain and Gibraltar would inflict on Britain's ability to defend her own shores, because it would sever her vital supply route from the Far East via the Suez Canal and the Mediterranean. He drew up plans to invade the Canary Islands as an alternative naval base but when he replaced Chamberlain as Prime Minister in May 1940 he decided that the best tactic was to bribe Franco's generals to stay out of the war. He discussed this with his new ambassador to Madrid, Sir Samuel Hoare, and briefed Alan Hillgarth personally, during a visit to London, setting him up with a slush fund of $10 million – later increased to $13 million – in an account at the Swiss Bank Corporation in New York. Down payments in pesetas were filtered to the targets through Juan March's Spanish companies.

The timing could not have been better. Within weeks of Hoare's arrival in Madrid Franco sacked his Air Minister, General Juan Yague. Yague had served Franco well in the past. When the Civil War started he led his troops from Ceuta across the Straits of Gibraltar to Seville and northwards to capture Badajoz where he was responsible for the massacre of thousands of prisoners and civilians, including women and children. He justified his action by claiming he could not leave them in his rearguard to launch a counter attack.

But Yague's outspoken support of the Falange and personal friendship with their leader, José Antonio Primo de Rivera, did not endear him to Franco. Yague, for his part, became frustrated by Franco's dilatoriness and made explicit criticisms. He opposed Franco's vengefulness against his enemies and began reinstating Republican officers in the air force, including freemasons. He became involved in a plot to remove Franco. It was exposed by the intelligence services and after a tense and emotional meeting with Franco on 27 June 1940 Yague was sacked and exiled to his native village, San Leonardo in Soria.[258]

On 20 June Hoare had been able to tell the Foreign Secretary, Lord Halifax, that Yague had received 20 million pesetas – about £500,000 – from the Germans to distribute among officers of the Spanish army and air force to encourage them to be loyal to the Third Reich. Franco had been shocked. Yague had also been on the verge of doing a deal to buy aircraft from Germany. His dismissal cleared the field for Hoare and Hillgarth to weigh in with their much larger slush fund.[259]

The effects were quickly apparent. On Christmas Eve 1940 Sir Samuel Hoare sketched out the situation in Spain to Anthony Eden, recently re-appointed as Foreign Secretary. He regarded Spain as the worst governed country in Europe. In the midst of anarchy there were 40,000 Germans organising things to their liking and the additional menace of the German army on the frontier across the Pyrenees. It was inevitable that Spaniards would put up a smokescreen of unfriendliness to Britain. They would not be grateful for economic aid but they would be hostile if it was refused.

While it was tempting to leave her people to starve and let the Spanish government take the blame, it was not in Britain's interests. That would be the excuse Hitler needed to occupy the country. Hoare insisted that ensuring Spain's independent economic survival was entirely in British interests and represented a strategy for winning the war. Public opinion was already turning against German domination and, crucially, so were the views of senior figures in the army. He explained:

> I put the Army view down to some extent to certain very
> confidential arrangements … that I made here about which I would
> ask you to inform yourself, and to an even greater extent to the
> growing resentment felt by the senior generals against German
> dictation. I think that you can also feel happy that … the British
> embassy is regarded as the centre of this growing feeling of Spanish
> independence.

He added a handwritten note saying that his 'excellent' naval attaché, Alan Hillgarth, was on his way to London and would give him a fuller briefing about the very secret matter in which the Prime Minister was taking such a great interest.²⁶⁰

Eden made arrangements to ensure that the operation of the slush fund was known by only a handful of people.

The biggest beneficiary was General Antonio Aranda, director of the Spanish military school, who received more than $2m. He had captured Oviedo for Franco in 1936 but was regarded as a potential leader of a coup if Franco showed any inclination to disregard his generals' advice and join the Axis powers. He was known to be pro-British and had been cultivated during the summer of 1939 by Wing Commander Archie James, the First Secretary in the embassy, and by David Eccles.

Aranda had been put in touch with Lord Lloyd, the president of the British Council, whose peacetime objective was to spread the country's cultural message around the world.²⁶¹ MI6, however, were not above using it as a vehicle. Lord Lloyd had once been Douglas Jerrold's protégé as a potential Tory 'dictator' but had been convinced of the Nazi threat since 1936 and was an opponent of appeasement. He became a roving ambassador to neutral countries, seeking to convince them that the war represented a defence of Christian civilisation against atheistic totalitarianism.²⁶²

Lord Lloyd paid a personal visit to Franco in October 1939 to persuade him to accept a British Institute in Madrid, and later other major Spanish cities, to share in Britain's cultural heritage. It seems an odd thing to do when war was about to engulf Europe but this was a battle for hearts and minds, even the hearts and minds of pre-school children. One of the most successful enterprises of the new Institute was a kindergarten, open to Spaniards, which was rapidly over-subscribed. This was a small coup against the Germans, whose own cultural offensive had a head start and a much bigger budget.

Franco insisted that senior staff of the Institute must be Catholic and this too, was turned to advantage. The inspired choice for director was Professor Walter Starkie, of Trinity College, Dublin, an anti-Republican Catholic Irishman. Starkie, an exceptional violinist, spent the early 1930s wandering Spain on foot in the company of 'raggle-taggle' gipsies. The tales of his adventures had a popular following and he knew more of Spanish culture than most Spaniards. His eccentric lifestyle was perfect cover for a British agent and the fact that he had supported Franco in the Civil War established his credentials. He and his part Italian, part South American wife Augusta played host in their Madrid flat to a procession of Jews and prisoners of war making their escape from occupied France.

The Institute was based in an aristocratic mansion close to *El Retiro*, Madrid's central park, and the Prado Gallery. It included a galleried baronial hall for lectures and concerts. Starkie kept up a varied programme of events to lure the Spanish elite into the British ambience and supplemented it with distinguished visitors who might appeal to Spanish sensibilities.[263] One of the first was Lord Sempill, a celebrated aviator who had collaborated with Juan de la Cierva on the development of the autogiro. One of Sempill's ancestors had been a courtier to King Philip II of Spain, and advised him not to send the Armada to confront Queen Elizabeth I, and another had been King James I's ambassador to Madrid. Sempill was a member of the Right Club, in political sympathy with the Franco regime. He had also been investigated by MI5 over his willingness to divulge Britain's aviation secrets to the Japanese while working for them as a military adviser and only escaped prosecution under the Official Secrets Act because the court case would have revealed that the Security Service had been interfering with diplomatic mail.[264]

The bald, rotund Starkie and the tall, lean embassy press and intelligence officer, Tom Burns, worked as a team – nicknamed Don Quixote and Sancho Panza – and were jointly involved in the ill-fated visit by the film star Leslie Howard.[265] By October 1941 Starkie was able to report back to London:

> The best tribute to the growing sympathy for England among all classes in Spain is the ceaseless Gestapo watchfulness against us. We are full of spies and counter-spies and hardly a day passes without the Embassy informing me that I am being followed and tracked. Some tell me that I am regarded as a spy, others that we are fomenting plots in the Institute.

German attempts to discredit Starkie personally foundered on his record during the Civil War. He had been on the Franco side in the thick of two of the bloodiest battles: the Christmas 1937 siege of Teruel and the summer 1938 battle of the Ebro.[266]

The Catholic contingent, Starkie, Burns and his deputy, Professor Bernard Malley, also held sway over the influential Spanish Catholic community. Starkie considered that some of Britain's best friends were in the priesthood and Sir Samuel Hoare sent back a number of despatches of inside information gleaned, apparently by Malley, from leading churchmen. A senior member of the Augustinian order in the monastery at El Escorial – a former royal palace – confided snippets of government gossip elicited from Juan Beigbeder during his occasional retreats there; the Jesuits expressed their apprehension at German influence.[267]

General Aranda earned his backhanders by consistently opposing the pro-Nazi policies of Franco's brother-in-law, Serrano Suñer, who replaced Beigbeder as Foreign Minister.

Eccles recalled a meeting he and Wing Commander James had with Aranda in November 1940 in which the Spaniard came across as so pro-British that Eccles began to worry whether he could deliver on his promises, or that the Germans might become aware of his loyalties and have him removed. Aranda said he and other generals had been warning Franco that economic survival must take priority over politics, leading Eccles to the view that 'they possess the only shred of common sense in a fool's purgatory'. The generals were fed up with Suñer behaving like an incipient dictator and Aranda was hoping to be brought into the government as Defence Minister. Eccles added:

> He would take charge of administration and orientate Spanish economic policy in our direction instead of the present rudderless higgledy-piggledy (his gestures and language here were delicious). The guiding principle would be anti-Axis. I said this sounded fine.[268]

General Aranda was a fervent monarchist. Franco was well aware of that, and of his pro-British attitude. He was eventually arrested by Franco in 1943, but later released, for plotting to bring back Prince Juan. His co-conspirator, and fellow beneficiary of British bribes, General Luis Orgaz had been prepared to lead a coup against Franco if he was guaranteed Allied recognition, but at the last minute concluded that he was not certain of sufficient support in the Spanish army. He contented himself with joining others in a petition to Franco asking him to consider a restoration of the monarchy.

Orgaz had been well-known to Hugh Pollard as the general who had helped him arrange Franco's flight from the Canaries to Morocco in 1936. He was one of the old school of army officers, jealous of their own positions and resentful of the influence of the Falange whose members also had a reputation for corruption when placed in positions of power.

Suñer was a leader of the Falange and the bane of Sir Samuel Hoare's life. So the ambassador was only too happy to see his career undermined. It was fortunate then that he was despised by many of the army officers who made up Franco's closest circle, who were emboldened by the rustle of British money to criticise Suñer to their leader.

He had been Interior Minister before he was Foreign Minister and still exerted influence in his old department. At the beginning of May 1941 Suñer arranged for a decree to be issued exempting the Falange press from the strict government censorship; he made public speeches attacking Britain and supporting Germany in far stronger terms than Franco would tolerate, particularly in the wake of an extra £2.5m of trade credits Britain had agreed in April; he began to demand greater Falange representation in the government. It looked like he was building a rival power base and this thought was reinforced by an anecdote about Franco's 15-year-old daughter Carmen having asked, disingenuously, at dinner one day whether her father or her uncle ran the country.

It was a crucial moment for Britain. After recent reverses in Greece and Yugoslavia, with the United States unwilling to enter the war, Churchill could not afford to see German troops sweeping across Spain towards Gibraltar and North Africa.

Franco was always conscious that his own position was not secure and acted swiftly, without warning his brother-in-law. Two of Suñer's most persistent critics, Generals Kindelan and Orgaz, were given the key commands of Catalonia and Morocco respectively, a new anti-Falange Minister of the Interior was appointed, and a series of further re-shuffles followed that significantly diminished Suñer's influence.[269] The pro-Falange press hinted darkly at British machinations and Sir Samuel Hoare was more than happy to take the credit privately while insisting that no hint of satisfaction should appear in British newspapers. In a 'Most Secret' personal note to Eden he wrote:

> No doubt you have realised that the political changes here are directly due to the secret plan of which you and the Prime Minister are aware. This makes it all the more necessary to stop any publicity that may give the impression that we are greatly interested in what has happened.[270]

There was a sub-plot of which Hoare was remarkably well-informed. Suñer was married to Zita Polo whose sister Carmen was married to Franco. Gossip to the effect that Suñer was having an affair with the Marqués de Llanzol's wife Consuelo had reached Franco's ears and probably Carmen's. In November 1941 Hoare was able to report from a most secret and special source that Suñer had a five-hour crisis meeting with Franco which culminated in a family reunion during which he went into the chapel and swore on oath that he had never slept with Consuelo. This written pledge had to be presented to the Marqués to clear his name in a court of honour but it was not going to save Suñer. He was, said the source, 'safe in the family nest for the moment but the nest is in a state of siege'.[271]

It took nearly a year for the siege to end in the final humiliation of Suñer. He was held personally responsible for a Falange bomb attack on a Carlist memorial service for their members who had died in the Civil War. Franco used the subsequent outrage as a cue to dismiss Suñer and replace him as Foreign Minister with General Francisco Jordana, who was more sympathetic to the Allies.[272]

In 1997 it was revealed that Suñer's name appeared on a list of dormant Swiss bank accounts along with a number of Hitler's supporters including concentration camp deputy director Willy Bauer, Hitler's photographer Heinrich Hoffmann, and Hermann Schmitz of I G Farben, the company responsible for Zyklon B, used in the gas chambers. Suñer, who lived to be 103, responded that it was an account used to pay college fees in Switzerland for his six children.[273]

One of the more bizarre acts of espionage took place in Spain in the summer of 1941. Lt Col. Dudley Wrangel Clarke, who used a position as war correspondent for *The Times* as cover for MI6 work, was arrested in a Madrid street dressed as a woman, right down to his brassière. He first claimed to be a novelist attempting realistic research for a character and then to be taking the clothes as a gift to a lady friend in Gibraltar, which made it all the more curious that they fitted him so well.

Hillgarth had the job of persuading the Spanish police to take a light-hearted view of the episode and release the surprisingly uncontrite agent. The naval attaché obviously hoped that the Prime Minister might be similarly amused. He sent him personal copies of the police before-and-after photos, the first portraying Dudley

Clarke in a loud floral-pattern V-neck dress with short puff sleeves, elbow length black gloves and white turban, black stockings, high heeled shoes, white clutch handbag, dark lipstick and mascara, with tell-tale unplucked eyebrows. By contrast the latter photo showed him in pinstripe suit, houndstooth check bow tie, with white handkerchief in his breast pocket and clutching a briar pipe in his hand in determinedly masculine fashion.

When Clarke was safely back in Gibraltar he was interviewed by the governor, Lord Gort, ex-Grenadier Guardsman, former Chief of the Imperial General staff and holder of the Victoria Cross, who came to the conclusion that Clarke was in all other respects mentally stable and showing no signs of insanity but had undertaken a foolhardy and misjudged action. He was practising 'cover' for a false information channel to the Germans in the Middle East. He was allowed to return there and pursued a brilliant career in deception and undercover work.[274]

Clarke wrote his own account of his intelligence work without mentioning his arrest in Spain in 1941. He does describe events in May 1940, at the time of Dunkirk after Hitler's invasion of France, just as Churchill assumed the Premiership and began his secret campaign to keep Hitler out of Spain and Spain out of the war. Clarke was summoned by his commanding officer in London and told that he had to go very quickly, under elaborate conditions of secrecy, to co-ordinate last-minute plans with a very important group in a neutral country. It was feared the Germans might extend their attack at any moment. He was instructed to go in disguise.

He and his contact from the foreign resistance group were to leave immediately. They met at the staff entrance of the Piccadilly Hotel and:

My disguise met with approval and I was paid the doubtful compliment of being assured that I might be taken for almost anything but an officer of the British Army!

They flew from Hendon to an unobtrusive spot a long way from their real destination – almost certainly Spain – and completed the journey by train, travelling in separate carriages. Clarke went to a hotel and waited for hours until his courier turned up and took him by car to what looked like an engineer's depot. They went along twisting underground corridors to a conference room where about a dozen men were present. There were no handshakes or introductions. There was a second meeting the next day after a rendezvous in a museum. They went through a store room and back into the underground tunnels for another conference. He returned to London after a weekend which had 'a dreamlike quality'. Clarke adds:

> As things turned out it was just an episode which had no effect at all upon the prosecution of the war, for the German invasion of that particular country never in fact took place. Perhaps we may have helped a little bit to halt it, but in the interests of a group of clear-sighted and courageous patriots I have felt it best to cloak the episode with anonymity.[275]

Clarke's role as commanding officer of 'A' Force put him in charge of strategic deception for Middle East Forces, including misleading Rommel about Montgomery and the Eighth Army's assault on El Alamein. In 1943 he began an elaborate series of manoeuvres to convince the Germans that the Allied push into Europe would begin in Greece, the Balkans or France, thereby drawing their attention and their military reserves away from the intended target in Sicily.

He was therefore required to give his approval to Operation Mincemeat, overseen from London by Hugh Pollard's cousin, Lieutenant-Commander Ewen Montagu of naval intelligence. It involved disguising the body of Welsh labourer Glyndwr Michael, who died of liver failure as a result of swallowing rat poison in a suicide attempt, as William Martin, a fictitious major in the Royal Marines acting as a courier between London and the Middle East. He was floated into the sea from the submarine HMS *Seraph* near the port of Huelva in southern Spain on Friday 30 April 1943 and, as the deception planners hoped, picked up by local fishermen. A briefcase containing documents apparently relating to a British offensive in Greece was attached to the body. These duly found their way, via the Spanish military authorities, to the Germans, who fell for the ruse, believing that Major Martin had been a passenger in a crashed aircraft.

The choice of Huelva as the best location was made on the advice of Alan Hillgarth's deputy, Lieutenant-Commander Salvador Gomez-Beare, who knew the coastline and that Huelva was the most likely place for the body to be handled by the Spanish, who would be less meticulous in their examination, rather than handed directly to German agents. Hillgarth's role, in co-operation with the local British consul Francis Haseldon, was to show sufficient concern for the proper formalities for a British war victim, and the return of his personal effects, without giving the Spaniards reason to think they were being set up.[276]

Hillgarth referred to his $13 million slush fund as the Knights of St George, an allusion to the figure of England's patron saint depicted on one side of a gold sovereign – the coinage traditionally used when Britain needed to pay allies in earlier European wars. Other British officials preferred the French expression 'pots de vin' but whatever the name, the intention was the same – to buy power and influence over the course of Spanish politics with old-fashioned bribery and corruption. Hugh Dalton wrote in his diary on 16 May 1941:

> In Spain, the Knights of St George have charged, that is what has brought about the recent changes; that is also what has caused the disquiet of attaché H about the tinplate of J. M.

Hillgarth, in other words, was anxious that Juan March should get the cash which the generals had been promised and which he was to disburse. The technicalities proved complicated. The Knights were almost unhorsed in late summer 1941 when the US government froze the New York account where the money was held, suspecting it was being used by Juan March for pro-Nazi purposes.

By September, after six weeks in which the Foreign Office failed to resolve the problem, Sir Samuel Hoare regarded the American blockade of the bribery payments as so critical that he sent Alan Hillgarth back to London to deal with it.[277]

Hillgarth spent the weekend with the Prime Minister at Chequers and wrote out for him on two sheets of Chequers notepaper the nub of the problem. The ten million dollars had been transferred from Geneva to the Swiss Bank Corporation in New York who knew nothing of its purpose. The Foreign Office said that it was impossible to explain to the Americans what was going on and the Treasury had a convoluted scheme to route the suspect money through Canada. The quickest way to resolve the problem was to get President Roosevelt to unblock the money without telling the US Treasury or the Swiss Bank the reason.

Churchill dispatched a copy of the note, and Hillgarth in person, to the Foreign Secretary and the Chancellor of the Exchequer, Sir Kingsley Wood, who tried to stall him. He told Churchill that he was concerned that transferring the money via Canada might cause a leak with serious consequences for the Spanish recipients. A personal appeal to the President would put him in the awkward position of having to issue instructions to his Treasury Secretary, Henry Morgenthau Jr, without explanation. Wood suggested rather naively that it would be much better for the recipients if the money stayed in the US until the end of the war, with an assurance that it would not be confiscated by the Americans. Churchill commented:

> Can't you give them something on account? We must not lose them now after all we have spent – and gained. Vital strategic issues depend on Spain keeping out or resisting. Hillgarth is pretty good.

Sir Samuel Hoare himself returned to London to sort it out. The ambassador in Washington, Lord Halifax, approached Morgenthau at the US Treasury with a personal appeal from the Prime Minister that the money was due to unnamed individuals for political services rendered and there could be serious consequences if it remained blocked. To their relief Morgenthau agreed that the money should be moved to a new unblocked account.[278]

In 1942 in Madrid Hillgarth briefed the newly arrived representative of the American Office of Security Services, Colonel Robert Solberg. He reported back to his chief, William Donovan, that Hillgarth's instructions to create a hostile attitude in Spanish army circles toward Spain's entry into the war had come from Sir Stewart Menzies, head of MI6. According to Solberg, Juan March was well known to Menzies and had approached thirty Spanish officers on Britain's behalf.

The initial tranche of ten million dollars had been intended to last for the six months up to May 1941. It had then been topped up with another one million dollars 'for new members' and in the autumn of 1941 a further two million dollars was added to see them through to the summer of 1942. At that point the generals asked for a written pact guaranteeing British support when they decided to overthrow the Franco regime, restore the monarchy and throw in their lot with the Allies.[279]

This caused some consternation in London and Hillgarth was recalled for discussions. The position remained, as it always had been, that from London Franco looked like the best practical option. The Foreign Secretary, Anthony Eden, spelled it out in a letter to Hoare on 3 June 1942:

> As I see the position, we have decided that, in the event of an invasion of Spain by the Germans, or of the Spanish government throwing in their lot with the enemy, it would be in our interests that a Free Spanish Movement should be formed, capable and willing to carry on the fight from overseas. We think that a movement which aimed at a restoration of the Monarchy would at present seem likely to obtain a wide measure of support in Spain … Hitherto we have not felt that it is necessarily in our interest to bring about the early overthrow of the existing Spanish Government … we run the risk that the new Government may be rapidly overthrown by the Germans or be forced to give way to their demands. The

present Government, although it permits many un-neutral acts in its territory and is by no means ideal from our point of view, has so far maintained a sufficiently independent policy where our major interests are concerned.[280]

One reason for maintaining the status quo was that planning for Operation Torch, the joint British and American invasion of North Africa, was well advanced and a closely guarded secret. Toppling Franco might have had some peripheral attraction but the last thing the Allies needed was for Hitler to start taking renewed interest in Spain.

Churchill expressed concern that the build up to the huge operation would become evident in Gibraltar where ships and aircraft would gather. He was worried that Hitler would demand intelligence or action from Franco.[281]

Britain and America had the advantage of knowing how the dictator's mind was working when it came to Hitler. British agents had been breaking into the Spanish embassy in Washington and stealing diplomatic traffic and cipher codes. William Donovan's new organisation took over the operation, despite an attempt to sabotage it by the all-powerful head of the FBI, J. Edgar Hoover, who did not want other agencies trespassing on his territory. The supply of ciphers enabled code-breakers at Bletchley Park in Buckinghamshire to read Spain's diplomatic telegrams. They showed that Franco would not allow the Germans into his territory prior to Operation Torch and he maintained that position after the success of the North African landings, accepting personal assurances from Churchill and Roosevelt that Spanish sovereignty would be respected.[282]

The Bletchley Park decrypts had already come up with a dossier, overseen by Kim Philby at MI6's Iberian section, revealing a secret German surveillance scheme that would have jeopardised Operation Torch. With Franco's acquiescence they had installed a seabed sonic detection system across the Straits of Gibraltar using relay stations in Spain and Morocco. Commando raids to destroy it were considered but a diplomatic solution was preferred.

The ambassador, Sir Samuel Hoare, with his embassy staff in full uniform, presented themselves in Franco's office and laid the dossier before him, explaining that a likely consequence was the complete cessation of oil supplies which would bring Spain to its knees. After some prevarication, Franco ordered the Germans to dismantle it.[283]

Philby, incidentally, was not an admirer of Alan Hillgarth's work and in his autobiography describes rather sneeringly how the naval attaché spent large amounts of money bribing Spanish officials to give him details of German agents in Madrid when Philby already had the information from other sources. Philby's view may have been coloured by the fact that he had been cut out of the loop. Hillgarth, at the Prime Minister's insistence, reported directly to Sir Stewart Menzies using the code name Armada.

On 8 November 1942 more than 100,000 US and British troops, commanded by General Eisenhower, began the successful invasion of French Morocco, Algeria and Tunisia and its capture from the Vichy French government. As a consequence, the Germans occupied Vichy France.

Even after the success of Operation Torch, with the war swinging in favour of the Allies and making Franco's publicly pro-German stance more precarious, the British government did not want the distraction of a coup against him. Plans for the next phase of the war – the invasion of Italy – were in hand and Eden again warned Hoare, in response to renewed monarchist activity, that they should expect no assistance from the Allies. He did, however, ask Hoare to try to keep Don Juan out of Italy's clutches.[284]

Sometime around July 1944 Hugh Ellis Rees, the Treasury's man in Madrid, wrote an appraisal of wartime financial relations with Spain.

There had been three agreements: a £5.5 million loan repayable over twelve years; an understanding that products allowed through the blockade would not be re-exported to Germany; and a financial clearing agreement which would pay off Spain's accumulated £7m of pre-war trade debts. They had achieved those targets while simultaneously raising the standard of living and suppressing any

Spanish inclination to go over to Hitler's side. An additional £2m in sterling was about to be paid to keep wolfram supplies out of German hands. The Anglo South American Bank held 220 million pesetas for use in the wolfram deals although it was not all needed and the Spanish had agreed to convert about 80 million pesetas back into sterling, a decision which found particular favour with the Treasury. The official exchange rate at the time was 44.5 pesetas to the pound.[285]

Many years later David Eccles also reflected on what he admitted had been a life of Humphrey Bogart style glamour: flying boats to Lisbon, intrigue, lovers, rogues, jewels and finery.

He told *The Guardian* newspaper that his main responsibility was to persuade Franco, by means of trade, that it was better to remain neutral than to join Hitler. That might seem obvious with hindsight, and Churchill recognised it, but half the government was against him, particularly Hugh Dalton. The greatest mistake of the war was the failure of the military to work with the economics people to plan war strategy. Total war meant that rather than send an army division, or a squadron of bombers, you could bribe people to come on to your side. President Roosevelt had understood that the first time they discussed it. Eccles implied that there had been kick-backs on everything from cases of oranges to tins of Spam and that the Ministry of Food in London had not understood that there had to be extra money on the table as part of the bribery war. He had not handled the money himself, simply directed where it should go. It was supplied by the Treasury and channelled through the Bank of Portugal.

> I saw we couldn't fight for Gibraltar. Nothing to fight with. So we bribed. I was an apostle of bribery.

Spanish generals, ambassadors and politicians – anyone who was any use – had been paid millions. But he was evasive about whether any of it had found its way to Franco or his family. On Franco he replied: 'Not from us.' But on his brother Nicolás, the ambassador in Lisbon, he added: 'Well ... his brother was a jolly man.'

Eccles credited his wife's charm at 'seducing' the powerful figures in London whom she met through her father Lord Dawson – men like the Foreign Secretary Lord Halifax and senior Foreign Office officials – with getting him extra leeway to subvert the Spanish leaders with the Knights of St George.[286]

Hillgarth's success is attributed to his ability to exploit a large circle of influential friends in Spain. In that, his wife Mary played a crucial part in the great deception. According to her son Jocelyn, she became a very popular hostess, thanks to her social standing and command of Spanish. She found the overtly pro-German feelings of many of her guests repulsive and personally hoped for a restitution of the Spanish monarchy. But she helped in the running of the escape lines for Allied airmen and escaped prisoners of war making their way home from occupied France and she had the comfort that both daughters from her first marriage, Joan and Elspeth, were brought out from London, reluctantly, to work in the embassy because as family they could evade the visa restrictions imposed by the Spanish on diplomatic staff. Nevertheless, she told Jocelyn in 1943: 'I hate being here. Life in London is hard and grim but at least it's real, not completely false.'[287]

In 1942 Mary's daughter Elspeth married one of Alan Hillgarth's SOE assistants, David Muirhead, who would go on to be an ambassador to Peru and Portugal and head of Foreign Office personnel. He had served in an infantry regiment at the start of the war and been evacuated from Dunkirk before going on special operations and parachute training at Lochailort, a remote village on the west coast of Scotland in February 1941. He was the adjutant to Operation Relator – also known as Ali Baba and the Twenty Thieves – preparing resistance and sabotage teams in case Hitler tried to occupy Spain.[288]

At Lochailort, Muirhead met Peter Kemp, one of the few members of the team with any previous knowledge of Spain or the language. They spent three weeks on intensive training – forced marches, pretending to blow up bridges with dummy explosive, small arms and unarmed combat – before embarking for Gibraltar. There they found themselves kicking their heels because the ambassador, Sir Samuel Hoare, insisted that he would not have sabotage squads in Spain unless Hitler actually invaded.[289]

Operation Relator was a combined SOE, MI6 and naval intelligence operation run by Admiral Godfrey's personal assistant Ian Fleming. Fleming went out to Gibraltar to oversee the preparations and to liaise with the newly arrived head of American secret operations, William Donovan. The team of around twenty men were to work in pairs, spreading out across Spain to galvanise local resistance to German occupation and carry out sabotage missions. It was renamed Operation Golden Eye, the name Fleming later used for his villa in Jamaica.

After Hitler invaded Russia the threat to Spain receded and most of the Golden Eye team was withdrawn but Fleming continued liaising with Alan Hillgarth in Madrid and Muirhead moved there full-time. Fleming and Hillgarth's friendship continued after the war.[290]

Kemp asked to be parachuted into the Basque country to organise a Resistance movement there but when that was vetoed he transferred to SOE's Balkan operations, going on to fight behind the lines in Albania and in Poland, spending three weeks as a prisoner of the NKVD, the Russian secret police, before transferring to the Far East and seeing action against the Japanese in Thailand and Laos. His appetite for warzones was not satisfied and he later turned up in the guise of journalist in many of the world's trouble spots – Hungary in 1956, Vietnam, Rhodesia and various Central and South American countries.[291]

Vice-Admiral Godfrey, whose protégé Hillgarth was, had been replaced as director of naval intelligence at the end of 1942 and appointed flag officer commanding the Royal Indian Navy. The new DNI was Rear Admiral Edmund Rushbrooke. During 1943 Hillgarth was transferred to Asia, apparently at the special request of Admiral Sir James Somerville, commander of the Eastern Fleet, to become his chief of intelligence and later chief of naval intelligence for the whole eastern theatre.

When he was told of the move at the end of October Churchill exploded. He wrote to the First Sea Lord, Albert Alexander:

I cannot in any circumstances approve the transference of Captain Hillgarth. There is no truth in the suggestion that he mentioned such a thing to me. I have very high ideas for him in Spain, as his work is of altogether special and exceptional value. As a retired officer living in Majorca and acting as our consul general, he has a knowledge of Spain extending over nearly ten years, and has seen every phase of the Civil War. There can be no question whatever of his being moved and all his special knowledge and contacts wasted. But he should certainly be promoted.

Rear Admiral Rushbrooke replied to explain that there were more personal considerations behind the posting.

It had come to my notice that all was not well with Captain Hillgarth's matrimonial affairs ... he had been seen in the company of a lady attached to the embassy at Lisbon ... and did not want Mrs Hillgarth to remain with him in Spain. He told me that he could no longer carry on his work in Spain if Mrs Hillgarth remained there with him.

Knowing that Capt Hillgarth and Mrs Hillgarth were prominent figures in Madrid society, I feel that if Mrs Hillgarth had not returned and carried on her social activities, it would soon have become a matter of comment. I also knew that she was very anxious to return there and was extremely unhappy about the whole position. Such being the case, I felt apprehensive that sooner or later a most uncomfortable situation might arise wherein the Ambassador, to avoid a scandal, might have felt obliged to have asked for Captain Hillgarth to be relieved.

Churchill was not mollified. He complained again to Alexander that it was very wrong and seriously damaging but, since it had already been announced, the move could not be prevented.

Alexander replied, rather abjectly, that neither he nor Rushbrooke had known until a few days previously that Hillgarth was on a special mission for the Prime Minister.[292] As late as 30 May 1945, when Churchill was asked if he wished to meet Hillgarth for lunch, he wrote to his private secretary: 'Yes, but he ought not to have left Spain.'[293]

With Alan Hillgarth's transfer, Mary Hillgarth returned to London, working unpaid for the Soldiers, Seamen and Air Force Association by day and as an air raid warden at night.

By late 1944 Sir Samuel Hoare's successful mission was drawing to a close and he was preparing to return to London, relinquishing the Chelsea constituency he had represented as a Conservative MP for thirty-four years for a seat in the House of Lords as Viscount Templewood. Franco, conscious of the need to re-align his political sympathies, sent a letter to his ambassador in London, the Duke of Alba, to pass on to Churchill proposing an Anglo-Spanish anti-Bolshevik alliance. Glossing over his frequent endorsements and support for the Axis cause he suggested that the only significant blemish on relations between the two countries had been British Secret Service interference in Spain's internal affairs.[294]

He wrote, foreshadowing a scandal that would unfold after the war's end:

> I consider that we ought not to conceal from the British the fact that the activities of their secret service and propaganda, involving a clash with the nation's most live and most sensitive elements – the army, the police and the Falange … have had throughout the past five years a deplorable affect on our relations… There has been no petty intrigue nor minor disorder … which has not in some way or other been traced back to British agents.
>
> Not one of the political and diplomatic stratagems contrived abroad against Spain has passed unnoticed in our country; even those matters that might have been thought to be the most confidential and secret have come providentially to our knowledge.[295]

An exasperated Hoare saw the opportunity he must have longed for – finally to tell Franco what he really thought. In a memo to Eden he suggested that the response should be firm and explicit, delivered face to face and backed up with an official copy already translated into Spanish so that it could not be watered down. Nothing short of high explosive would dent Franco's complacency.

He recommended acknowledging that Franco had not opposed them at the time of the fall of France or the invasion of North Africa but had frequently been guilty of un-neutral behaviour in regard to submarines, shipping, sabotage and agents. His speeches had disparaged the Allied democracies and regarded their defeat as desirable and inevitable. The suggestion of an anti-Bolshevik alliance implied that Britain and America would be guilty of disloyalty to their Russian ally. Franco should be reminded of the democratic deficiencies of his regime and warned that he must choose between complete isolation and conformity with the basic principles of the new world.[296]

Eden agreed and proposed inviting the United States to re-iterate the message and back it up with an oil embargo. Churchill did not agree. Pointing out that he would rather live in Spain under Franco than Russia under Stalin, he told his Foreign Secretary:

> What you are proposing to do is little less than stirring up a revolution in Spain. You begin with oil: you will quickly end in blood. Should the Communists become master of Spain, we must expect the infection to spread very fast through Italy and France.[297]

Although Churchill acknowledged Eden's strong feelings in the matter by agreeing to write an 'insulting' response to Franco's message he had not done so by the time Hoare took his leave of El Caudillo on 12 December. The ambassador delivered a critical appraisal of the country he was leaving behind but the sting was missing.[298]

When Churchill did reply, in January 1945, he reminded Franco of Spain's frequent un-neutral acts and hostile attitude; welcomed the improvement in relations that had occurred after Serrano Suñer's dismissal as Foreign Minister; but made clear that Britain would not betray its wartime Russian ally for some future alignment with Spain, a country which would still be excluded from any international organisation formed when peace was achieved.[299]

The justification in British eyes of Franco's coup in 1936 carried equal conviction in 1945. He was a bulwark against Communism and with the Cold War already looming Britain and America were searching for men like Franco in satellite countries around the world: leaders who would hold the line against Stalin. Eastern Europe would be lost to them but across the Middle East, Asia and Africa there were secret battles to be fought with the weapons that Hillgarth and Eccles had shown could be deployed to great effect.

CHAPTER 13: PAYBACK

A t the end of the Second World War many of the protagonists went their separate ways, into the anti-climax of peace. For some, like David Eccles, it was the opening of a new chapter. For Juan March and Alan Hillgarth it was payback time: the scheming and fixing, the dodgy deals and the dubious contacts with government officials went on just as before except that this time March was the principal beneficiary.

Douglas Jerrold had remained at Eyre and Spottiswoode, as chairman, with the novelist Graham Greene as his deputy. Greene had returned to Britain after working for MI6 in Sierra Leone in the early stages of the war. He had been recommended to the firm by fellow Catholic Tom Burns, press officer and intelligence agent of the Madrid embassy.[300] Burns in due course returned to his family publishing firm, Burns and Oates, and later took over as editor of the Catholic weekly *The Tablet* which he co-owned.

Shortly before he died, in 1966, Hugh Pollard gave an interview to *The Guardian* in which he rehearsed the story of the flight to the Canaries. He claimed only to have been paid expenses. In full Colonel Blimp mode he declared:

I wasn't interested in Spanish politics. My objection was to a lot of Communists. I haven't a serious political belief one way or the other except that the Communists are better put down than anything. They're so bloody silly. Quite incapable of governing. Oh they're worse than the Fascists.

But perhaps more tellingly he also justified his role in the following terms:

> The Church was in support of the uprising *and there were good reasons from the British point of view not to have a Communist government in Spain* [my italics]. Anyway I'm a Catholic and it's the duty of a good Catholic to help fellow Catholics in trouble.[301]

According to surviving relatives, when Hugh Pollard died some of his personal papers disappeared in a burglary committed while the family was attending his funeral. Pollard was not a wealthy man. He and his wife Ruth were living in a cottage at West Lavington near Midhurst. He left £12,500 – equivalent to £160,000 in 2010 – but specified in his will that his estate was to be held in trust and invested to produce an income shared equally between his widow and his friend Olivia Paterson.

Olivia was his long term mistress, ensconced in a flat in Chelsea. She was a painter, draughtswoman and printmaker, a member of the Paterson family of artists from Helensburgh, near Glasgow. She had studied at the Slade School of Fine Art in London and then in Paris in the 1920s. At the outbreak of the Second World War she was living in the south of France and returned in 1941 to make her own contribution to the secret war effort, working for the Admiralty's inter-services topographical department run by Margaret Godfrey, wife of Admiral John Godfrey, director of naval intelligence. Artists and draughtsmen provided the top secret maps, topographical outlines and false documentation that invasion forces needed.

Ruth Pollard reluctantly tolerated the division of her husband's affections – and subsequently his assets – persuaded by Pollard's sister Rosamund that Miss Paterson was discreet and would not cause her unnecessary embarrassment.[302]

Pollard's bequest was to last for the lifetimes of the two women and then to revert to his two daughters, Diana and Avril, but again there was a codicil. It appears he did not approve of Diana's husband

Yorick Smythies. So although Diana would receive income in trust she could not receive a capital sum unless Yorick had died. If Diana were to die her share would automatically revert to Avril.

Diana had married Yorick in Oxford early in 1944. It is easy to see why he and Hugh Pollard might not get along. Yorick was a pacifist philosopher, Ludwig Wittgenstein's star pupil while at King's College, Cambridge and a friend of the novelist Iris Murdoch, who described him as a cross between Hamlet and the grave-digger – thin, stooped, myopic, tall and pure of heart. The character Hugo Belfounder in her first novel *Under the Net* was based on him.[303]

Diana's cousin Colin Davis has fond memories of her:

> As a small boy I used to go and stay with Diana in Oxford, after we got doodle-bugged in London during the war, and she came to visit us once or twice later when we lived in Italy. Diana's politics were very much to the left of her father's. She was much more liberal. She was certainly not an admirer of Franco. She said to me that they had fallen on the wrong side. I think she had the idea [on the flight] that she was not being told everything that was going on. Yorick was a very pleasant man and a great philosopher but my uncle was very much a military man and he didn't want to fraternise with Yorick.[304]

The marriage did not last but Diana Smythies continued to live in North Oxford for the rest of her life. She died in 2003.

The saddest fate befell the most innocent of all the participants – Dorothy Watson. In 1938, on the anniversary of the uprising, Franco sent her a signed photograph acknowledging her contribution and later awarded her the Order of The Yoke and Arrows, the insignia of which was passed on by his ambassador in London. This may not have impressed her new husband, Harry Gauntlett, who was strongly anti-Fascist. In 1939 he went off to France with the British Expeditionary Force, escaping at Dunkirk and then serving with the Eighth Army in North Africa and Italy. He and Dorothy separated before the end of the war. Then in the 1950s she suffered a serious brain tumour and the operation to remove it left her severely paralysed. Her bachelor brother cared for her in a cottage in Surrey but, embarrassed by the disfiguring effect of the operation, she became increasingly reclusive, reserving her affection for a pet bush baby she kept in the kitchen. She died in a nursing home in 1999.[305]

Cecil Bebb returned to his job with Olley Air Service in 1936 almost as if nothing had happened. He turned down a chance to take part in an attempt to break the London to Cape Town flight record and from 1939–43 he was chief test pilot to Cunliffe-Owen Aircraft. Post-war he joined British South American Airways and then British United Airways where he was divisional operations manager. He returned to Spain in the 1950s to receive the Spanish Order of Merit from Franco personally.

Gordon Olley returned to Croydon after the war and attempted to resurrect his company but by 1953, in financial difficulties, he was taken over by Morton Air Service, run by his former chief pilot Sammy Morton. He in turn sold out to Airwork Ltd which in due course became part of British United Airways.

Walter Petre spent the war in the RAF, rising to the rank of Wing Commander, in charge of a unit that recovered crashed aircraft for salvage. He worked for Olley again and then progressed via Imperial and British South American Airways to BEA and BOAC where he was chief engineer until his retirement. He died in 2004.

David Eccles had returned to London in 1942, after an affair in Madrid threatened to break up his marriage, and worked on the government's munitions programme. In 1943, with Churchill's encouragement, he became Conservative MP for Chippenham, Wiltshire and a front-bench spokesman on economics. In 1953, as Minister of Works, he played a part in the organisation of the coronation of Queen Elizabeth II and was rewarded with a knighthood. He moved to education, approving the introduction of comprehensive schools and the expansion of university education, had a spell at the Board of Trade and then went to the House of Lords after a falling out with the then Prime Minister Harold

Macmillan. He returned to office under Edward Heath as Arts Minister and was closely involved in the running of the British Museum and the creation of the new British Library.[306]

Alan Hillgarth had spent the last years of the war in the Far East. In 1943 he became chief of intelligence for the Eastern Fleet and a year later chief of naval intelligence for the eastern theatre. He developed a high grade intelligence organisation, including the code-breaking station at HMS *Anderson*, a shore base on a golf course just outside Colombo, the capital of Ceylon – now Sri Lanka – where Lord Mountbatten had set up his south-east Asia command. The cryptographers made significant breakthroughs against the Japanese navy. Hillgarth also made diplomatic efforts to improve relations with the American military who dominated the Pacific war. Ian Fleming paid him an official visit in Colombo over Christmas 1944 and the two of them went on a liaison mission to Australia. They maintained their friendship after the war and toyed with the idea of launching an English language newspaper in Tangier but it came to nothing.

Hillgarth and Mary divorced in 1946 and the following year he married Jean Cobb, whose father Frank owned a silverware manufacturing firm in Sheffield. They had met in Lisbon during the war, while Jean was working for the Red Cross, and settled in County Tipperary, in the Irish Republic. Intent on semi-retirement, Hillgarth decided to turn his hand to forestry.

He had not severed his connections with Juan March, and replaced Arthur Loveday as his business representative in London. Loveday was nearly seventy by the end of the war but from 1946–47 took up duties as British representative on an intergovernmental committee on refugees in South America. He became a Commander of the Chilean Order of Merit and a Knight Commander of the Spanish Civil Order of Merit. He died in December 1968. His son George, a stockbroker with Rowe and Pitman, had served in the Royal Artillery during the war and went on to be chairman of the London Stock Exchange from 1973–75.

Hillgarth also took a directorship with Rio Tinto. And he found he could not lay down the duties of intelligence officer that easily either. Churchill, having lost the election of 1945, was out of office but ever eager for the secret intelligence on which he thrived. Hillgarth became an occasional lunch guest at Churchill's country home, Chartwell, and fed his anxiety that a Labour government lacked the determination to confront their former allies, the Soviets, over their ever-expanding espionage network.

Hillgarth somehow managed to get access to reports of secret government business at the highest level. After a lunch with Churchill on 3 December 1948 he wrote to him the next day from the Army and Navy Club in Pall Mall – his regular haunt while in London – pointing out that there were 150 staff at the Russian embassy in London, plus seventy to ninety trade delegates, compared with eighty-five in the British embassy in Moscow including the commercial counsellor but no trade mission. The Russians were given free rein to roam Britain spying and buying up British technology because MI5 had no staff to keep them in check. He warned:

> The chief trouble is that there is no-one concerned to fight this quiet, cold-blooded war of brains in the background. The facts exist. No-one will use them.

In September 1949 he was able to tell Churchill that a visit by the US Chiefs of Staff had shaken everybody. They made clear that they were prepared to use atom bombs against Moscow but there was no agreed plan of action and the British military felt that the Cabinet had no clear policy that would give them support or guidance. The US was treating Spain as an important part of its network of strategic bases despite the objections of the British Foreign Secretary, Ernest Bevin, who had tried and failed to stop an American delegation from visiting Franco.

In July 1950 Hillgarth provided a detail account of the proceedings of a Foreign Office committee on Communism overseas, advised by the Chiefs of Staff and the head of MI6, Sir Stewart Menzies. No action was being taken, Hillgarth complained, for fear of upsetting Russia's leaders or of losing vital foreign trade. He also reported that Bevin believed that the teaching profession and the Trades Union Congress in Britain were already deeply penetrated.

Simultaneously Churchill was warned by his own party's military spokesmen that the Joint Chiefs of Staff were concerned about dwindling recruitment, the loss of experienced men and the lack of readiness to defend the country in the event of war. They asked Churchill to intervene personally with the Labour Prime Minister Clement Attlee.

Hillgarth clearly felt he knew the wartime Prime Minister well enough to talk to him about troubles in his personal life. In August 1946 he had turned up, uninvited, in Switzerland where Churchill and his wife were taking a well-earned vacation on the shores of Lac Léman. Hillgarth was staying in Geneva and Churchill invited him over to lunch the next day. Hillgarth explained that he was trying to resolve his marriage problems with Mary but later wrote to say it had proved impossible and they were getting divorced. Hillgarth accepted that the fault was his.

The previous month Hillgarth had tried to set up a meeting in London between Churchill and Juan March, who wanted to express his pleasure at the result of past events. The financier did not want anything in return, Hillgarth insisted. Churchill may have had his doubts. In any case he could not find time for an appointment.[307]

March did meet Admiral Godfrey, whose only previous encounter had been in September 1939. In 1952 he paid a courtesy call on March at the Ritz and agreed that everything had turned out as he had advocated. Godfrey later went to Spain to meet March's two sons who were taking over his business interests.[308]

Churchill also received regular bulletins about Hillgarth's visits to Spain and copies of lectures he gave to private audiences. He was not exactly a cheerleader for Franco but he questioned the Allied policy of political ostracism as counter-productive. Franco, he added, was personally honest but had suppressed every other honest man. He knew that many of his generals were lining their pockets, running brothels and using army transport for black market goods, but he did not clamp down on them because it gave him a hold on them. The worst thing Franco had done was to undermine what little sense of moral probity existed in public affairs:

> Franco has created, or allowed to be created, a vast number of vested interests in his regime, through jobs and privileges, and nearly all the interests are actively and continually corrupt. And the effect of what he has allowed, plus the circumstances of the time, is that almost everyone in Spain, from top to bottom, is living on corruption whether they like it or not.[309]

These views would hardly have surprised Churchill, knowing as well as he did the corrupting influence that Hillgarth himself had exercised on his behalf over Spanish generals during the war. But he may not have known that Hillgarth had become actively involved with Juan March in a financial coup of breathtaking audacity and dubious propriety.

In April 1944 Tom Burns had a rather one-sided conversation with Juan March. The old rogue spoke non-stop for six hours and never wasted a word, the Madrid embassy press officer reported. 'One should never ask anyone how he made his first million,' March admonished him, before claiming to be worth 300 million pesetas. Other sources had told Burns the figure was more like 1,000 million – and at that time the official exchange rate was fewer than 50 pesetas to the pound. March kept his fortune in gold, sterling, dollars and other stable currencies spread around the world's financial centres.

Burns took his simple statement as evidence of his cynicism, discretion, sagacity and wit and was given ample evidence of all four. March admitted bankrolling the Republican movement to the tune of several hundred thousand pesetas before falling out with them over their constant demands for more.

Just about every general, monarchist and right-wing revolutionary also beat a path to his door with the begging bowl and Franco found particular favour, collecting twenty million pesetas and five million in sterling. Once the 1936 uprising began March committed his entire fortune and would have been ruined if it had failed. He did, however, take out a small insurance policy. He went to Mussolini and told him that his home territory of Majorca was 90 per cent pro-Franco and that if the Republicans prevailed in Spain the islanders would prefer to be ruled by Italy. Il Duce, recognising a 'heads I win, tails you lose' opportunity, sent the planes, ships and militiamen needed to secure the island the moment Franco's uprising began.

Naturally March had expected to see a financial return on his investment and he had acquired it during the Second World War. Some of Franco's ministers had taken exception to this and wanted him indicted for treason. March warned Franco that if he was obliged to defend himself against the charge he would identify publicly the many other corrupt leaders of the administration, not least the Industry Minister Demetrio Carceller, who had made his fortune from backhanders on trade deals including the sale of wolfram, where David Eccles had been handing out bribes to keep the vital ore out of German hands.[310]

Burns characterised March's strictures as rather like a bank robber criticising a pickpocket but it is possible that March chose his line of defence with characteristic panache. It has since been suggested that Carceller helped Franco salt away money in Switzerland against the possibility that he might one day be overthrown.[311]

During the war Juan March had accumulated 236,686.391 ounces of fine gold at the Bank of England. It had been put there by the Treasury on the understanding that he could not touch it until the war ended. It was his payback for acting as intermediary on the bribery scheme.

The money was held in a Treasury account on behalf of March's Swiss company, Société Financière Genora. In exchange March had provided the embassy in Spain with pesetas for use in various secret transactions.

His representative at Kleinwort's was now Norman Biggs who had recently become a director after nearly twenty years at the Bank of England. The Bank and Biggs agreed that London was the most flexible place to stash March's fortune and he was considering transferring more gold and Swiss francs from Geneva. Biggs and the Bank discussed other boltholes for the March fortune including South America, South Africa or the British colonies of Northern and Southern Rhodesia.

By 1954 the value of March's wartime stash of gold in London had increased from £2m to £2.9m – equivalent to £50m in 2010.[312] His interests at the Treasury were looked after by the assistant secretary, Kenneth Southwold Weston, who had been financial adviser at the Madrid embassy from 1943 to 1945. After his retirement, in 1962, Weston became a director of J. March & Co. until his death in 1971. Alan Hillgarth had joined the company after the war and was its chairman up until his death in 1978. He was also chairman of another March company, Helvetia Finance.

On 5 February 1970 the International Court of Justice in The Hague delivered its 500-page verdict on one of its longest running cases, originally launched in 1958. The case was nominally between two countries, Spain and Belgium, but in reality it was between Juan March and a club of wealthy international investors. Juan March won, although he had been dead for seven years by the time he got the verdict.

It was, in the words of one American commentator:

The successful legalised theft from its foreign owners of a company that supplied 20 per cent of all electrical power produced in Spain … it had been accomplished by a series of manoeuvres perhaps as reticulated and Machiavellian as anything in the whole chequered history of world finance.

… March stands as one who in some ways outdid all our Carnegies, Rockefellers and Vanderbilts: he was bolder, more guileful and less inhibited by restraints of either prudence or conscience. March's outstanding characteristics as a financier were patience, nerve, subtlety at negotiation, crude skill at bribery, and prodigious political adaptability.[313]

March did not achieve this alone. He had the help of leading figures in British intelligence, the Foreign Office and the Treasury. Alan Hillgarth was his principal spokesman, backed up by some of the best advice money can buy from the leading City law firm Slaughter and May. They were legal advisers to the Council of Foreign Bondholders, responsible for representing the interests of British investors trying to recover pre-war overseas investments. This was an apt choice. The lawyer most closely involved in the case was Jack Beevor who had recently returned to his peacetime job with the firm after service with the Special Operations Executive. Up until 1942 he had been head of operations in Lisbon – Hillgarth's direct contemporary – and had worked closely with David Eccles, who was responsible for the secret trade deals in Spain and Portugal. These deals were now coming back to haunt them. Jack Beevor spent the later stages of the war working alongside Sir Charles Hambro, SOE's director, and then took charge of SOE operations in Italy.

Another of the bondholders' representatives was Jack Beevor's old friend Ralph Jarvis, director of the Hill Samuel merchant bank, wartime head of counter-espionage for MI6 in Lisbon and the man who recruited Britain's most celebrated double agent – Juan Pujol, codenamed Garbo – who successfully deceived the Germans about the location of the D-Day landings.[314]

The International Court confirmed what an obscure judge in the small Spanish town of Reus in Catalonia had decided twenty-two years earlier when he accepted a winding up petition brought against the Barcelona Traction, Light & Power Company in 1948 by a mysterious stranger. The company had been hugely profitable but when Catalonia eventually fell to Franco's forces the new regime imposed currency restrictions that prevented the company paying interest in sterling to its bondholders – international investors who had originally put up £8m capital to build the hydro-electric power stations. By 1948 these payments had been outstanding for twelve years.

The company had more than enough assets to cover its liabilities, and would have done so, but the judge decided the arrears were justification to declare Barcelona Traction bankrupt. Trustees were appointed to oversee its assets. Barcelona Traction's own managers and staff knew nothing of the court order until the trustees turned up and started taking over their offices. The trustees declared all the old shareholdings invalid, and issued new ones, which they sold at rock-bottom prices to … Juan March.

In 1952 a Foreign Office résumé of the case estimated that March had acquired a company worth £52m for just £2,091,000. An American law firm, acting for some of the original owners, later estimated that the company was worth 85 million US dollars and that Juan March's shares had cost him just $250,000.[315]

Needless to say, the original litigant, the trustees in bankruptcy and the obscure provincial judge were all Juan March's placemen. What puzzled people then, and will puzzle people still, is why the British Treasury went out of its way to help him, especially given that many of the original bondholders who lost fortunes were British.

Barcelona Traction had been founded in 1913 by the pioneering American engineer Fred Stark Pearson who had started his career on the Metropolitan Street Railways of New York. Finance for Barcelona Traction came from Canada, principally through stockbroker and banker James Dunn, business partner of Alfred Loewenstein and Hugo Cunliffe-Owen. Pearson died in the sinking of the *Lusitania* by a German U-Boat in 1915 and never saw his Barcelona project fully operational.

The ownership passed to Dunn and Loewenstein's Belgian company Sidro and they in turn sold a chunk of their company to American-born engineer Daniel Heineman, also based in Belgium. His company Sofina built tramways and electrical systems in major cities around the world and employed 40,000 people.

Juan March had approached Heineman in 1940 and again in 1944 trying to buy the company at a knock down price and was rebuffed. Heineman had been in touch with Sir Samuel Hoare about the company's future. Hoare reported back to London:

He told me very confidentially that he was starting a negotiation for the transfer of the ostensible control of the Barcelona Light and Power Company to a Spanish board and Spanish shareholders. It was clear he had a very cunning scheme for reconciling Spanish opinion with British and Canadian interests in the company. I would guess that having started this negotiation he will carry it through.[316]

Heineman maintained friendly contact with Sir Samuel Hoare and in July 1944 did his best to ingratiate himself by offering to send the ambassador facsimiles of letters he owned, written by Napoleon to the Empress Josephine. They were not, he confided, suitable reading for young ladies and might be held up by the censor. He was complimentary about Sir Samuel's achievements in Madrid and briefed him about the latest developments with his various power companies in the Iberian peninsular and South America. He also, very pointedly, reminded him that he had influential British friends, among them the flamboyant industrialist Sir Bernard Docker, the King's private secretary Lord Wigram, the Conservative Party treasurer Viscount Greenwood, Lord Swinton and Sir Edward Peacock of Baring's Bank.[317] It would soon emerge how badly he needed their influence and how little they could offer in opposition to the incorrigible Señor March.

At the end of the war Barcelona Traction tried to find a way of paying off the bondholders, using money from its parent companies' worldwide income to overcome the difficulty of converting its Spanish profits from pesetas to pounds sterling. This compromise was approved by the bondholders in London in October 1945 and then by a court in Ontario where Barcelona Traction's ultimate parent company was based. Juan March objected and so did the British government. They took the view that the bondholders were being asked to accept a return which represented only half the true value. But the reality was that rejecting the compromise meant that the bonds had virtually no value since they could not be redeemed. March began to buy them up from the other bondholders for about one quarter of their face value while secretly preparing to launch his bankruptcy petition. The bonds were held by March's company Helvetia Finance – chairman Alan Hillgarth – and ownership was transferred from London to Tangier.

When March later purchased the shares for £91,000 to gain control of the company he also took on the responsibility for its debts to the bondholders. Since he was now the largest owner of those bonds he was able to pay himself – in pesetas from the supposedly bankrupt company's huge financial reserves – far more than he had spent buying them in the first place.

In the Foreign Office in London these financial manoeuvrings were viewed with considerable alarm. The insouciant attitude of the Treasury was greeted with anger and distaste. But they, along with Juan March and Alan Hillgarth, knew a guilty little secret – Britain had plundered the Barcelona Traction bank balances during the war to help pay for the bribery and corruption that kept Spain neutral and guaranteed that Germany did not get its hands on the wolfram ore it needed for its armaments industry.

When March first launched his bankruptcy petition in 1948 the consul general in Barcelona, Henry Hobson, described it as a complete outrage and a travesty of justice. The Foreign Office immediately sought to absolve itself of responsibility: it was a Treasury operation, they decided. In the National Archives at Kew, south-west London, more than sixty years after the event, there are twenty-three Foreign Office files on the case but not one single Treasury file has been released. The Treasury says it does not have any.[318]

The Foreign Office files do contain some internal correspondence, mainly with two Treasury officials: Hugh Ellis-Rees and Kenneth Southwold Weston – the two men most closely involved in wartime Madrid with the trade deals and bribery payments that Juan March facilitated.

While the Foreign Office might try to lay off the blame it still had to bear the brunt of the diplomatic exchanges with the Spanish government and thereby arose a further complication. Canada had no embassy in Madrid; Britain looked after her interests. The Treasury could airily dismiss the furore by pointing out that it was only a British problem as far as the British bondholders were concerned – and since Juan March quickly became a bondholder too, what was good for Señor March must also be good for the other bondholders. The Canadians, on the other hand, represented the original owners of the company, and their interests were quite different. Whatever was good for Señor March was bad news for them.

The owners, naturally, attempted to challenge the bankruptcy ruling. Every time they tried to get a hearing March entered a counter claim and the case was delayed. Barcelona Traction's Spanish subsidiary Ebro, whose assets had been seized, applied for the decision to be overturned. The same judge who had ruled that their assets could be seized now ruled that they had no standing before the court and could not challenge his order.

Messrs Hillgarth and Beevor were quick to make sure that the Foreign Office understood the merits of Juan March's case. They turned up in Henry Hobson's office in Barcelona in company with Sir Arthur Page, who had been in charge of blockade intelligence at the Ministry of Economic Warfare and was a former Chief Justice of Burma. These three had been nominated as representatives of the British bondholders. Hobson complained:

> He [Hillgarth] dwelt at some length on the question of the alleged misappropriation of funds, and I could not help feeling (although I may be wronging him) that he had prior knowledge of the facts of the case and that by asking me questions which I was unable to answer, he was attempting to embarrass me. It was a difficult interview and Hillgarth did nothing to ease the situation.

Hobson went on to report that a pamphlet, apparently generated by the Heineman camp, was circulating among prominent people in Spain, attacking Juan March and alleging that the Minister of the Interior was in his pay. Hobson's three visitors went on to a meeting with Francisco Gambús who had been appointed receiver. George Lawrence, the company accountant, was present and Gambús began to ask questions about 40 million pesetas worth of 'defalcations' – money thought to have been misappropriated during the war.[319]

Hobson was uncomfortably aware that a cache of wartime Barcelona Traction documents had been hidden in the consulate for safekeeping. He was told by the Foreign Office to keep them there and on no account send them back to London, still less hand them over to the new owners of the company or the Spanish authorities. The Spanish government officially remained aloof: the law must take its course. It then maintained that Barcelona Traction had taken far more money out of Spain than it had put in. This was ominous.

The Canadians demanded an independent audit of that Spanish claim. The Foreign Office neglected to put this proposal to the Spanish government, while behind the scenes the Treasury manipulated the situation. Hillgarth scurried about consulting his employer, Juan March, and adding to the confusion and delay. At the last minute the Spanish government came up with their own proposal for an inquiry. The Foreign Office breathed a collective sigh of relief and told the Canadians that diplomatically this was a much better option.

Two Spaniards, one Briton and one Canadian conducted the audit and divided neatly on predictable lines. The Spanish investigators said Barcelona Traction had been guilty of profiteering and extracting large sums of money from Spain; and the British and Canadian experts said it had invested a balance of £19.5 millions.[320]

Before this stalemate could be revealed, the Spanish government issued an 'Agreed Minute' in June 1951, endorsed by the British government, declaring that Spain had been 'fully justified' in refusing to permit the currency exchanges that would have paid the bondholders.

The British signatory to the Agreed Minute was the then ambassador in Madrid Sir Jock Balfour, with Treasury authorisation. Sir Jock did not want to sign the document and protested to the

Foreign Office that he was being asked to preside over a meeting on a subject about which he did not know enough and had no opportunity to learn. He was instructed from London just to follow the advice given to him by the Treasury representative Henry Eggers, who had served in the Ministry of Economic Warfare from 1940–45, and to lend the proceedings 'a high diplomatic tone'.[321]

The Treasury professed to think that this massaging of the Spanish position would prevent further revelations, including damning but not entirely accurate accusations from the Spaniards. They were wrong. Juan March took the documents to the Spanish court. It authorised the new share issue through which March was able to acquire the company.

The Heineman camp made their objections clear to the Foreign Office and began putting the word around the City of London that the banktruptcy proceedings were completely illegal. Alan Hillgarth and Jack Beevor hurried to the Foreign Office to assure them this was not so, backed up by a Spanish lawyer's report. They argued that it was the receivers' duty to sell assets and that new shares had to be issued because the existing ones were held outside Spain. The Foreign Office found these arguments unconvincing but concluded that there was no need 'to go into the matter too deeply.'[322]

Simultaneously the Spanish government turned the screw on Britain in quite dramatic fashion. Spanish judges started to ask questions about the wartime finances of Barcelona Traction. In 1948 they began interrogating the company's chief cashier, who was likely to admit some of the missing money had gone to the British government for 'pre-emptive purchases' as a contribution to the war effort.

The Foreign Office, on Treasury advice, admitted to Henry Hobson that £40,000 had gone to the embassy in Madrid from Barcelona Traction's secret reserves without ever appearing in the company accounts. Later payments were disguised as 'general capital expenditure'.

Hobson recommended that Britain could avoid a scandal by making an admission to the Spanish government, accusing the

Germans of behaving just as badly and requesting a diplomatic cover-up. This was a humiliation too far for the Foreign Office. Instead, they persuaded the cashier to skip the country.

But there were too many people who knew the secret. The embassy warned Ellis-Rees at the Treasury that it was the talk of Madrid that Britain had taken 41 million pesetas out of the company during the war for information and intelligence purposes. They blamed Heineman's representative Charles Wilmers for the outrageous rumours. Wilmers for his part threatened to use the information in court in support of his clients.[323]

The temperature rose as it was announced that the former president and managing director of Barcelona Traction, Fraser Lawton, and the treasurer, Frederick Clark, both British, were to face 262 criminal charges of illegally transferring millions of pesetas, gold and foreign currencies out of the country to deposit in London. They were safely out of the country, beyond Spanish jurisdiction, but liable to have their Spanish property and personal bank accounts sequestered by the courts. Their British lawyer complained to Weston at the Treasury:

> It is really a most shocking thing that these gentlemen should be publicly branded as common criminals and should go about in fear of arrest mainly for having done what they could for their country during the war without thinking too much of the risk they might be running, and in any case relying on the assurances of protection they were given then.[324]

The lawyers also hinted that if the men's property were seized they would sue the Foreign Office to recover their losses. Behind the scenes Foreign Office officials protested forcefully. John Curle wrote to Weston:

> It seems intolerable that the careers and livelihood and even the liberty of British subjects should be imperilled because Juan March, whose own financial dealings have been just as illegal *vis à vis* the

Spanish government, wishes to use them as pawns in blackmailing the Heineman group... Would it be possible for you to tell him [March] that we will not tolerate this sort of conduct and that he must arrange to call off the investigation into these funds.[325]

Weston's response was to call the defendants' bluff. The British government had only, he pointed out, received a fraction of the 100 million pesetas which it was now rumoured had been siphoned off from Barcelona Traction's Spanish bank balances. The company's defalcations had started before the government got involved and continued long after, so the defendants could not hide under the Treasury's skirts.[326]

Mr Wilmers backed down and acknowledged that it would be unwise to invite questions about who else had benefited from the scam. The Spanish lawyer who conducted the defence case was Serrano Suñer, former Falangist Foreign Minister and Franco's brother-in-law.

Charles Wilmers was a curious character, an Englishman whose Jewish parents came to Britain from Augsburg in Germany. He studied at Cambridge but spent most of his life abroad, working for Sofina in Brussels and in the United States. His wife, Cecilia Eitingon, came from the wealthy American branch of a family of Russian fur traders. One of her relatives, Leonid Eitingon, became an agent of the Cheka, Stalin's security police. He was based in Spain during the Civil War, helping to remove the country's gold reserves of 500-600 million dollars to Russia for safekeeping. They were never seen again. He also recruited Ramon Mercader, the man who assassinated Stalin's most charismatic rival, Leon Trotsky, by burying an ice-pick in his skull. There does not, however, seem to be any Soviet intelligence connection to the Barcelona Traction scandal.[327]

That was very much the work of Juan March, whose malicious hand was seen to be once again pulling the strings of the Spanish judiciary. The Foreign Office accused Weston at the Treasury of 'acquiescing blandly in the persecution of British subjects by a blackmailing scoundrel'. Weston, unfazed as ever, pointed out that while he disapproved of Juan March's unscrupulous methods, he had taken care to ensure that the charges against Lawton and Clark were only announced when they were safely out of the country. And this was no empty gesture. The men were found guilty and fined sixty-six million pesetas – double the amount they had supposedly transferred illegally to London. They could have been fined ten times the original amount. But, because they were out of the country, responsibility for paying the fines fell on their former employer Barcelona Traction. So the company, now controlled by Señor March, handed over a lump sum to the Spanish court and, effectively, to the Spanish government.

A significant amount of cash also moved in Señor March's direction. Manuel Pinilla, the chief cashier of the subsidiary company Ebro, swore an affidavit saying that after the bankruptcy order was made he had opened an account for Ebro at March's bank in Palma de Majorca. Ebro had no business interests in Majorca and he did not know the reason for opening the account. Nor could he explain why twenty-three million pesetas were transferred into it from Barcelona.[328]

It had by now dawned on the Foreign Office that General Franco and his government knew full well what had gone on during the war. The court case enabled Franco to be seen publicly confronting foreign capitalists accused of bleeding his country dry while privately British diplomats faced excruciating embarrassment. The Foreign Office official responsible for extricating them from this dilemma was David Muirhead, Alan Hillgarth's former deputy in SOE in Madrid.

The Canadian Foreign Affairs Minister and future Prime Minister Lester Pearson said from the start that he found the British attitude 'very fishy'. The Americans, who had no immediate axe to grind, also became involved. In 1954 Arthur Dean of the New York law firm Sullivan and Cromwell was retained by Barcelona Traction and went to see Franco to impress on him how much damage the case was doing to Spain's image in the United States. Dean was a senior partner in the Wall Street firm and had been President Eisenhower's personal envoy to the peace talks at Panmunjeom which ended the Korean War. John Foster Dulles, Eisenhower's Secretary of State, was a former partner. Dean explained to Franco that the scandal had gone beyond a commercial stigma; it was affecting US defence strategy. In 1953 the Americans agreed to develop three major bases in Spain at Morón, Zaragoza and Torrejón, near Madrid. USAF bombers, fighters and support services were stationed there. The bases required more modern industrial infrastructure and power supplies than Spain could provide but American contractors would not invest if their assets were going to be seized. Franco listened politely to Mr Dean for three hours, referred him to another minister ... and did nothing.[329]

For the next fifteen years lawyers chased each other round in circles. And at the end of it: anti-climax. The International Court ruled that Belgium, where Sofina and Sidro had been based, had no standing before the court because Barcelona Traction was registered in Canada. And with that the case collapsed.

Juan March enjoyed the profits and new-found respectability that came with being the proprietor of one of Spain's essential industries. He demonstrated his gratitude in 1955 by establishing the Fundación Juan March, run by his family and dedicated to research and public appreciation in the fields of science and the humanities. It organises art exhibitions, concerts, lecture series and seminars and administers the Spanish Library of Contemporary Music and Theatre in Madrid, the Museum of Spanish abstract art in Cuenca and the March Music Foundation in Majorca. It ensures that Juan March will be remembered long after the source of his wealth has been forgotten.

Luis Bolin, with whom this story began in Simpson's in the Strand, became Franco's director of tourism. The Balearics and the Costa del Sol began to open up to the package holidaymakers. Germans and Britons fought over nothing more controversial than the sun beds. Bolin died in 1969 but by the time Franco died in 1975 the number of tourists had grown from fewer than one million in

1950 to thirty million, bringing in the equivalent of 3.5 billion US dollars.

Like Alan Hillgarth, Hugh Pollard, Douglas Jerrold, Arthur Loveday, MI6, even Winston Churchill, they were all, in their own way, Franco's Friends.

BIBLIOGRAPHY

Archive Sources

CA – Churchill Archives, Churchill College, Cambridge CB3 oDS

CUL – Cambridge University Library, West Road, Cambridge CB3 9DR

GRO – General Record Office (Register of Births Marriages and Deaths)

Institution of Mechanical Engineers, 1 Birdcage Walk, London SW1H 9JJ

IWM – Imperial War Museum, Lambeth Road, London SE1 6HZ

NMM – National Maritime Museum, Greenwich, London SE10 9NF

TNA – The National Archives, Kew, Richmond, Surrey TW9 4DU

ADM – Admiralty

BW – British Council

CAB – Cabinet Office

FO – Foreign Office

HS – Special Operations Executive

J – Supreme Court of Judicature and related courts

MEPO – Metropolitan Police

PREM – Prime Minister's Office

(Monetary valuations in the text to 2010 equivalents were calculated using the National Archives currency converter)

Parliamentary Records

The Labour Party Commission to Ireland 1921 Hansard

Books and journal articles

(Published in London unless otherwise stated)

Alpert, Michael: *A New International History of the Spanish Civil War* (Macmillan, 1994)

Andrew, Christopher: *The Defence of the Realm, The Authorized History of MI5* (Allen Lane, 2009)

Anonymous (Bolin et al): *The Spanish Republic, A Survey of Two Years of Progress* (Eyre and Spottiswoode, 1933)

Beesly, Patrick: *Very Special Admiral: The Life of Admiral J H Godfrey CB* (Hamilton, 1980)

Bennett, Gill: *'A most extraordinary and mysterious business': the Zinoviev Letter of 1924* (Foreign and Commonwealth Office, 1999)

Bolin, Luis: *Spain, The Vital Years* (Cassell & Co, 1967)

Brown, Anthony Cave: *The Last Hero, Wild Bill Donovan* (New York, Times Books, 1982)

Burns, Jimmy: *Papa Spy* (Bloomsbury, 2009)

Churchill, Winston S: *The Gathering Storm* (Cassell & Co, 1950)
Their Finest Hour (Cassell & Co, 1951)
The Grand Alliance (Cassell & Co, 1951)
The Hinge of Fate (Cassell & Co, 1951)

Cierva, Juan de la and Rose, Don: *Wings of Tomorrow* (New York, Brewer, Warren & Putnam Inc, c1931)

Clarke, Dudley: *Seven Assignments* (Jonathan Cape, 1948)

Cluett, Douglas: *Croydon Airport, The Great Days 1928–39* (Sutton Publishing, 1980)

Dictionary of National Biography

Diplomatic Service Year Book

Dorril, Stephen: *MI6 Fifty Years of Special Operations* (Fourth Estate, 2000)

Eccles, David: *By Safe Hand, Letters of Sybil & David Eccles 1939–42* (The Bodley Head, 1983)

Edwards, Jill: *The British Government and the Spanish Civil War, 1936–1939* (Macmillan, 1979)

Foot, M R D: *SOE The Special Operations Executive 1940–1946* (Pimlico, 1999)

Fox, Rosalinda Powell: *The Grass and the Asphalt* (Cadiz, J S Harter and Associates, c1997)

Gilbert, Martin: *Winston S. Churchill Official Biography Volume VI Finest Hour, 1939–1941* (Heinemann, 1983)

Gonzáles-Betez, Antonio: *Franco y el Dragón Rapide* (Madrid, Ediciones Rialp, 1987)

Griffiths, Richard: *Fellow Travellers of the Right* (Constable, 1980)

Hastings, Macdonald: *The Other Mr Churchill* (George G Harrap & Co, 1963)

Haxey, Simon (Pseudonym): *Tory M.P.* (Victor Gollancz, 1939)

Hillgarth, Alan: *The War Maker* (Thomas Nelson & Sons, 1926)

Hillgarth, Mary: *A Private Life* (Privately printed, 1984)

Howard of Penrith, Lord (Esmé): *Theatre of Life* (Hodder and Stoughton, 1936)

Jeffery, Keith: *MI6 – The History of the Secret Intelligence Service 1909–1949* (Bloomsbury, 2010)

Jerrold, Douglas: *Storm Over Europe* (Ernest Benn, 1930)
Georgian Adventure (Collins, 1937)
England, Past, Present and Future (J M Dent & Sons, 1950)

Joll, James: *Europe Since 1870* (Pelican, 1976)

Keene, Judith: *Fighting for Franco* (Leicester University Press, 2001)

Kemp, Peter: *The Thorns of Memory* (Sinclair-Stevenson, 1990)

Koestler, Arthur: *The Invisible Writing* (Collins, Hamish Hamilton, 1954)

Lewis, Jeremy: *Shades of Greene* (Jonathan Cape, 2010)

Little, Douglas: 'Red Scare, 1936: Anti-Bolshevism and the Origins of British Non-Intervention in the Spanish Civil War' (*Journal of Contemporary History*, Vol. 23, No. 2, April 1988) pp 291–311

Loveday, Arthur F: *World War in Spain* (John Murray, 1939)

Lycett, Andrew: *Ian Fleming* (Weidenfeld & Nicolson, 1995)

McCormick, Donald: *Pedlar of Death, The Life of Sir Basil Zaharoff* (MacDonald, 1965)

McGinty, Stephen: *Churchill's Cigar* (Macmillan, 2007)

McIntosh, R H: *All Weather Mac* (MacDonald, 1963)

McKercher, B J C: "A dose of fascismo" Esme Howard in Spain 1919–1924' (*The International History Review*, Vol. 9, No. 4, November 1987)

Maiz, B Felix: *Mola, Aquel Hombre* (Barcelona, Planeta, 1976)

Middlemass, Keith and Barnes, John: *Baldwin, A Biography* (Weidenfeld & Nicolson, 1969)

Mills, William C: 'Sir Joseph Ball, Adrian Dingli, and Neville Chamberlain's "Secret Channel" to Italy, 1937–1940' (*The International History Review*, Vol. 24, No. 2, June 2002)

Moloney, Thomas: *Westminster, Whitehall and the Vatican, The Role of Cardinal Hinsley, 1935–43* (Burns & Oates, 1985)

Montagu, Ivor: *The Youngest Son* (Lawrence & Wishart, 1970)

Noel, Gerard: *Ena, Spain's English Queen* (Constable, 1984)

Norris, William: *The Man Who Fell from the Sky* (New York, Harmondsworth: Viking, 1987)

Olley, Captain Gordon P: *A Million Miles in the Air* (Hodder and Stoughton, 1934)

Petrie, Sir Charles: *Chapters of Life* (Eyre & Spottiswoode, 1950)

Pocock, Geoffrey A: *One Hundred Years of the Legion of Frontiersmen* (Phillimore, 2004)

Pollard, Hugh B C: *A Busy Time in Mexico* (Constable & Co, 1913)
The Story of Ypres (McBride, Nast & Co, 1917)
The Secret Societies of Ireland (P Allan & Co, 1922)

Preston, Paul: *Franco* (HarperCollins, 1993)
A Concise History of the Spanish Civil War (Fontana, 1996)
Doves of War (HarperCollins, 2002)

Reith, Lord: *The Reith Diaries* edited by Charles Stuart (Collins, 1975)

Rowe, Dr V A: *Hertfordshire People, Vol 25, 1925*

Sanchez Maurandi, Antonio: *Don Juan de la Cierva, Estudio biográfico del político murciano* (Murcia, San Francisco, 1962)

Sánchez Soler, Mariano: *Ricos por la guerra de España* (Madrid, Raices, 2007)

Sanders, Michael L and Taylor, Philip M: *British Propaganda during the First World War, 1914–18* (Macmillan, 1982)

Scott-Ellis, Priscilla: *The Chances of Death* (Michael Russell, 1995)

Shute, Nevil: *Slide Rule* (William Heinemann, 1954)

Smith, Denys: *Deathly Deception, The Real Story of Operation Mincemeat* (Oxford University Press, June 2010)

Southworth, Herbert R: *Conspiracy and the Spanish Civil War* (Routledge, 2002)

Spender, J A: *Weetman Pearson, First Viscount Cowdray* (Cassell & Co, 1930)

Stafford, David: *Churchill and the Secret Service* (John Murray, 1997)

Strang, G Bruce: 'Once More unto the Breach' (*Journal of Contemporary History*, October 1996)

Smith, Denys: *Deathly Deception, The Real Story of Operation Mincemeat* (Oxford, Oxford University Press, 2010)

Thomas, Hugh: *The Spanish Civil War*, 3rd edition (Penguin, 1986)

Waugh, Evelyn: *The Diaries of Evelyn Waugh* edited by Michael Davie (Weidenfeld & Nicolson, 1976)

Welsh Biography online/National Library of Wales

Westminster School Almanac

Whealey, Robert H: 'Economic Influence of the Great Powers in the Spanish Civil War' (*The International History Review*, Vol. 5, No. 2, May, 1983)

Who Was Who

Wilmers, Mary-Kay: *The Eitingons, A Twentieth-Century Story* (Faber and Faber, 2009)

Newspapers and magazines

ABC, Madrid

Flight Magazine, London (Wing Commander Reginald Brie, former *Autogiro* test pilot: *The Rise of the Helicopter*, 23 January, 1953)

The Times, London

The New Yorker Magazine (John Brooks: 'Annals of Finance', 21 May & 28 May, 1979)

NOTES

1 Diana Smythies (née Pollard): Imperial War Museum sound archives, IWM 7371

2 *Diplomatic Service Year Book*

3 *ABC* profile, 13 January 1967

4 Luis Bolin: *Spain, The Vital Years* p11

5 *Dictionary of National Biography*

6 CA Weir 19/12

7 *Dictionary of National Biography*

8 Richard Griffiths: *Fellow Travellers of the Right* pp47-49

9 Douglas Jerrold: *England, Past, Present and Future* pp245-246

10 Anonymous (Bolin et al): *The Spanish Republic, A Survey of Two Years of Progress*

11 G Bruce Strang: 'Once More Unto the Breach' (*Journal of Contemporary History*, October 1996) p733

12 Sir Charles Petrie: *Chapters of Life* p100

13 Stephen Dorril: *MI6, Fifty Years of Special Operations* p430

14 Geoffrey A Pocock: *One Hundred Years of the Legion of Frontiersmen* pxvii, p28

15 TNA FO 371/488

16 Hugh B C Pollard: *A Busy Time in Mexico*

17 TNA FO 371/1148

18 J A Spender: *Weetman Pearson, First Viscount Cowdray* p187

19 *The Times*, 25 March 1927

20 1911 Census

21 Institution of Mechanical Engineers Archives

22 Diana Smythies: Imperial War Museum sound archives, IWM 7371

23   Institution of Mechanical Engineers Archives

24   TNA HS9/1200/5

25   General Record Office marriage certificate

26   Douglas Jerrold: *Georgian Adventure* p95

27   *Army List*

28   Institution of Mechanical Engineers Archives

29   Macdonald Hastings: *The Other Mr Churchill* p98

30   Geoffrey A Pocock: *One Hundred Years of the Legion of Frontiersmen*

31   Michael L Sanders and Philip M Taylor: *British Propaganda during the First World War, 1914–18* p107

32   Ivor Montagu: *The Youngest Son* pp31-32

33   Sanders and Taylor: *British Propaganda during the First World War, 1914–18*

34   Macdonald Hastings: *The Other Mr Churchill* p98

35   The Labour Party Commission to Ireland 1921 pp47-50

36   Hansard, 2 December 1920

37   Macdonald Hastings: *The Other Mr Churchill*

38   Macdonald Hastings: *The Other Mr Churchill* p99

39   Diana Smythies: IWM 7371

40   Luis Bolin: *Spain, The Vital Years* pp18-20

41   Douglas Jerrold: *Georgian Adventure* pp372-373

42   Luis Bolin: *Spain, The Vital Years* pp20-23

43   Douglas Jerrold: *Storm Over Europe* pp88-89

44   Paul Preston: *Franco* pp18-19

45   Arthur Koestler: *The Invisible Writing*

46   B J C McKercher: "A dose of fascismo" Esmé Howard in Spain 1919-1924' (*The International History Review*, Vol. 9, No. 4, November 1987) pp517-688

47   Esmé Howard: *Theatre of Life* Vol. II p425

48   TNA FO 371/7131

49   TNA FO 371/8369 W9737 & FO 371/9490 W7602

50   Paul Preston: *A Concise History of the Spanish Civil War* pp28-29

51   Paul Preston: *A Concise History of the Spanish Civil War* pp 86-87

52 TNA FCO 371/20520 W2869

53 TNA FCO 371/20520 W1677

54 TNA FO 371/20558 W1744, W2203

55 TNA FCO 371/20520 W2678

56 CUL: Baldwin papers Vol. 124, 13 April 1936

57 Jill Edwards: *The British Government and the Spanish Civil War, 1936-1939* p3

58 Douglas Little: 'Red Scare, 1936: Anti-Bolshevism and the Origins of British Non-Intervention in the Spanish Civil War' (*Journal of Contemporary History*, Vol. 23, No. 2, April 1988) pp291-311

59 Winston S Churchill: *The Gathering Storm* p24

60 James Joll: *Europe Since 1870* p276

61 Christopher Andrew: *The Defence of the Realm, The Authorized History of MI5*

62 Sir Charles Petrie: *Chapters of Life* p177

63 Michael Alpert: *A New International History of the Spanish Civil War* pp15-16

64 TNA FO 371/20475 W11340

65 John Brooks: 'Annals of Finance' (*New Yorker* Magazine, 21 May 1979)

66 Esmé Howard: *Theatre of Life* Vol. II p469

67 TNA FO 371/20560 W576

68 *Dictionary of National Biography*

69 John Brooks: *Annals of Finance* (New Yorker Magazine, 21 May 1979)

70 TNA FO 371/17435 W13240

71 Mariano Sánchez Soler: *Ricos por la guerra de España* pp31-32, 38-39

72 Arthur F Loveday: *World War in Spain* pp55-56

73 Herbert R Southworth: *Conspiracy and the Spanish Civil War* p87

74 TNA FO 371/20538 W10767

75 Arthur F Loveday: *World War in Spain*

76 Gill Bennett: *'A most extraordinary and mysterious business': the Zinoviev Letter of 1924* pp91-92

77   TNA KV2/677
78   *Dictionary of National Biography*
79   TNA FO 1093/56-56; HO 382/49
80   Welsh Biography online/National Library of Wales
81   *Dictionary of National Biography*
82   TNA ADM 196/122; ADM 196/147
83   TNA ADM 196/122; ADM 196/147
84   *Lloyd's Register of Yachts*, 1925; *Lloyd's List & Shipping Gazette*, casualty reports 13 April 1926; *ABC* newspaper, Madrid, 10 April 1926
85   Alan Hillgarth: *The War Maker*
86   TNA J77/2513/8265
87   Evelyn Waugh: *The Diaries of Evelyn Waugh*, ed Michael Davie, 1 July 1927
88   *Dictionary of National Biography*
89   *Dictionary of National Biography*
90   Mary Hillgarth: *A Private Life* p193
91   Mary Hillgarth: *A Private Life* p87
92   TNA FO 369/2285 K14554
93   TNA FO 369/2374 K11251
94   Paul Preston: *Franco* pp90-96
95   TNA FO 369/2430
96   Keith Middlemass and John Barnes: *Baldwin, A Biography* p872
97   Jimmy Burns: *Papa Spy* p22
98   Winston S Churchill: *The Gathering Storm* pp160-161
99   Richard Griffiths: *Fellow Travellers of the Right* p242
100 Lord Reith: *The Reith Diaries* 6 December, 1936, p191
101 Captain Gordon P Olley: *A Million Miles in the Air*
102 William Norris: *The Man Who Fell from the Sky*
103 Douglas Cluett: *Croydon Airport, The Great Days 1928-39* pp82-84
104 Olley Air Service Ltd: Official report to government, 1939 (British Airways Museum and Archives)
105 The aircraft is now in a military museum in Madrid. There is a Spanish feature film immortalising its exploits.

106 Paul Preston: *Franco* pp120-137

107 Diana Smythies: Imperial War Museum sound archive IWM 7371

108 IWM 11497 01/28/1

109 Personal interview, March 2011

110 *News Chronicle*, 7 November 1936; *The Guardian*, 25 June, 1966; *Aeroplane Monthly*, August 1986

111 *Sunday Dispatch*, 8 November 1936

112 Antonio Gonzáles-Betez: *Franco y el Dragón Rapide* pp129-130

113 *Sunday Dispatch*, 8 November 1936

114 Paul Preston: *Franco* pp137-143

115 Luis Bolin: *Spain, The Vital Years* pp24-48

116 The *Morning Post*, 20 July 1937 p10

117 *ABC* newspaper (Madrid), 1 April 1975 p17

118 Croydon airport archives, Sutton library, south-west London

119 Brian Bridgman: *Croydon Airport Society Journal*, Autumn 2002

120 Hugh Thomas: *The Spanish Civil War* p254

121 Hugh Thomas: *The Spanish Civil War* pp338-342, 370

122 Olley Air Service Ltd: Official report to government, 1939 (British Airways Museum and Archives)

123 TNA FO371/20525 W7476

124 TNA CAB 83/5 54(36)

125 Keith Middlemass and John Barnes: *Baldwin, A Biography* p961

126 Winston S Churchill: *The Gathering Storm* pp182-183

127 Hugh Thomas: *The Spanish Civil War* p388

128 TNA: FO 371/20527 W7745

129 TNA: FO 371/20525 W7400

130 TNA: FO 371/20530 W8628

131 TNA FO 371/20729 W8263

132 TNA CAB 23/85 56(36) Appendix I

133 TNA CAB 24/264 CP 233(36)

134 TNA CAB 23/85 56(36)

135 TNA: FO 271/20537 W10439

136 Antonio Sanchez Maurandi: *Don Juan de la Cierva, Estudio biográfico del político murciano*

137 TNA FO 371/20537 W10422

138 *The Times*, 21 September 1936

139 TNA FO 371/20530 W8545

140 Stephen Dorril: *MI6, Fifty Years of Special Operations* pp436-448

141 *Dictionary of National Biography*

142 TNA FO 371/20527 W7911

143 B Felix Maiz: *Mola, Aquel Hombre* pp317-322

144 TNA FO 371/20579 W12847

145 Keith Jeffery: *MI6 The History of the Secret Intelligence Service* p286

146 *Dictionary of National Biography*

147 TNA FO 371/20538 W11263

148 Nevil Shute: *Slide Rule* pp232-233

149 TNA FO 371/20530 W8635

150 Hugh Thomas: *The Spanish Civil War* pp381-383

151 Patrick Beesly: *Very Special Admiral: The Life of Admiral J H Godfrey CB* p85

152 TNA FO 371/20533 W9191

153 TNA FO 371/20578 W10418

154 TNA FO 371/20538 W10865

155 TNA FO 371/20527 W7781

156 TNA FO 371/20587 W17441

157 TNA CAB 23/87 2(37)

158 TNA CAB 56/6

159 TNA CAB 23/89 36(37)

160 NMM GOD/169

161 TNA FO 371/24146 W1404, 1668, 1857, 2096, 2366, 2499, 2630

162 TNA ADM 196/122

163 TNA FO 371/21386

164 TNA FO 371/21386 W16146/138/41

165 Judith Keene: *Fighting for Franco* pp4-7

166 TNA FO 371/24508

167 Peter Kemp: *The Thorns of Memory passim*

168 Judith Keene: *Fighting for Franco* p46

169 Stephen Dorril: *MI6, Fifty Years of Special Operations* p129

170 TNA FO 371/21287 W5279

171 Priscilla Scott-Ellis: *The Chances of Death* p233

172 Paul Preston: *Doves of War* p84

173 Thomas Moloney: *Westminster, Whitehall and the Vatican, The Role of Cardinal Hinsley, 1935-43* p71

174 Simon Haxey (Pseudonym): Tory MP (Victor Gollancz, 1939) p216

175 *Dictionary of National Biography*

176 Jill Edwards: *The British Government and the Spanish Civil War, 1936-1939* p66

177 Simon Haxey (Pseudonym): Tory M.P. pp109-110

178 TNA FO 425/413 pp58-60

179 TNA FO 371/22673

180 TNA FO 371/21317

181 Robert H Whealey: 'Economic Influence of the Great Powers in the Spanish Civil War' (*The International History Review*, Vol. 5, No. 2, May 1983), pp229-254

182 TNA FO 371/21394 W2091

183 TNA FO 800/323 HXXXIV/16

184 TNA CAB 24/268 CP80(37)

185 *Dictionary of National Biography*

186 Lord Reith: *The Reith Diaries* edited by Charles Stuart, 9 March 1937

187 TNA CAB 24/68 CP 80 & 82 (37), CAB 23/87

188 William C Mills: 'Sir Joseph Ball, Adrian Dingli, and Neville Chamberlain's "Secret Channel" to Italy, 1937-1940' (*The International History Review*, Vol. 24, No. 2: June 2002)

189 Hugh Thomas: *The Spanish Civil War*, 3rd edition p856

190 TNA FCO 73/265 SP/38/1-4

191 TNA FO 800/323 HXXXIV/7

192 Simon Haxey (Pseudonym): Tory M.P. pp222-223

193 TNA FO 371/24129 W6796

194 TNA FO 371/24129 W5827

195 Robert H Whealey: 'Economic Influence of the Great Powers in the Spanish Civil War' (*The International History Review*, Vol. 5, No. 2, May 1983), pp229-254

196 TNA FO 371/24132 W12029

197 TNA FO 371/24132 W12114

198 TNA FO 371/24132 W7050

199 TNA FO 800/323 HXXXIV/13

200 Gerard Noel: *Ena, Spain's English Queen* pp1, 234-237, 246-252

201 TNA FO 185/1753

202 TNA MEPO 2/3290

203 TNA FO 371/24129 W5393

204 TNA FO 371/24129 W6678

205 Gerard Noel: *Ena, Spain's English Queen* pp254-256

206 Keith Jeffery: *MI6 – The History of the Secret Intelligence Service 1909-1949* p352

207 M R D Foot: *SOE The Special Operations Executive 1940-1946* pp5-8

208 David Eccles: *By Safe Hand* p25

209 TNA HS6/942

210 Paul Preston: *Franco* p134

211 TNA HS6/942

212 Keith Jeffery: *MI6 – The History of the Secret Intelligence Service 1909 -1949* pp383-385

213 Keith Jeffery: *MI6 – The History of the Secret Intelligence Service 1909 -1949* p402

214 Jimmy Burns: *Papa Spy* p116

215 TNA KV 2/2823

216 TNA FO 800/323 HXXXIV/39

217 CUL Templewood Papers XIII/16

218 CUL Templewood Papers XIII/2

219 CUL Templewood Papers XIII/16

220 TNA FO 371/26974

221 Jimmy Burns: *Papa Spy* pp118-123

222 TNA HS 9/1200/5

223 TNA HS 9/1200/5

224 Stephen McGinty: *Churchill's Cigar*

225 TNA FO 371/24502 C9355/G

226 TNA HS 9/1200/5

227 TNA ADM 223/490

228 TNA ADM 223/490

229 CA MLBE 1/16/4

230 David Eccles: *By Safe Hand* p45

231 TNA ADM 223/490

232 Winston Churchill: *The Gathering Storm* pp556-557

233 TNA ADM 223/490

234 TNA HS7/163

235 TNA ADM 223/490

236 TNA ADM 1/9809

237 TNA FO 371/24145

238 TNA FO 371/24145 W13281

239 David Eccles: *By Safe Hand* p15

240 CUL Templewood papers XIII/16

241 Jimmy Burns: *Papa Spy* p352

242 Rosalinda Powell Fox: *The Grass and the Asphalt* p87

243 Rosalinda Powell Fox: *The Grass and the Asphalt* p189

244 Robert H Whealey: 'Economic Influence of the Great Powers in the Spanish Civil War' (*The International History Review*, Vol. 5, No. 2, May 1983) pp229-254

245 Winston S Churchill: *Their Finest Hour* p412

246 TNA FO 800/323 C12295

247 TNA FO 371/24508 C11460

248 TNA FO 371/26982 C4298/4298/41

249 TNA KV2/3489

250 Martin Gilbert: *Winston S Churchiill Official Biography Volume VI Finest Hour, 1939-1941* p630

251 TNA FO 800/323 HXXXIV/32 & 35

252 TNA CAB 66/12/12 20 September 1940

253 TNA FO 800/323 HXXXIV/70

254 David Eccles: *By Safe Hand* p205

255 Anthony Cave Brown: *The Last Hero, Wild Bill Donovan* p162

256 Winston S Churchill: *The Grand Alliance* pp22-25

257 *Dictionary of National Biography*

258 Paul Preston: *Franco* p365

259 TNA FO 371/24508 C7164G

260 TNA FO 954/27 SP/40/8

261 TNA FO 371/24145 W11300

262 *Dictionary of National Biography*

263 TNA BW 56/2

264 TNA FO 371/11355

265 Jimmy Burns: *Papa Spy* pp253-254

266 TNA BW 56/3

267 TNA FO 371/24508 C9677-8

268 David Eccles: *By Safe Hand* p197

269 Paul Preston: *Franco* pp427-437

270 TNA FO 954/27 SP/41/22

271 TNA FO 954/27 SP/41/64

272 Paul Preston: *Franco* pp467-468

273 Mariano Sánchez Soler: *Ricos por la guerra de España* pp119-120

274 Keith Jeffery: *MI6 – The History of the Secret Intelligence Service 1909-1949* pp406-407 and CA CHAR 20/25

275 Dudley Clarke: *Seven Assignments* pp181-184

276 Denys Smith: *Deathly Deception, The Real Story of Operation Mincemeat*

277 TNA FO 954/27 SP/41/58 & 59

278 TNA PREM 4/32/7

279 Anthony Cave Brown: *The Last Hero, Wild Bill Donovan* p225

280 TNA FO 954/27 SP/42/26

281 Winston S Churchill: *The Hinge of Fate* p439

282 Anthony Cave Brown: *The Last Hero, Wild Bill Donovan* pp226-235

283 Paul Preston: *Franco* pp460-461

284 TNA FO 954/27 SP/43/17

285 CUL Templewood papers XIII/7

286 *The Guardian*, London, 15 January 1983, p15

287 Mary Hillgarth: *A Private Life* pp28-29

288 TNA HS 9/1646

289 Peter Kemp: *The Thorns of Memory* pp147-151

290 Andrew Lycett: *Ian Fleming* pp124-132

291 *Dictionary of National Biography*

292 TNA PREM 4/21/2B

293 CA CHAR 20/197B

294 Paul Preston: *Franco* pp519-520

295 TNA PREM 8/106 C17827/23/41

296 CUL Templewood papers XIII/7

297 TNA PREM 8/106

298 Paul Preston: *Franco* p521

299 TNA PREM 8/106 C17827/23/41

300 Jeremy Lewis: *Shades of Greene* p338

301 *The Guardian*, Saturday 25 June 1966

302 Interview with Hugh Pollard's nephew, Colin Davis, March 2011

303 Obituary, King's College, Cambridge annual report, 2008

304 Personal interview, March 2011

305 Personal interview, March 2011

306 *Dictionary of National Biography*

307 CA CHUR 2/36

308 NMM GOD/170 Godfrey's unpublished memoirs

309 CA CHUR 2/36

310 CUL Templewood Papers XIII/6

311 Paul Preston: *Franco* p510

312 TNA T 236/6354

313 John Brooks: *New Yorker* Magazine, 21 May 1979

314 Keith Jeffery: *MI6 - The History of the Secret Intelligence Service 1909-1949* p569

315 TNA FO 371/102038 WS1161/37 & FO 371/117895 A Report by Sullivan & Cromwell

316 CUL Templewood papers XIII/17

317 CUL Templewood papers XIII/7

318 Freedom of Information Act inquiry, 28 March 2011

319 TNA FO 637/87

320 TNA FO 637/89
321 TNA FO 371/102038 WS1161/37
322 TNA FO 371/102037 WS1161/14
323 TNA FO 371/102038 WS1161/43
324 TNA FO 371/73362 Z4399
325 TNA FO 371/73362 Z2856
326 TNA FO 371/102039 WS 1161/69
327 Mary-Kay Wilmers: *The Eitingons, A Twentieth-Century Story*
328 TNA FO 637/91
329 TNA FO 371/117895A RS 1161/1-3

INDEX

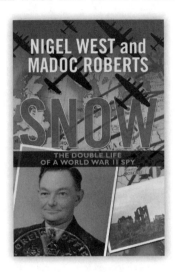